HOW EFFECTIVE IS STRATEGIC BOMBING?

THE WORLD OF WAR

GENERAL EDITOR
Dennis Showalter

SEEDS OF EMPIRE

The American Revolutionary Conquest of the Iroquois

MAX M. MINTZ

HOW EFFECTIVE IS STRATEGIC BOMBING?

Lessons Learned from World War II to Kosovo

GIAN P. GENTILE

GIAN P. GENTILE

HOW EFFECTIVE IS STRATEGIC BOMBING?

Lessons Learned from World War II to Kosovo

New York University Press
NEW YORK AND LONDON

NEW YORK UNIVERSITY PRESS
New York and London

Library of Congress Cataloging-in-Publication Data
Gentile, Gian P.
How effective is strategic bombing? : lessons learned from
World War II and Kosovo / Gian P. Gentile.
p. cm. — (World of war)
Includes bibliographical references and index.
ISBN 0-8147-3135-X (cloth : alk. paper)
1. Bombing, Aerial—United States. 2. World War, 1939–1945—
Aerial operations, American. 3. Kosovo (Serbia)—History—Civil War,
1998—Aerial operations, American. I. Title. II. Series.
UG633 .G46 2000
355.4'22—dc21 00-045267

New York University Press books are printed on acid-free paper,
and their binding materials are chosen for strength and durability.

Manufactured in the United States of America

10 9 8 7 6 5 4 3 2 1

CONTENTS

ACKNOWLEDGMENTS

British historian Eric Hobsbawm noted that a person can make a contribution to historical knowledge if he or she has the "capacity for very hard work and some detective ingenuity." While researching and writing this book I have had the capacity to work hard, yet without the patient mentoring and tutoring of Barton J. Bernstein of Stanford University I would have never pursued my topic of research or completed the book. I owe him a lot. I also owe a great deal to Lieutenant Colonel Conrad C. Crane of the United States Military Academy (USMA) History Department who read every chapter and through many discussions taught me a great deal about air power history. Colonel Robert A. Doughty, head of the USMA History Department, provided me with important advice and criticism along the way and with a semester off from teaching to research and write.

Many others deserve mention. Colonel Judith A. Luckett is a role model for me in scholarship and leadership. Colonel Charles F. Brower IV helped me to be a better teacher and historian. From my first days as a graduate student at Stanford through three years of teaching history at West Point, Colonel Gary J. Tocchet has been a mentor and friend. Gordon H. Chang of Stanford University forced me to think about the book as a whole and how to better tie the chapters together. A number of discussions with Dennis Showalter of Colorado College about bombing in World War II refined my overall argument in the book. Major Christopher Kolenda, Major Peter Huggins, and Major Edward Rowe provided valuable comments on all or portions of the book. Major Ian Hope of Princess Patricia's Canadian Light Infantry gave me an especially helpful reading of chapter 7 and the introduction. Steven Ross of the Naval War College critiqued an earlier version of chapter 6. Elizabeth Kopelman Borgwardt helped with some key passages in the book. Robert Newman of the University of Iowa (and World War II combat veteran) gave me very thoughtful readings of the chapters. Norris Hundley, former editor of the *Pacific Historical Review*, showed me how to sharpen prose that I already thought was sharp. Major Frank Huber solved many word-processing problems for me. My graduate cohort at Stanford, colleagues at the USMA History Department, and seminars at the Command and General Staff College and the School of Advanced Military Studies (SAMS) provided engaging intellectual environments. Colonel Robin Swan, Colonel Kim Summers, Robert Berlin, and the rest of the faculty at SAMS set the standard for me as progressive-minded defense intellectuals. Many lively and stimulating discussions with Roger Spiller of the Combat Studies Institute informed my thinking on history, culture, and theory. E-mail correspondence with Eliot Cohen, Emery M. Kiraly, Mark Mandeles, and Barry Watts, all former members of the Gulf War Air Power Survey, provided me with valuable criticism of chapter 7. Electronic and phone conversations with Barry Watts were especially helpful on air power history. Special thanks to the NYU anonymous reviewer for thoughtful ways to improve the book. Niko Pfund, director of the New York University Press, has pushed me toward precision and excellence.

I received help at numerous archival collections across the country: Dave Giardano and Wil Mahoney at the National Archives; the staff at the Library of Congress, Washington, D.C.; Joseph Caver and the staff of the Air Force Historical Research Agency (AFHRA) at Maxwell Air Force Base, Alabama; the Seely G. Mudd Library at Princeton University; the Naval Historical Center in Washington, D.C.; and the USMA Special Collections Department. Dennis Bilger of the Truman Presidential Library was the perfect "finding aide"; he somehow intuitively knew the documents that I needed to read. Grants from the Dean of USMA, the AFHRA, and the Truman Presidential Library helped to pay for a number of research trips.

My parents, Al and Betty Gentile, sparked my interest in history at a very early age by telling me stories about the Great Depression and World War II. My wife Gee Won and two children, Michael and Elizabeth, are the inspiration for all that I do. I could not have completed this book without their love and support.

INTRODUCTION

✦ ✦ ✦ ✦ ✦ ✦ ✦ ✦ ✦ ✦ ✦

I would like to again emphasize this Philosophy of the Survey . . . and that is with an open mind—without prejudice, without any preconceived theories—to simply gather the facts. We are simply to seek the truth.

FRANKLIN D'OLIER, December 1944

Remember that quote from the chairman of the Strategic Bombing Survey of World War II: "We wanted to burn into everybody's soul the fact that the [USSBS's] responsibility was . . . to seek truth. . . ." Nothing, but nothing, is more important than the integrity of our [Gulf War Air Power Survey] product.

ELIOT COHEN, March 1992

Air power has been one of the most controversial issues for American defense policy since it first came into being as a military force in the early part of the twentieth century. Moreover, a certain component of American air power—strategic bombing—has been especially controversial. Pundits have railed against its perceived *ineffectiveness,* advocates have praised its apparent *effectiveness,* and zealots have been seduced by its professed cheaper cost in national blood and treasure. Over time strategic bombing's contested nature has endured. Although not the only type of American air power, strategic bombing has provided the historical identity for airmen and their air force.

Other major forms of military power have not been so problematic, so contested in American defense policy. Why? Perhaps because for many people strategic bombing continues to be an ambiguous and even unproven military force in war and conflict.

Strategic bombing has evolved over the years. American airmen like Haywood Hansell and Muir Fairchild laid the conceptual groundwork for strategic bombing during the 1930s. The first crucible for the airmen and their strategic bombing concept was World War II, when high-flying bombers were used to attack the war-making capacity of Germany and Japan. The experience of strategic bombing in World War II helped the American Air Force prepare for "toe-to-toe nuclear combat"[1] against the Soviet Union during the cold war. Strategic bombing was tried in the limited wars of Korea and Vietnam, but it was a frustrating experience to airmen. More recently, technological improvements allowed the United States Air Force to conduct strategic bombing campaigns in the Gulf War and Kosovo using bombs guided to their targets by lasers.

Throughout its evolution, however, strategic bombing remained controversial because of the difficulty of proving its effectiveness. During strategic bombing operations, owing to the short amount of time over the target and the distance separating the airplane from the ground, it has been hard to determine success or failure simply in terms of physical destruction. And evaluating the effects of strategic bombing on vital enemy targets is especially difficult because that evaluation requires not merely an assessment of physical damage but an analysis of the entire enemy system. In short, the overall effect of strategic bombing on the enemy has not often been immediately apparent, sometimes taking an extended period of time to manifest itself. In early 1944, well aware of the problem of proving the effectiveness of strategic bombing, American airmen came up with a way to deal with one of their most vexing problems.

Secretary of War Henry L. Stimson officially established the United States Strategic Bombing Survey (USSBS) in November 1944 to analyze the effects of strategic air power in the European theater. Later, President Harry S. Truman expanded the Survey's scope to study all types of aerial war against Japan, including the effects of the atomic bombings of Hiroshima and Nagasaki. In an attempt to keep the Survey's findings impartial, prominent civilians were appointed as directors of most of the Survey's divisions. The key directors of the Survey were Franklin D'Olier (Chairman), Henry Alexander (Vice-Chairman), George Ball, Paul Nitze, John Kenneth Galbraith, Admiral Ralph A. Ofstie, and General Orvil Arson Anderson. The final studies, completed and published in late 1945 through 1947, numbered over 330 reports and annexes; the amount of research and statistical data is staggering. In 1991, forty-four years after the last USSBS reports were published, Secretary of the Air Force Donald B. Rice commissioned another extensive, civilian-led evaluation of American Air Force operations in the Persian Gulf War: the Gulf War Air Power Survey (GWAPS). The chairman for the GWAPS Review Committee was Paul Nitze.

Two scholarly writings on the combat use of the atomic bomb against Japan, and the Pacific Survey's counterfactual conclusion on Japan's surrender, sparked my interest in the evaluation of American air power. The argument that President Truman dropped the bomb on Japan not to end the war (because he knew Japan would surrender soon) but to intimidate the Soviet Union,[2] seemed flawed to me at an intuitive level. Moreover, the Survey's counterfactual conclusion stating that Japan would have surrendered, even without the atomic bomb, "certainly prior to 31 December 1945, and in all probability prior to 1 November 1945,"[3] also seemed incorrect. Such a sweeping conclusion—the atomic bomb was unnecessary in forcing Japan to surrender—struck me as missing the critical role the threat of a land invasion may have played in Japan's unconditional surrender. The other writing, arguing that the United States dropped the bomb on Japan primarily to end the war quickly and save American lives, and, as a secondary purpose, to intimidate the Soviet Union,[4] was a more reasonable explanation to me of America's combat use of the atomic bomb.

I then began to look at many of the other published Survey reports from Europe and the Pacific to see if they lent support to the counterfactual conclusion concerning Japan's surrender. I discovered that the Survey reports were not a single set of unified analyses and arguments, systematically grounded in data, but, rather, a loose amalgam of studies, sometimes prepared more to shape the future than to assess the past. I also came to realize that the conclusions brought out in Survey reports were informed by a common conception of strategic air power. That common conception became especially clear to me after reading through the American plans for war against the Soviet Union written from 1945 to 1950.

The World War II United States Strategic Bombing Survey contains conclusions that have influenced scholars, strategists, and journalists since its reports were first published in the two years following the end of World War II. Analysts like Bernard Brodie and P. M. S. Blackett used the Survey's conclusions and evidence to support their ideas on nuclear strategy and postwar defense policy and organization. The Survey's findings also played a role in the postwar debate over President Truman's decision to drop the atomic bombs on Hiroshima and Nagasaki. Beginning with Karl Compton, Henry L. Stimson, Hanson Baldwin, and continuing up through at least Herbert Feis and Gar Alperovitz and beyond, writers have used portions of the Survey to support their position in the debate over the 1945 combat use of the bomb. Further, USSBS reports have supported various positions over President Richard Nixon's bombing of North Vietnam, and, much more recently, the application of American air power in the Gulf War and Kosovo.

Because a presidential directive established the Survey and gave it an official status, and because the Survey was headed by civilians, ostensibly making it impartial, the Survey reports have taken on the aura of a document that contains the truth about strategic bombing in World War II. In fact, the Survey is a secondary source that interprets the past: yet analysts and pundits who have used the Survey in their postwar writings have instead tended to treat it as a primary source. In criticizing such views, retired Air Force General Haywood Hansell once cynically compared the Strategic Bombing Survey to the "Bible."[5] Yet as Clarence Darrow forced William Jennings Bryan to acknowledge in the famous 1925 Scopes trial, the Bible was only one of many truths that purported to explain the origins of man. And the Survey contains the truth about the effects of strategic bombing against Germany and Japan as the writers of its reports discerned that truth through their own attitudes and biases. Writing on the use of air power in the Persian Gulf War almost fifty years later, the analysts of the Gulf War Air Power Survey told the truth about air power, as they perceived it, but with a more subtle understanding of the policy implications of their published volumes.[6]

The first, and only, book-length study of the USSBS, David MacIsaac's *Strategic Bombing in World War II: The Story of the United States Strategic Bombing Survey*, did not appear until 1976.[7] It is ironic that such a study was so long in coming, considering the influence the Survey was having on postwar scholarship and journalism. MacIsaac accepted the official premise that the Survey conducted an objective and impartial study of strategic bombing because civilians headed it. Many analysts in postwar writings, therefore, have used MacIsaac's book as a scholarly confirmation of the Survey's purported impartiality, thereby reinforcing the aura of "biblical truth" surrounding the Survey's conclusions concerning strategic air power in World War II.

As a collection of documents, as an establishment organization, and through the ideas of its civilian and military analysts, the United States Strategic Bombing Survey reflected the American conceptual approach to strategic bombing. Two fundamental tenets formed the American conception: strategic air power should be used not to attack ground forces in battle directly but instead to attack the vital elements of the enemy's war-making capacity; and the air force must be independent of and coequal with the army and the navy. My study seeks to show how that conception informed and shaped the Strategic Bombing Survey's evaluation of American air power in World War II. Since the Survey accepted the American conceptual approach to strategic bombing and made it a framework for analysis, a truly impartial evaluation was never really a possibility. My study also explores the subtle interplay of advocacy and assessment throughout the Survey's formal evaluation from January 1945 to June 1946 and the use of the Survey's published reports in the postwar years. To bring into relief my analysis of the USSBS, I end with a chapter that compares the World War II USSBS and the 1993 Gulf War Air Power Survey.

By 1939, Major Muir Fairchild, an instructor at the Army Air Forces' (AAF) influential Air Corps Tactical School (ACTS), had refined a conception of air power that sought to use strategic bombers against the "vital elements" of the enemy's war-making capacity. Once strategic bombers had destroyed these "vital elements," Fairchild and other airmen believed that the enemy's will to resist would subsequently collapse. Air power theorist Guilio Douhet noted almost twenty years before Fairchild taught classes at ACTS that determining which "vital elements" to bomb would become the essence of air power strategy. But it was the civilian industrialists and economists, not the airmen, who were really the experts at air power strategy because the civilians better understood the workings of a modern industrialized economy. The American conceptual approach to strategic bombing, therefore, created a need to have civilian experts conduct target selection and evaluation—the essence of air power strategy. The United States Strategic Bombing Survey was an outgrowth of this requirement.

During World War II, when the AAF was using strategic air power over the present battlefield, they were also preparing for a future fight. But that future fight would not involve airplanes dropping bombs on targets in enemy cities. Instead, it would be a postwar crusade for an independent air force. The airmen knew that a civilian-led evaluation of the effects of strategic bombing against Germany could be very helpful in their upcoming postwar fight for independence.[8] Such an evaluation could provide the evidentiary base for proving the effectiveness of American strategic air power in World War II. As a result, the airmen took deliberate steps to shape the questions that the Survey would ask concerning the effectiveness of American air power against Germany.

The evaluation methodology that Survey directors like John Kenneth Galbraith devised, and the published reports produced by the European portion of the Survey, reflected the American emphasis on using strategic bombers to destroy the "vital elements" of the enemy's war-making capacity. For example, Survey analysts believed that the effects of strategic bombing on the morale of the German people were important only insofar as lowered morale may have reduced the productive capacity of the German industrial labor force. Moreover, many of the European Survey's published reports argued that American air power was "decisive" against Germany because it destroyed transportation facilities, which were "vital elements" that linked together many important industries in Germany's wartime economy.

Generals Carl A. Spaatz and Orvil Anderson believed that the European Survey's published reports confirmed the correctness of the American conceptual approach to strategic bombing. Those published reports would help them fight the future battle of air force independence.

Within the American conception, though, disagreements did occur over the most effective methods for strategic bombers to use when attacking the enemy's war-making capacity. Recommending a strategic bombing plan for the air campaign against Japan, Survey Director Paul Nitze concluded, based on his studies in Europe, that the best method would be precise attacks against Japanese transportation and electrical power facilities (precision bombing). Other AAF targeting agencies, however, believed that a more effective method would be to bomb large areas of Japanese cities using incendiary weapons (area bombing). The objectives of both these bombing methods could have been either to lower morale by killing Japanese civilians or to destroy Japanese war-making capacity. But in the minds of Survey analysts and targeting planners, morale as an objective did not necessarily have to be synonymous with area bombing.

When conducting its evaluation of air power in the Pacific, in addition to studying the effects of area bombing against Japanese cities, the Survey also assessed the navy's use of air power against Japan and the effects of the atomic bomb. The Pacific Survey had to wrestle with the fact that, unlike Germany, Japan was forced to surrender without a land invasion. But if it was not a ground invasion that ended the war, then what did force Japan to surrender? The airmen believed that Japan's surrender confirmed the decisiveness of the AAF's conventional bombing campaign and the war-winning potential of air power for the future. The Pacific Survey *Summary Report* supported the airmen's belief by calling for an independent "third establishment" that would be responsible for strategic air operations in postwar American security.

Airmen and navy officers used the published reports from the European and Pacific portions of the Survey during the postwar congressional hearings over unification of the armed services and the independence of the air force. The Survey's numerous published studies turned out to be very malleable sources, especially for airmen and navy officers arguing their respective cases before congressional committees. But the disagreements between the air force and the navy during the hearings were not over the soundness of the American conceptual approach to strategic bombing. Rather, the navy and the air force disagreed over the most effective methods for carrying out a strategic bombing campaign in a potential war against the Soviet Union. Because the Strategic Bombing Survey had its evaluation shaped by the American conception, and because both the navy and the air force believed in the correctness of that conception, the Strategic Bombing Survey proved to be a source of truth for both services when advocating their postwar parochial interests.

The clear perception of the soundness of strategic bombing in World War II, as manifested in the USSBS reports, became muddled in the limited wars of Korea and Vietnam. American airmen in those wars chafed at the restrictions placed on them by their political leaders. If the correct approach to strategic air power was to attack the war-making capacity of the enemy, in Korea and Vietnam that approach proved difficult to carry out. Since the use of air power in Korea and Vietnam did not fit the airmen's conception of strategic bombing, an extensive evaluation along the lines of the World War II USSBS was not conducted. It was not until the American Air Force perceived great success after the Persian Gulf War in

1991 that a USSBS-like assessment of air power was commissioned and carried out.

As efforts in history, the reports of the United States Strategic Bombing Survey (and the Gulf War Air Power Survey) are useful in providing data and interpretation about the value, problems, and ambiguities of strategic bombing in war and conflict. But are they unimpeachable authorities, closed to rigorous scrutiny and thoughtful analysis? To what extent was the Survey "objective" in its analysis of strategic bombing in World War II? To answer these questions by exploring the interpretive framework that USSBS analysts brought to their work is to open up for historical view the very object of their study: the effectiveness of strategic bombing.

CHAPTER 1

✦ ✦ ✦ ✦ ✦ ✦ ✦ ✦ ✦ ✦ ✦

The Origins of the American Conceptual Approach to Strategic Bombing and the United States Strategic Bombing Survey

> All this sounds very simple; but as a matter of fact the selection of objectives, the grouping of zones, and determining the order in which they are to be destroyed is the most difficult and delicate task in aerial warfare, constituting what may be defined as aerial strategy.
>
> GUILIO DOUHET, 1921

> There is that whole question of what is morale. . . . I confess I don't know what morale is.
>
> CARL BECKER, 1943

In his 1921 book *The Command of the Air,* Italian air power theorist Guilio Douhet argued that once strategic bombers had achieved command of the air, they could quickly force an enemy into submission by dropping bombs on key targets in its cities.[1] But he only loosely defined those targets, and he never explained how to select them. Indeed, Douhet went on to state that it would be impossible to determine enemy targets in aerial warfare systematically because the choice would "depend on a number of circumstances, material, moral, and psychological, the importance of which, though real, is not easily estimated. It is just here, in grasping these imponderables, in choosing enemy targets, that future commanders of Independent Air Forces will show their ability."[2] Considering the overwhelming confidence that Douhet had in the ability of a fleet of bombers to destroy enemy cities and break the will of the civilian population, one would think that target selection would have played a more important role in the Italian's theory of air warfare.[3] Douhet's reluctance to deal with target choice anticipated the problems that air commanders would have with target selection and evaluation during World War II.

Douhet challenged conventional military thought on warfare in the 1920s by claiming that the nation that owned an air force predominantly of strategic bombers could avoid costly naval and ground engagements by attacking the "vital centers" of enemy cities, thereby creating terror among the civilian population. The result, according to Douhet, would be a quick, decisive victory for the nation equipped with an independent strategic air force. A casual glance at the title of Douhet's book, *The Command of the Air,* leads one to think that gaining superiority in the air—the ability to fly at will over enemy territory—was the most important objective. But for the Italian, this was only the first, albeit essential, part of a theory of air warfare that ultimately envisioned using airplanes to bomb enemy cities.[4] Within those cities, Douhet argued, were primarily two types of objectives to bomb: the morale of the people and their material resistance. Munitions factories, transportation networks, and electric power plants, for example, made up material resistance—what commonly became know as the enemy's war-making capacity. But Douhet made clear that while it might be important to attack the enemy's industrial capacity to resist, the enemy's morale would ultimately have to be attacked. The way to break the morale—the will to resist—of the enemy was to bomb cities, killing large numbers of civilians.[5]

American airmen were aware of Douhet's theory. As early as 1923 a translation of *The Command of the Air* was being circulated at the Air Service Headquarters. In 1933 the Air Corps Tactical School (ACTS) at Maxwell Field, Alabama, maintained copies of Douhet's work.[6] Historians have debated how much direct influence Douhet had on the development of American air power strategy in the 1930s.

Some analysts argue that air power proponents like William Mitchell had greater influence on American thinking on strategic bombing than Douhet. Others argue that Douhet's prolific writings played an important role in shaping American views on air power.[7] Most scholars, however, would agree that Douhet's collective works gave a literary comprehensiveness to the ideas that shaped the American conceptual approach to strategic bombing.[8]

By 1939 American airmen had developed a conception of air power that envisioned using strategic bombers to attack the "vital links" of the enemy's war-making capacity, thereby breaking the enemy's will to resist.[9] But what were the "vital links" in the enemy's industrial structure essential to the capacity to resist? American airmen were soldiers, not experts in industrial economies. They were trained to fly aircraft and to drop bombs on critical targets. However, the targets to attack under the American conception were economic in nature. To assess how the destruction of any given target would affect the overall war capacity of the enemy nation required a level of analysis that airmen, by their training, were unable to provide.

Naval and ground commanders of the same period did not have the same problem. For an army officer commanding an infantry division, for example, the target or objective to attack was generally similar in nature to his own command. It would probably be another infantry division or smaller-sized unit trying to block his advance. To analyze the target and its importance, therefore, was something that the ground officer was trained to do. The ground commander could determine success or failure by the amount of ground gained and the level of destruction of the enemy and his own forces.

For American airmen, target selection and evaluation were a much more complicated and ambiguous task. Unlike the ground officer, airmen were generally not attacking targets similar to their own men and equipment.[10] Hence the uncertainties of target selection and evaluation, which were embedded in the American conceptual approach to strategic bombing, created a need for civilian experts to change "imponderables" to ponderables. Organizations like the Committee of Operations Analysts, the Committee of Historians, and the United States Strategic Bombing Survey were an outgrowth of this need.

I

The biggest problem for American air officers during the years following the end of World War I, however, was not so much target selection (that problem would present itself more fully in the 1930s when they began to develop a strategic bombing concept) as achieving a coequal status with the army and navy. The leading proponent in the 1920s for an independent air arm was Army General William Mitchell.[11] Conventional thinking concerning air power during that decade saw it mainly as an adjunct, or supporting arm, of ground and naval operations. Since air power, according to this line of thinking, could not win a war, it did not require independent status. Mitchell, conversely, argued that an independent air force could win by itself. He also posited that the United States should rely on an independent air force, not the navy, for its first line of defense.[12] For publicly criticizing his superiors and their respective services, Mitchell was court-martialed in 1925 and convicted of "conduct prejudicial to good order and military discipline."[13] After the conviction Mitchell resigned from the service but continued his air power crusade with greater zeal.

Throughout the court-martial ordeal Mitchell had the strong support of his fellow air officers. For example, Lieutenant Orvil Anderson, who later became a major general and served as a director on the Strategic Bombing Survey, testified on behalf of Mitchell's ideas for an independent air arm. One year prior to Mitchell's court-martial, the House of Representatives created a committee led by Representative Florian Lampert to determine air power's role in the national defense. The committee received testimony from many air officers who argued that the air corps should have an independent role in defending the continental United States from naval and air attack. The navy also presented its case to the committee. Lieutenant Ralph A. Ofstie testified that the nation's defense was in good hands with the navy and therefore an independent air force was not needed.[14] Ofstie, like Orvil Anderson, became a director of the Strategic Bombing Survey at the end of World War II. His testimony in 1924 anticipated the bitter interservice rivalry between himself and Anderson over air power issues in the post–World War II unification debates.

During the Depression years of the 1930s, airmen had to show caution when advocating their conceptual approach to strategic bombing. Mitchell and other American airmen believed that strategic bombers were fundamentally offensive weapons designed to strike quickly, violently, and preferably with *surprise* at key targets in enemy territory.[15] In the logic of air power theory that Douhet, Mitchell, and other airmen of the time understood, there was a need to strike first at the enemy's homeland to destroy its aircraft and production facilities *before* they could be brought to bear against the United States. Defense of the continental United States, however, was the ostensible justification that airmen used when calling for an independent air force. Continental defense fit comfortably with isolationist American attitudes. It would have been unpalatable for air officers to advocate air power in an offensive role after the American experience with German aggression in the Great War and the nominal support for the Kellogg-Briand Pact of 1929 that purportedly outlawed war. The Depression years focused American attention on internal domestic problems. Arguing for a fleet of long-range strategic bombers designed to attack the homeland of a foreign nation obviously smacked of direct American military involvement in foreign affairs. Air officers, therefore, had to couch their crusade for an independent air force (an air force that they understood fundamentally as an offensive weapon) in the rhetoric of defensive military policy that coincided with the isolationist temper of the American public.[16]

In 1937, Major General Frank M. Andrews, commanding general of the Army Air Forces, supported a congressional bill to make the air arm independent from the army. The general stated in a memorandum to the army adjutant general that the rapid evolution of bombardment aviation in other threatening nations throughout the world had convinced him "that a safer state of national security and peace can be insured more positively and sooner, through the development of air defense and the Air Forces which make possible such defense . . . on a basis coequal in authority with the Army." The implication of General Andrews's statement was that the proposed independent air force would use its airplanes in a defensive role: to engage and destroy enemy aircraft in the air as they attempted to bomb American cities. This was not primarily the way General Andrews and other airmen intended to use an independent air force. The general went on to acknowledge in the same memorandum that the modern bombardment airplane existed to attack the enemy nation's "vital organs." To keep a potential enemy from attacking the "vital centers" of the United States, General Andrews argued that

> the airplane is an engine of war which has brought into being a new and entirely different mode of warfare—the application of Air Power. . . . It is another means, operating in another element, for the same basic purpose as ground and sea power, the destruction of the enemy's will to fight. It is a vital agency, to insure in peace, the continuation of our nation's policies and existence, or in war, the destruction of the enemy's will to invade our defensive jurisdiction.[17]

According to the American conceptual approach to strategic bombing that by 1937 was reaching maturity at the influential Air Corps Tactical School, the way to break the enemy's will to resist was first to destroy its war-making capacity by bombing key economic-industrial targets.[18] Once those key targets had been selected and bombed, the will of the enemy would most likely collapse.[19] General Andrews's rhetorical allusion to the defensive use of airpower nevertheless was grounded in an offensive conception for an independent air force. To destroy the enemy's "will to invade," as the general suggested, the United States would have to launch a strategic bombing offensive that would prevent the enemy nation from using its war-making capacity first to attack American soil with strategic bombers.[20]

The Munich conference of 1938 and Hitler's subsequent march into Czechoslovakia created a more conducive atmosphere for air officers forthrightly to advocate their conceptual approach to strategic bombing.[21] Air Corps Tactical School officer Lieutenant Colonel Donald Wilson pointed out to other members of the school that the United States needed to develop a long-range bombardment force that could threaten an enemy nation's "home territory." Although he did not explicitly mention Germany as the "home territory" that the United States should be able to threaten, the thrust of his argument made clear that Germany was the nation he had in mind. Wilson asked what would be the result if this "upstart dictator" (presumably Adolph Hitler) could threaten America's home territory with strategic bombardment. According to Wilson the United States had the greatest "ability to secure, manufacture, and organize the men and materials required for war." Why then, inquired Wilson, should the United States itself be "vulnerable to such a new theory as air attack?" He answered: "Simply because an industrial nation is composed of interrelated and entirely interdependent elements. The normal every day life of the great mass of the population is basically dependent upon the continuous flow and uninterrupted organization of services, materials, and food." Wilson then brought out a clear example of why American air officers thought that attacking "vital links" in the enemy's industrial structure with strategic bombers would destroy their capacity to resist:

> The industrial nation has grown and prospered in proportion to the excellence of its industrial system, but, and here is the irony of the situation, the better this industrial organization for peacetime efficiency the more vulnerable it is to wartime collapse caused by the cutting of one or more of its essential arteries. How this is accomplished is the essence of air strategy in modern warfare.[22]

Since the individual was so closely linked to the industrialized state, airmen believed that by attacking the key components of that industrial state, the enemy's will to resist would almost certainly collapse. This became axiomatic among American airmen. But airmen offered only a loose explanation of the link between strategic bombing attacks on industrial capacity and the purported breakdown of the enemy's will to resist. Instead they focused more clearly on objectives, or targets, that were tangible and easy to quantify: the "vital links" of the enemy's war-making capacity. Determining these "vital links" became the "essence" of air strategy. Wilson, quoting Douhet, stated: "The art of air strategy consists mainly in choosing the objectives."[23]

ACTS instructor Major Muir Fairchild, who later became the chief of plans for the Army Air Forces (AAF) in World War II, had refined the American conception of air power in classes to officers at the Air Corps Tactical School. In a 1939 lecture to ACTS students titled "National Economic Structure," Fairchild argued that there were two types of objectives to attack with strategic airpower: the morale of the people and the "national economic structure." Fairchild acknowledged at the beginning of the lecture that "it may well be possible for air attack directly on the civilian populace to destroy morale—provided of course that the air force can strike soon enough and hard enough." But, Fairchild asked, "how hard, is hard enough?" Whether it was possible to break the will, or morale, of an enemy nation, based on the limited experience with Japanese attacks on Chinese cities, was in the realm of an imponderable, asserted Fairchild. In fact attacking morale directly by killing people, as he put it, might have the effect of increasing "the morale of the nation as a whole." Fairchild thus concluded that "for all of these reasons the School advocates an entirely different method of attack. This method, is the attack of the National Economic Structure."[24]

According to Fairchild, a nation had to possess "a highly organized and smoothly functioning economic system, to carry on war in the modern way. The capacity to wage modern war is definitely fixed by the capacity of the national economic structure to provide the raw materials and to connect these materials into the sinews of war." Although efficient in peacetime, the economic structure in war would be highly susceptible to the application of strategic bombing. Air power could apply, as he put it, "the additional pressure necessary to cause a breakdown—a collapse—of this industrial machine by the destruction of some vital link or links in the chain that ties it together, constitut[ing] one of the primary, basic objectives of an air force—in fact, it is the opinion of the School that this is the maximum contribution of which an air force is capable towards the attainment of the ultimate aim in war."[25] The dominant theme of the American theory of air power was not to attack civilians directly but to separate the enemy population from the sources of production by attacking their war-making capacity.[26]

Based on a study of the American industrial system, ACTS instructor Major Haywood Hansell, who a few years later would assist in writing the plan for the American air war against Germany, determined that the "vital links" common to the United States and most other industrialized nations were, "in order of importance," electric power, rail transportation, fuel, steel, and armament and munitions factories. Muir Fairchild concluded that if an enemy equipped with strategic bombers were to attack electrical power facilities in major American cities, for example, the will to resist of the Americans living in those cities would almost assuredly be broken because their links to the sources of goods and production would have been severed.[27]

But once this set of general objectives was established, determining target priority, their location in enemy countries, their protection, and assessment of the damage inflicted required a level of expertise that airmen did not posses. Hansell stated that these problems "were beyond the competence of the Tactical School. Strategic air intelligence on major world powers would demand an intelligence organization and analytical competence of considerable scope and complexity."[28] Muir Fairchild realized that his own analysis of the American industrial system was somewhat "amateurish" and that target selection and assessment of "vital links" in the enemy's industrial structure called for analysis by "the economist—the statistician—the technical expert—rather than a strictly military study or war plan."[29]

II

Since according to Douhet and Wilson the essence of air strategy was target selection, and since according to Hansell and Fairchild target selection for strategic bombing must rely heavily on civilian experts, the logical conclusion then was that civilians—economists, industrialists, and technicians—were the most qualified to plan and evaluate strategic air warfare. As air officers became immersed in organizing and operating the Army Air Forces to fight Germany and later Japan, there was a growing reliance on civilian experts for target selection and evaluation within the Army Air Forces.

Air officers also realized that evaluations would become the evidentiary base establishing the efficacy of strategic bombing and, they hoped, an independent postwar air force. General Henry H. Arnold, air power pioneer during the interwar years and AAF commanding general during World War II, noted that the Strategic Bombing Survey's evaluation of American air power in the European theater would "prove to be the foundation of our future national policy on the employment of air power."[30] Civilian experts would come to play a crucial role in formulating air strategy, and their evaluations would assist the airmen in their postwar crusade for an independent air force.

The fledgling Air Intelligence Section of the AAF was one of the first agencies that brought in civilian experts to work on strategic target selection and evaluation. After leaving the Tactical School in 1940, Haywood Hansell joined the section and was placed in charge of determining the critical links in the German and Japanese industrial systems. With the growing threat of Nazi Germany and the availability of a more robust AAF budget, Hansell was able to bring a number of prominent civilian experts into the Air Intelligence Section. One was Malcolm Moss, who held a Ph.D. in industrial engineering. Moss produced an analysis of Germany's electrical power system that, according to Hansell, provided the information needed to put together an extensive target plan for attacking German electrical power.[31] Hansell and other air force officers would draw heavily on analyses like Moss's as war with Germany became a reality.

A year later in 1941, responding to a request from President Roosevelt to the service secretaries, General Arnold directed Hansell along with Lieutenant Colonels Harold George, Kenneth Walker, and Laurence Kuter to write the AAF's portion of "the overall production requirements required to defeat our potential enemies." [32] In order to determine production requirements the AAF needed to develop an air strategic concept. The result after nine days of intense, demanding work by the four men was Air War Plans Division/1.[33]

AWPD/1, as it became known, posited that a massive strategic air offensive attacking German war-making capacity might make an invasion of the European continent unnecessary by forcing Germany to surrender early. At a minimum, argued the planners, the air offensive would weaken German war-making capacity to a point that would allow for a successful land invasion, if that became necessary.[34]

The plan called for a massive strategic bombing offensive against "German military power" that would attack what it determined to be an already weakened social and economic structure:

> [Destruction] of that structure will virtually break down the capacity of the German nation to wage war. The basic conception on which this plan is based lies in the application of air power for the breakdown of the industrial and economic structure of Germany. This conception involves the selection of a system of objectives vital to continued German war effort, and to the means of livelihood of the German people, and tenaciously concentrating all bombing toward destruction of those objectives.

The specific target systems to attack within the German industrial and economic structure would be, in order of priority: electrical power; transportation; oil and petroleum production; and the undermining of morale by air attack.[35] Just as enemy morale in the ACTS lectures of the late 1930s was seen as a potential target to attack, so too was it a potential target in AWPD/1. Yet after the planners acknowledged it in the plan as a possible target, morale received very little attention. Indeed, AWPD/1 bore striking similarity to Muir Fairchild's ACTS lecture on the "National Economic Structure," with the emphasis on attacking "vital links" in the war-making capacity of the enemy. Once under way in 1945, the Strategic Bombing Survey would continue to emphasize, through its evaluation, the use of strategic bombers to attack war-making capacity while downplaying its effect on morale.

The authors of AWPD/1 acknowledged that the strategic concept brought out in the plan and the estimates derived from that concept required "continuing study" and refinement.[36] They pointed out to Army Chief of Staff General George C. Marshall that even though target selection might need adjustment based on further evaluation, the overall conceptual approach would not "result in any appreciable change."[37] In August 1942, one year after the submission of AWPD/1, air planners produced AWPD/42, "Requirements for Air Ascendancy." AWPD/42 added to the older list of objectives the destruction of German submarine construction and the depletion of the German air force, but maintained the same conceptual base as the earlier plan. As Haywood Hansell later noted about AWPD/42, the primary strategic purpose was still to use strategic bombing to destroy "the capability and will of Germany to wage war." This would be accomplished, according to Hansell, by "destroying the war-supporting industries and economic systems upon which the war-sustaining and political economy depended."[38]

III

From late 1942 to the end of 1943 the AAF put into practice its theory of strategic bombing in the skies over France and Germany. The AAF's Eighth Air Force began bombing operations out of bases in Britain in August 1942 by attacking German submarine pens in the coastal waters of France. While conducting these early operations, American airmen realized that their prewar idea of having large bombers fly over enemy territory without fighter aircraft protection was wrong. In August and October 1943, respectively, the Eighth Air Force conducted two large-scale bombing missions against ball-bearing factories in Schweinfurt, Germany. But without their own fighter protection the bombers suffered prohibitive losses to German fighters. With the arrival of substantial numbers of new American fighters, the P51 Mustang, the airmen were able to resume their full-scale attack on the German war economy in February 1944. As the airmen of the Eighth Air Force worked through the tactical and operational procedures of strategic bombing, they gave more attention to strategic target selection and evaluation.[39]

But the selection of targets produced by the AAF's military and civilian intelligence sections created a good deal of controversy. Some airmen believed that the analyses were too pessimistic in their appraisal of the effect that target destruction would have on German industry. Others argued that much more analysis was required of German industry if the AAF wanted to attack the most vital targets contributing to the German war effort.[40]

Realizing the importance of target selection for the AAF, General Arnold in December 1942 established the Committee of Operations Analysts (COA). The general wanted an organization that could streamline the process of target selection and somewhat separate itself from the existing disputes over intelligence within the AAF.[41] The group was made up predominantly of civilian personnel, most of whom were industrial experts. For example, Elihu Root, Jr. was a senior member of a New York financial firm, Edward Mead Earle was a Princeton scholar of history and economics, Edward S. Mason was an economics professor at Harvard, and Guido R. Perera was a lawyer with an elite Boston law firm and would later occupy influential positions in the Strategic Bombing Survey. The heavy reliance on civilian experts reflected the AAF belief that its staff officers did not have the professional training or ability to conduct sophisticated economic analysis that could produce strategic target recommendations.[42]

In his first directive, General Arnold asked the "group of operational analysts" to

> Prepare and submit to me a report analyzing the rate of progressive deterioration that should be anticipated in the German war effort as a result of the increasing air operations we are prepared to employ against its sustaining sources. This study should result in as accurate an estimate as can be arrived at as to the date when this deterioration will have progressed to a point to permit a successful invasion of Western Europe.[43]

Contained in this directive was the explicit desire on the part of General Arnold to have the committee come up with a prediction as to when the progressive destruction of the "German war effort" due to strategic bombardment would allow for a successful land invasion of the European continent. In order to predict when this future event might occur, the committee would necessarily have to undertake a detailed, systematic evaluation of German war-making capacity. Predicting decisive events brought about by strategic bombing would come to be part of most AAF directives for analyses and evaluations of the German and Japanese war efforts during World War II. The imperative for predicting decisive events would also set the precedent for the Strategic Bombing Survey's historical counterfactual speculation about events that did not occur in the past.

COA members never questioned the American conceptual approach to strategic bombing. Their evaluation of the effects of AAF strategic bombing attacks on Germany, their target recommendations, and their predictions were grounded in the American conception. The committee's preliminary report argued that it was better to use strategic bombers to attack a "few really essential industries or services" rather than cause a minor amount of destruction to many industries. According to this early report, critical targets, once selected, should be attacked with "relentless determination," which would probably cause "grave injury" to German war-making capacity.[44]

The COA did not consider German morale a target. Their analysis was directed at evaluating the effects of strategic bombing on Germany's "economic system." Likewise, when they later studied the potential effectiveness of "urban area attacks" against Japan, it was in the context of overall war production, not morale.[45] The committee analyzed the impact of British area attacks on German cities, but only insofar as those area attacks related to the industrial targets that American strategic bombers were attacking.[46] The COA's dismissal of German morale as a target reflected the American emphasis on attacking industrial targets, and it demonstrated a continuing desire on the part of airmen to separate themselves from British morale attacks on German cities.[47]

General Arnold's request for a prediction as to when strategic bombing attacks would reduce German war-making capacity to a point where a land invasion would be possible drew an ambiguous response from the committee. Perera's group stated that they could not give a "precise answer to this question." But they went on to say that the destruction of a number of key targets "would gravely impair and might paralyze the Western Axis war effort. . . . In view of the ability of adequate and properly utilized air power to impair the industrial sources of the enemy's military strength, only the most vital considerations should be permitted to delay or divert the application of an adequate air striking force to this task."[48] On the one hand, the committee would not offer General Arnold a firm date for a land invasion made possible by strategic bombing. Yet on the other hand, the committee concluded strongly that at some point in the future, with relentless determination and dedication of resources, American strategic bombers "might" produce the result the general desired.

IV

Various agencies working for and within the AAF would produce more studies evaluating the effects of strategic bombing on the ability of Germany and Japan to continue fighting. Indeed the Committee of Operations Analysts recommended to General Arnold that "there should be a continuing evaluation of the effectiveness of air attack on enemy industrial and economic objectives in all theatres for the information of the appropriate authorities charged with the allocation of air strength."[49]

Mirroring the work of the Committee of Operations Analysts was the Economic Objectives Unit (EOU) of the Office of Special Services (OSS) in Europe. In late 1942, during the early days of the American strategic bombing campaign against Germany, the EOU began to develop detailed intelligence on critical elements of the enemy's war economy. As the bombing campaign progressed, so did the work of the EOU in assisting the Eighth Air Force, and later, the United States Strategic Air Forces (USSTAF) in target selection for operations over France and Germany.[50]

The EOU also took part in the debate over the best employment of air power to support the upcoming D-Day landings in Normandy. USSTAF Commander General Carl Spaatz believed that the optimal approach would be to use his strategic air forces to bomb oil facilities in Germany, which, as he believed, would provide air superiority over the Normandy beach landings by grounding the German air force. Others, however, wanted Spaatz's bombers to attack German tactical targets that could quickly interdict the Allied landings. General Dwight D. Eisenhower decided in favor of using USSTAF bombers to hit tactical targets; this decision went against the recommendation of EOU members, who argued that the role of the strategic bomber was to attack the vital centers of "German military strength."[51]

EOU analysts were thus in line with the AAF's approach to strategic bombing. One such analyst, Major Walt W. Rostow, argued that "in strategic bombing the enemy consists of the vast structure of economic and civil life which supports the military effort." The way to attack the "enemy structure" was to hit small segments of the "vital elements" in great detail. Indeed, Rostow noted that the "weighing of alternative target systems was the essence of the problem of air planning." Rostow and other EOU personnel would later help the AAF organize and train the USSBS.[52]

Another study group brought together by the AAF back in Washington, D.C., was the Committee of Historians (COH). In late 1943,

General Arnold asked the committee to evaluate the effects of allied bombings on German war potential and morale and to determine whether or not Germany "could be bombed out of the war during the first three months of 1944." General Arnold desired the committee's report to be a "completely objective study, from a civilian and not a military point of view."[53] What made this study significant was not so much the instructions, which followed along the same lines as those given to the COA for its evaluations, as the historians who made up the committee and the conclusions that they produced. They included some of America's leading historians in the fields of American and European history: Carl L. Becker, professor of European history at Cornell University; Henry S. Commager, professor of American and European history at Columbia University; Edward Mead Earle, member of the COA, special AAF advisor, and scholar at the Institute for Advanced Studies at Princeton University; Louis Gottschalk and Bernadotte Schmitt, professors of history at the University of Chicago; and Dumas Malone of Harvard University.[54]

Their report, "Germany's War Potential, December 1943: An Appraisal," was different in its analytical approach and assumptions from those written by groups like the COA that preceded it and the Strategic Bombing Survey that would follow. In his directive to the committee, General Arnold wanted the historians to examine secret and confidential intelligence material to evaluate the "effect of Allied bombings . . . on Germany and German morale and attempt to appraise future developments under continuation of Allied military and economic pressure."[55] But in the transmittal letter that accompanied the historians' completed report to General Arnold, they stated forthrightly that

> their conclusions were based primarily upon the information and opinions to which they had access. The committee was acutely aware of various inadequacies and gaps in the information the members would greatly like to have had. The members recognize that there are intangibles and imponderables in war which cannot be assessed but which may be more nearly decisive than any of the purely military, economic, or psychological factors now apparent. Not all the truth

can be discerned in even the best intelligence reports, since we always operate through the "fog of war."[56]

Here the historians were distinguishing themselves from the industrial experts that predominantly made up the other target selection and evaluation agencies. Historians, by nature, usually allow for complexity and uncertainty in their analysis: When can the historian ever collect "all" the evidence on a given historical problem? Physical scientists, conversely, operate differently in that "all" the facts—or at least all the necessary representative facts—pertaining to a given line of inquiry can usually be gathered and systematic conclusions can thus follow based on those facts.[57]

In a series of meetings held between the committee and members of the Office of Special Services (OSS) and the Office of War Information (OWI) from October to November 1943, the historians wrestled with problems of evidence. In one such session a representative from the OSS, Hajo Holborn, presented his agency's findings on the effects of bombing on German morale. But Louis Gottschalk was concerned about the evidence that Holborn was presenting to the committee. The historian argued that if his committee was going to try and evaluate the effects of bombing on the enemy, then they needed "some notion of what it is that creates a fact and some notion of how you measure that fact."[58] And the committee members realized that once they determined what exactly the facts were, they still would be unable to collect and analyze "all of the facts." Since General Arnold had given them only about two months to complete their report, there simply was not enough time.[59]

Not only did the historians chafe under the deadline imposed on them, they also had to deal with security restrictions on classified evidence. The chairman of the committee, Major Frank Monaghan, told the historians that there was no question concerning the "loyalty, integrity or the discretion of any member." But Monaghan pointed out to them that their evidence was still of a classified nature. He then went on to remind them that "professors have a habit of speaking (and more or less widely) their opinions."[60]

In their final study of 18 January 1944, the Committee of Historians expressed their opinion to General Arnold that by its nature modern war using strategic bombers was filled with imponderables that could "not be assessed." The historians acknowledged that they could evaluate the effects of strategic bombing on certain German economic, military, and political factors. Yet they also realized that the relationship between cause and effect in war (in their report the cause being strategic bombing attacks on Germany and the effect being Germany's possible surrender) was filled with complexity and nuance, and in its essence impossible to determine.

The historians also differed from other AAF agencies in their methodological approach to evaluating the effects of strategic bombing. The COA, for example, broke its members down into analytical subsections that reflected the American emphasis on attacking "vital links" in the enemy's industrial structure.[61] The Committee of Historians not only studied strategic bombing's impact on German military and economic factors (like the COA), but also included a systematic analysis of its effect on the German political situation and on German morale, areas that the COA did not address.

Analyzing the German economy, the historians stated that it was "suffering from critical shortages and qualitative deterioration of consumer goods—the result both of a rigid war economy and of devastating air attacks." Even though Allied air attacks had greatly damaged the German consumer economy, the report argued that the deterioration did not "extend to essential war materials; at no point has direct war production suffered a crippling blow." Even so, the German military and civilian economy had "reached and passed its peak." But because "the German people are totally mobilized for total war and therefore possess an element of strength which has not yet been achieved," as they put it, strategic bombing attacks had yet to produce conditions in Germany that would allow for an early termination of the war.[62]

When considering the impact of strategic bombing on Nazi political control over the German people, the historians asked whether or not the Nazi government was "likely to collapse from internal weakness." The committee members acknowledged two relevant facts. The first was that there was "no widespread desire in Germany to get rid of the Nazi Government." Second, argued the historians, even if such a desire existed, "no organized power except the Army could get rid of it." They thus concluded that "there is no conclusive evidence that British and American bombings of German cities have effectively weakened the general hold of the Nazi Government on the German people."[63]

If the committee downplayed the decisive effects of strategic bombing on the German economy and political situation, it viewed attacks on morale with much greater optimism. During the sessions on evidence with the OSS and the OWI, discussion was almost always centered on the effects of bombing on the individual and collective morale of the German people. In their final report to General Arnold, when considering the impact of the British area attack on Hamburg in July 1943, the historians admitted that its psychological effects could not yet "be fully measured, but bombing of this scope and intensity is already producing a situation in which fear of the consequences of continuing the war is becoming greater than fear of the consequences of defeat." The report argued that even though the limits of endurance of the German people had not been reached, "the German will to resist, already subjected to the cumulative effect of years of strain, is almost certain to be broken as the result of intensified mass bombing, and further defeats on land, at sea, and in the air."[64]

It was the committee's focus on the effects of bombing on morale that infuriated airmen like General Laurence Kuter, the assistant chief of staff for plans. In a memorandum to General Arnold, Kuter recommended that the historians' report be returned "for filing," to keep it from getting to President Roosevelt's desk. In a shrill comment General Kuter told General Arnold that what he received was a "cold, unimaginative report by professional historians." Kuter then drove straight to the crux of the difference between the airmen's conceptual approach to strategic bombing and the conclusions drawn by the Committee of Historians in their final report:

> [The historians'] approach, one of housing, morale, and manpower, makes operations by the RAF Bomber Command their principal interest, considers only specific factories known to be smashed. Very little consideration is given to the intricate industrial and economic machine behind the German effort and dislocation that must have been caused when obscure ex-sewing machine factories, etc., have been hit. Had the full utilization of the bombardment offensive been directed against vital targets such as aircraft, ball-bearing, rubber and oil production, the German position today would have been extremely critical.[65]

With the airmen's focus on the use of strategic bombers to attack "industrial systems" and the historians' emphasis on enemy morale and political decision making, they were both, in a sense, talking past each other.

But even more troubling to Kuter than the focus on morale and the British area bombings of cities was the central thesis to the historians' forty-two page report: even though morale attacks held the greatest possibility for strategic bombing, there was still "no substantial evidence that Germany [could] be bombed out of the war during the early months of 1944. The final collapse of Germany requires large-scale invasion operations against the continent of Europe." Germany would then "be unable to maintain a prolonged resistance to Anglo-American ground operations or to prevent the complete destruction of her industries, her cities and her communications by aerial bombardment." But the decisive event that would create the conditions inside of Germany to compel surrender would be the land invasion of the European continent, argued the historians.[66]

This was not the conclusion that either General Kuter or General Arnold wanted to hear, because it placed air power fundamentally as an adjunct, or supporting arm, to ground power. In fact Edward Mead Earle, who had been overseeing the historians' work, complained that the historians had been "one big headache" to him. Their final report, lamented Earle, was "highly unsatisfactory" to him and also to General Arnold.[67] Although General Arnold agreed with the overall Allied strategy that called for an invasion of the European continent, he along with the senior ground commanders maintained the lingering hope that air power alone could force Germany to surrender.[68] General Arnold also asked the Committee of Historians to compare the condition of Germany in 1943 with that of Germany in 1918 on the eve of its surrender in World War I. Perhaps he was trying to find a historical precedent for the surrender of a major power in war before its home territory was invaded.[69] The historians, however, concluded rather bluntly that the German surrender of 1918 afforded "no real analogy with the present military situation" of Germany.[70]

In his cover memorandum to President Roosevelt that went along with the historians' report, General Arnold made a subtle but important change to their conclusion. General Arnold in fact tried to salvage from the report the notion that there was still a possibility of forcing German surrender without a land invasion, a possibility that the historians thoroughly argued against. General Arnold agreed with the committee's conclusion that Germany could "not be bombed out of the war in the next three months" but added that

> surrender will come when, through lack of adequate air defense, Germany finds herself unable to maintain resistance to ground operations or prevent destruction by aerial bombardment of her industries, cities, and communications. . . . I believe the report tends to confirm our essential theses of the use and effect of air power and our own findings as to the results of operations to date.[71]

By stating that surrender would come about *either* when Germany was unable to resist ground operations (a land invasion of Germany) *or* when it could no longer stop destruction of its "cities, industry, and communications" by strategic bombardment, General Arnold subtly, but profoundly, changed the conclusion of the historians. They argued conversely that the land invasion was a necessary condition for Germany's surrender. Strategic bombing, according to the historians, had to be coupled with a land invasion of the European continent to force German capitulation. Strategic bombing was not, therefore, a discrete option along with a land invasion,

either of which might force Germany to surrender, as General Arnold contended in his letter to the president.[72]

Historian David MacIsaac, author of the only book-length study of the Strategic Bombing Survey (1976), praised the Survey for doing "a good job" in its evaluation of strategic bombing in World War II, but its analysis, according to MacIsaac, would have benefited "from the presence in their councils" of a historian like Carl Becker.[73] There is subtle irony here. When writing his book MacIsaac apparently was not aware that in January 1944, just a few months before the bureaucratic wheels would start to turn establishing the Survey, General Arnold received an analysis by Carl Becker and other distinguished historians that examined the same problems the Survey would later address. Yet the report by the Committee of Historians was brushed into the dustbin of the past because it contained just what MacIsaac later argued the Survey needed: "The presence of a questioning and persuasive historian [who would] have had the effect of bringing into better balance the collection and interpretation of evidence . . . [who was] never very sure that he [could] discern the complicated relationships between cause and effect. . . ."[74] In short, the historian would have recognized the existence of imponderables in evidence and analysis, as did Carl Becker and his fellow members on the committee.

The AAF, however, wanted its civilian experts to produce target recommendations, predictions, and evaluations of strategic bombing that used scientific "calipers" instead of historical analysis.[75] "Calipers" grasped the imponderables of strategic bombing, took them apart, and discerned from them cause and effect. Historical analysis, like the one produced by the Committee of Historians, acknowledged the existence of imponderables but allowed them to remain intact. The civilian experts who would come to fill the analytical positions in the United States Strategic Bombing Survey, being fully in line with the American conceptual approach to strategic bombing, adopted the "caliper" framework of analysis for their evaluation of American strategic bombing in World War II.

CHAPTER 2

The United States Strategic Bombing Survey and the Future of the Air Force

> We can be sure that this concept will not be accepted by the nations of the world unless air power proves itself during the course of this war.
>
> FRANK M. ANDREWS, March 1943

> Our entire future air policy might well be determined from the [Survey's] report.
>
> LAURENCE KUTER, April 1944

Establishing the facts that proved the effectiveness of American air power in World War II would lay the foundation for a postwar independent air force. Senior AAF leaders like Major General Laurence Kuter, the assistant chief of staff for plans, therefore, committed themselves to proving the efficacy of air power through a civilian-led, scientific evaluation of the American strategic bombing effort against Germany. Civilian experts would be able to tackle the complex problems of strategic target analysis that the airmen were unable to grasp while at the same time providing an aura of objectivity in their evaluation. But the conclusions of an evaluation of such importance would have to vindicate, not discredit, the use of American strategic air power in World War II, if the airmen were to use it to justify a postwar policy that embraced an independent air force.

In November 1944, Secretary of War Henry Stimson made an

official request to Franklin D'Olier, the president of Prudential Life Insurance, to become the chairman of the United States Strategic Bombing Survey, a large organization that would conduct a "scientific investigation of all the evidence" of strategic bombing in the European theater and help to evaluate "the importance and potentialities of air power as an instrument of military strategy, for planning the future development of the U.S. Air Forces, and for determining future economic policies with respect to the national defense."[1] Secretary Stimson, in his letter to D'Olier, wanted the Survey to evaluate the fundamental relevance of strategic bombing in warfare and national defense policy. But during the course of its lengthy evaluation of American strategic bombing in Europe, the Survey did not question the relevance of air power but only assessed the degree of strategic bombing's effectiveness.[2]

From March to November 1944, AAF officers shaped the questions that the Survey would answer and constructed an organizational framework that reflected the American strategic bombing emphasis on attacking national economic structures. By the time Survey directors like lawyer George Ball, financier Paul Nitze, and economist John Kenneth Galbraith began their evaluation in early 1945, the AAF had already established the parameters for an evaluation of strategic bombing. Those parameters would fundamentally shape the conclusions that the Strategic Bombing Survey would reach in its evaluation of the effectiveness of strategic bombing against Germany (and later, Japan). A truly impartial and unbiased report, therefore, was never really a possibility.

I

In May 1944, Edward Mead Earle, special consultant to General Arnold and the AAF, toured the European theater of operations discussing operational and strategic problems with AAF commanders. Earle had been a member of the Committee of Operations Analysts and the Committee of Historians and by mid-1944 was an influential civilian analyst within the AAF.[3] During the tour, Earle met with Major General F. L. Anderson and Colonel Robert Hughes of the United States Strategic Air Forces (USSTAF). Hughes, a senior intelligence officer for the command, told Earle that target selection was a continuing challenge and he was convinced that military people were not properly qualified to conduct that kind of analysis; it was a job for civilian experts.

USSTAF's deputy commander for operations, General Anderson, also pointed out to Earle that he was very eager to establish a civilian-led group that would evaluate the effects of strategic bombing. Such a study, according to Anderson, was "important for a variety of reasons: for the historical record [and] for the guidance of the air staff in the formulation of overall policies during the rest of the war and during the post war period."[4]

Anderson in fact had been part of the early planning for the Survey that began back in March and April within AAF headquarters in Washington, D.C., and England. Lieutenant Colonel James B. Ames, assistant to General Anderson, proposed on 28 March that once hostilities in Europe had ceased there should be an "intensive survey in Germany and occupied countries of the results achieved by the Combined Bomber Offensive."[5] In Washington, D.C., a similar proposal appeared on the desk of the assistant chief of air staff for intelligence, Brigadier General Thomas D. White. One of White's intelligence assistants, Major Ralph A. Colbert, recommended to the general on 27 March that plans should be drawn up for a commission of experts to "conduct an investigation inside Germany which will disclose the true facts concerning the Strategic Aerial Bombardment of Europe and, on the basis of such facts, to prepare a report analyzing the accomplishments and potentialities of Air Power as an independent instrument of military policy."[6] These two memorandums initiated a series of letters, more memorandums, and proposals between senior AAF leaders and the Joint Chiefs for a scientific evaluation of the effects of strategic bombing against Germany that would culminate in the official establishment in November 1944 of the United States Strategic Bombing Survey.

The documentary record of the roots of the Survey can be traced back to the memos of Ames and Colbert, but its intellectual origins go back much further. The Survey's chronicler, Major James Beveridge, argued (most likely based on contemporaneous interviews with air force officers) that discussions had been occurring informally at AAF headquarters in England and on the European continent prior to the first two memorandums.[7] The notion of an expert evaluation of strategic bombing was nothing new for the AAF. It was not a radical departure and it did not surprise anyone. Airmen had been using civilian experts to make strategic target recommendations and evaluate AAF operations prior to and during the war. The Strategic Bombing Survey was a logical and natural continuation of this concept.[8]

Airmen like Hap Arnold and Carl Spaatz put forward the idea that having a civilian in charge would insure that the Survey's report would "be received as an unbiased and completely impartial study based solely on fact and not on opinion." Because of its great importance, Spaatz argued, "careful consideration should be given to the selection of the head of this committee." According to Spaatz, the AAF should try to find "a well-known American publisher, jurist, or university president" for the post.[9] A civilian-led, impartial study became the leitmotif of the AAF because its conclusions would ostensibly have an air of objectivity that could be used to support the postwar crusade for an independent air force.

In the main, the Survey would accomplish three goals for the AAF: first, it would serve as the AAF's primary historical record that would help it establish postwar independence and lay the foundations for future air policy and theory; second, it would determine the effects of strategic bombing on Germany's war-making capacity; and last, it would yield lessons that could be applied to the strategic air campaign against Japan.

General Arnold proposed to the Joint Chiefs of Staff that the Survey ought to determine the facts and lessons learned from German experience so that they "may be applied without delay to the strategic bombardment of Japan. . . ."[10] Because the air campaign against the

Japanese home islands was still in its early stages in mid-1944, any relevant lessons learned from the European theater could prove helpful in the war against Japan.[11] But the AAF had other evaluation agencies like the COA to conduct those types of studies, many of which demonstrated that there were differences between the industrial structures of Germany and Japan. There would be limits, therefore, to the usefulness of the German experience for fighting Japan.[12]

But the need for applying the lessons learned in Germany against Japan did, however, give the Survey a sense of wartime urgency. General Spaatz agreed with General Arnold in June that the airmen should "stress the time factor and the operational requirements of the war against Japan, leaving until later the detailed evaluations and sifting of evidence that will be necessary for the formulation of future Air Force doctrine." In this way, General Kuter noted to Spaatz, the airmen could avoid "lengthy debate along abstract lines."[13]

By setting aside the "issue" of postwar air force doctrine, and the desire to avoid debate along "abstract lines," Kuter, Arnold, and Spaatz implicitly recognized the potential for controversy over the application of Survey results. They knew that if the AAF presented the Survey primarily as a way to establish the need for postwar independence, it could lose its urgency. The Army, and especially the navy, would criticize the AAF for being more concerned with the future of the air force than with victory.

Other airmen also understood that the controlling reason for creating the Survey would be to use its results for the future of the air force. General Anderson told General Spaatz that the Survey's results "might well prove to be the foundation of our future doctrine on the employment of air power." Spaatz, using the same language as Anderson, told Arnold that the Survey would have a profound influence on the "future employment of air power." Arnold agreed with Spaatz, and by June had recognized the "ever increasing importance" of the Survey.[14] Airmen below Spaatz and Arnold appreciated the Survey's potential for establishing the theoretical base for a future independent air force. The assistant chief of staff for personnel, Colonel John H. McCormick, pointed out to General Kuter:

> Although a survey of results of the Combined Bomber Offensive appears highly desirable with respect to post war air policy, this office questions its advisability with respect to future offensives in the Japanese theater for several reasons: The full weight of the Air Force will be thrown against Japan regardless of the relative value of strategical bombing [against Germany].

McCormick's report went on to lament how the Survey would draw away manpower from other AAF missions.[15] Yet the thrust of his argument to Kuter was emblematic of the desire of senior AAF officers to use the Survey's results as a tool for creating a postwar independent air force.

II

The Americans, however, would have to conduct their survey separately from the British, who were also creating an organization to evaluate the effects of strategic bombing against Germany. The British wanted the Americans to conduct a joint investigation of the Combined Bomber Offensive carried out by the RAF and AAF.[16] But differences with the British over bombing doctrines and the desire by the American airmen to use the Survey's results for postwar defense policy kept both countries from conducting a joint evaluation. For the Americans, a joint U.S./British survey would end up as a "mark of self-justification" for Britain's own bombing methods and target selection.[17]

The notion of comparing the effects of RAF area bombing and American precision bombing permeated the early correspondence between air officers considering the objectives for the Survey. General Thomas D. White, the assistant chief of staff for intelligence, put it rather bluntly when he recommended to Kuter that the Survey should determine "the respective contributions of the USAAF precision bombing and the RAF area bombing to the result[s] achieved."[18] General Spaatz was beginning to sense in May growing pressure from the British to establish a joint survey rather than separate endeavors. Spaatz told Arnold:

> In the last few days, there have been growing indications that the British may press for a combined U.S.-British post-hostilities investigation of the bombing results. My view is that we should resist any such pressure, whether brought to bear over here, or in Washington through the Combined Chiefs of Staff or otherwise. In my opinion, the investigation we propose should be set up as a completely independent American survey, staffed from American personnel from top to bottom.

By the end of May, Spaatz had come to an agreement with the British that would allow the British and the Americans to share data but conduct independent evaluations. The reason, according to General Spaatz, was obvious: "The whole purpose of the American survey is to arrive at the plain facts upon which our future air force doctrines, both tactical and strategic, can be based. These doctrines will be an essential ingredient of our national defense policy. A complete community of interest in the survey and its results cannot be assured to exist between ourselves and any other country."[19]

American airmen perceived a fundamental difference between the AAF's precision bombing and the RAF's area bombing. The AAF used its strategic bombers in Europe for the precise destruction of specific industrial targets.[20] The RAF, conversely, had developed a different doctrine of strategic bombing. By 1942, the RAF was committed to using strategic bombers to attack German morale directly by bombing large areas of German cities.[21] A reporter asked General Ira Eaker, commanding general of the Eighth Bomber Command in Europe, about the apparent opposite approaches to bombing practiced by the RAF and AAF. The general responded by arguing that both RAF and AAF bombing doctrines were in harmony, because as he put it: "There are two ways to win a war. One is to break the enemy's will to fight and the other is to remove his means of waging war. Either way wins a war. Use both and you do it much quicker." Implicit in Eaker's response was that British area bombing directly attacked the will to resist while American precision bombing attacked the means of making war. Although the RAF and AAF were working together to attack Germany by air, they were carrying out two fundamentally different doctrines of air power, according to Eaker.[22]

As the war progressed in Europe, the AAF conducted limited area attacks against the German war economy (and later, on a much larger scale, against Japan). The RAF, beginning in 1942, also used area bombing to attack the enemy's war economy, but its primary purpose was to undermine the morale of the German population, specifically the industrial workers.[23] When American airmen themselves conducted area raids, they understood those raids to be a *method* of using strategic bombers to attack the war-making capacity of the enemy, which was the *objective* of the attacks. In the American conception, area or precision attacks would ideally also lower the morale of the enemy population, but morale was not the primary objective for precision or area bombing, according to American airmen.[24] Strategic Bombing Survey analysts would carry out this conception in their analytical approach and published reports.

III

In the earliest correspondence within the AAF over the primary questions that the Survey should answer, senior airmen posited that the Survey ought to determine the overall relevance of air power as a means of modern war. The Survey would provide the country with an evaluation of the "potentialities of Air Power as an independent instrument of military strategy."[25] But once the airmen began to think through the questions that the Survey would address, the relevance of air power to military strategy was never really challenged. Instead, they began to construct an organization designed to evaluate the effectiveness of strategic bombing against German war-making capacity. The airmen were confident that the level of destruction visited on Germany by American bombers would provide ample grounds for a positive evaluation of the AAF's performance during the war.

A few months prior to the Normandy landings, General Kuter directed the Deputy Air Chiefs of Staff to submit questions concerning strategic bombing that the Survey should try to answer.[26] The agencies responding to the request emphasized in their proposed questions that the Survey should direct its evaluation toward studying the effects of strategic bombing on the economic structure of Germany.

The Economic Objectives Unit (EOU) pointed out that an important objective for the Survey would be to determine "repair times for damaged processes [and] the ability of German producers to pool output in to damaged 'complexes' and continue production at a reduced level. . . ." It also addressed directly the fundamental question about the relevance of air power to national defense policy. The Survey might, according to the EOU, "eventually lead to the formulation of answers to the wider question: has the allocation of resources by the United States to air power been justified. . . ." But the EOU concluded that this "more ambitious undertaking," which could lead to "broad historical and even sociological speculation, should, in our view, be subsidiary to the initial more limited and definitive task."[27] That limited task would be to evaluate the degree of strategic bombing's effectiveness against the German war economy.

The airmen certainly recognized the possibility that a Survey evaluation could be very critical of the AAF's strategic bombing efforts against Germany. To the airmen, the prize that the Survey would produce for them would be justification, in the form of Survey evidence, for a postwar independent air force. The airmen, therefore, did not want the Survey to answer the question of whether or not there should be an independent air force. As a result, they left alone the "more ambitious undertaking" of questioning the relevance of air power to national strategy and focused instead on strategic bombing's effectiveness. Moreover, the airmen were confident that a group of civilian industrialists and economists serving as Survey analysts would undoubtedly find plenty of positive evidence of the effectiveness of the AAF strategic bombing campaign against German war-making capacity. That is why in so many of the letters, memorandums, and directives establishing the Survey, the airmen often noted that the Survey would bring out "the accomplishments and potentialities of Air Power as an independent instrument of military strategy."[28] The Survey would do this by evaluating the effects of strategic bombing on the German war economy.

Once the Joints Chiefs of Staff had formed the Joint Target Group (JTG) in the fall of 1944, it too provided Survey planners with a set of questions that it desired to have answered concerning the effectiveness of strategic bombing. Since the JTG's purpose was to provide centralized strategic target planning for the AAF in the Far East, it appreciated the opportunity for a "scientific evaluation of the effectiveness of air attack under battle conditions against strategic targets" that could be applied to "target selection and damage assessment in the Far Eastern Theater." The JTG was most interested in a comparative study of American precision attacks and RAF area attacks against German cities. The JTG wanted the Survey to determine the "loss of production in plants and industries from precision attacks by U.S. Strategic Air Forces [and the] loss of production from RAF area attacks."[29]

Although the JTG did not ask the Survey to study strategic bombing effects on German morale, other AAF agencies did. But interestingly, they wanted the Survey to study morale not in terms of the collective will to resist of the German people, or the political will of the Nazis to continue fighting under strategic bombing attacks. Instead they thought the Survey should determine how lowered morale among individual German workers affected Germany's war economy. The AAF's air inspector, for example, wanted to know "what effect strategic and tactical bombing had upon morale as it affected war production." When recommending the types of civilian experts that should man the Survey, the air inspector called for a number of sociologists "to study the effect of bombing on the capacity of families to productively work in industry."[30] Although AAF agencies would often include more general questions about the effects of strategic bombing on the German will to resist, when it came to the details of the proposed analysis, the effects of strategic bombing on morale were usually understood in terms of war production.[31]

Throughout the summer months and into the fall of 1944 the appointed executive director of the Survey, Colonel Theodore J. Koenig (assigned by General Kuter in July to do the preliminary organizational planning), took the questions from the various agencies, along with the recommendations from General Spaatz, and designed the core of what would become the organizational structure of the Strategic Bombing Survey. By September, Koenig envisioned the Survey as consisting of five evaluation divisions: physical damage, strategic operations, economics, political and morale, and military analysis.[32] Although this organizational structure would undergo a few more modifications as the Survey began its work in early 1945, the basic structure would remain as Koenig had planned it.[33]

IV

Koenig and his assistant, Major Thomas D. Upton, had wrestled with the many objectives and questions circulating within AAF headquarters since April 1944, trying to bring together the most important ones that supported the organizational structure they devised. Upton had prepared an extensive review of the proposed questions and objectives for Koenig. According to Upton, the primary purpose of the Survey would be to study the "overall effects of strategic bombing in the industrial, economic, political, and military fields, with a view towards evaluating the relative importance of strategic bombing in the sphere of military operations as a whole." Secondary objectives would include the more detailed evaluations of the effectiveness of precision versus area bombing in destroying the German capacity to wage war and the correctness of target selection and damage assessment methodology. But without the aim of evaluating the relevance of strategic bombing to military strategy, it would be unrealistic, according to Upton, to get the president to appoint "a well known, impartial, public figure to head the survey committee and write the report. Any lesser objective than this would fail to give proper weight to both the historical importance of such a survey and its importance in the long term formulation of Air Force policy."[34]

Downplaying Upton's emphasis on the Survey's overarching goal and demonstrating a shrewd understanding of what his AAF leaders wanted, Koenig argued that the Survey, once it began its evaluation, should not pursue the broader question of the relevance of air power to military strategy. Instead, the Survey should confine itself to "an intensive survey of bombing effects," and not a "lengthy study of the war, and the part of the AAF in it."[35]

A formal, written request to authorize the Strategic Bombing Survey may have reached President Roosevelt in the form of a memorandum, written by General Spaatz, for General Arnold's signature on 20 April 1944, recommending "an intensive survey, in Germany and German occupied countries, of the results achieved by the Combined Bomber Offensive."[36] General Arnold on one hand admitted that the "air forces will be dependent on the results of the proposed study." But on the other hand he proclaimed:

> I do not propose in any way to attempt to influence the conclusions of the [Survey] and I believe they should be strong enough to resist any partisan influence, that may be brought to bear upon them. What I want is to get at the facts, and if mistakes have been made in the past, I want to know about them, so that we can be even more effective in the future. . . . In order to guarantee that the report of the [Survey] will be received as an unbiased and completely impartial study based solely on fact and not opinion, I am most anxious to have as the head of the [Survey] some outstanding American civilian, whose reputation for impartiality and good judgment is beyond question.[37]

General Arnold's proposed memorandum encapsulates the dilemma that senior airmen faced when they were establishing the Survey: How do you create a truly impartial study of strategic bombing when you are taking deliberate steps to shape the conclusions that the Survey would reach?

Framing the questions that the Survey would answer and then setting up an organizational structure designed to answer those questions would indeed influence its conclusions. (Consider the markedly different approach that General Arnold took when he allowed the Committee of Historians to evaluate the effects of strategic bombing without an established organization for its analysis.) But as General Arnold acknowledged in his memorandum to the president, the future of the AAF was bound up in the Survey's results, and therefore it had to have a strong aura of impartiality. An aura was enough, however: the airmen never wanted the Survey to question the relevance of strategic bombing to military strategy.

Survey director George Ball, in his memoirs, confirmed that the Survey's "frame of reference" was limited to studying the effect of the American "air offensive on the Germany economy."[38] Paul Nitze would later point out that his and the Survey's task in regard to strategic bombing "was to measure precisely the physical effects and other effects as well, to put calipers on it. . . . I was trying to put quantitative numbers on something that was considered immeasurable."[39] The Survey would be able to make imponderables ponderable by limiting its analysis to the effectiveness of strategic bombing against German war-making capacity, exactly what the airmen wanted.

President Roosevelt sent a letter to Secretary Stimson on 9 September 1944 formally requesting that he organize a study of the Combined Bomber Offensive; its value, according to the president, "depends on the quality and impartiality of the group selected to make the study. . . ."[40] About two months later, on 3 November, Stimson in turn sent a formal request to Franklin D'Olier asking him, "pursuant to the President's letter [of 9 September]," to head "an impartial and expert study of the effects of our aerial attack on Germany and report thereon." D'Olier agreed, and the Survey was officially under way.[41]

V

Franklin D'Olier, president of Prudential Life Insurance and first national commander of the American Legion, however, was not the first choice for chairman of the Survey. Arnold and Spaatz had initially tried to get Harvard University president and National Defense Research Committee member James B. Conant to take the post.[42] Conant declined because Vannevar Bush, director of the Office of Scientific Research and Development, would not approve his release.[43] Other prominent civilians considered by Arnold and Spaatz were *New York Times* publisher Arthur Sulzberger; Donald David, dean of the Harvard Business School; Robert Sproul, president of the University of California; and Karl T. Compton of MIT.[44] They all declined for various reasons. Some may have turned down the job out of doubts about the very impartiality the senior airmen were claiming. John Kenneth Galbraith, who would become head of the Economic Division of the Survey in February 1945, explained after the war that a certain Harvard professor who was working for the Office of Strategic Services (OSS) in England advised against taking the post because he thought the air force would make a "heavy-handed" attempt to influence the results of the Survey.[45] Some of the civilians who were offered the position of chairman may have declined owing to these reasons; others probably did so because they had more pressing concerns at the time. By late October, the AAF ended up with Franklin D'Olier, number 15 on their list of prospects.[46]

Although appointed as chairman of the Survey, D'Olier would remain, as George Ball described him, only its "nominal leader." Galbraith politely referred to D'Olier as an "amiable figurehead."[47] For the day-to-day running of the Survey once it began operations,

D'Olier would come to rely heavily on his vice-chairman (and de facto head), New York banker and lawyer Henry Alexander. D'Olier would not make any meaningful intellectual contributions to the Survey's work. That would be done by key Survey directors like Ball, Galbraith, Alexander, and Nitze, and the many civilian and military experts who would fill the Survey's ranks and carry out the evaluation of strategic bombing.[48]

For its civilian experts, the AAF wanted individuals who had a strong scientific or industrial background. After the experience that General Arnold and Edward Mead Earle had had with the Committee of Historians in late 1943, it was no wonder that historians were not considered for positions on the Survey's staff (except for the Survey's chronicler, Major James Beveridge). Instead, the Survey sought experts who had experience "in economic research and analysis, and with either a college background indicating work in this field and/or research experience with an organization like the National Bureau of Economic Research . . . or other groups occupied with the collection and analysis of data in the economic and industrial field."[49] Civilian experts with a strong background in economics and industry would fit comfortably into the organizational structure that the airmen had constructed for the Survey's analysis. They could be counted on to provide a "scientific evaluation of all the facts" without the "headaches" that the Committee of Historians had given to General Arnold when they conducted their evaluation of strategic bombing a year earlier.

Colonel Guido R. Perera, an original COA member and an elite Boston lawyer before the war, would be instrumental in influencing Chairman D'Olier in selecting the division directors and in making modifications to the organizational structure that Koenig had set up. Perera first met D'Olier in late October in Washington, D.C. Perera, along with another COA analyst, Major W. Barton Leach (formerly a professor of law at Harvard University), recommended to D'Olier that the Survey be divided into eight to ten analytical divisions that closely paralleled those of the COA. Perera also made suggestions to D'Olier for the division heads. Most of the men that

Perera recommended he had known before the war or during his time with the COA.[50]

George Ball had worked with Perera on certain COA reports, and in September 1944 the AAF had assigned him to help Major General Jacob E. Fickel's Air Evaluation Board study the operational and tactical aspects of the AAF's strategic bombing campaign against Germany.[51] Prior to his work with the AAF, Ball had served as a legal advisor to Lend-Lease administrator Edward R. Stettinius. From that position Ball moved into the newly formed Foreign Economic Administration and acted as the chief economic advisor for a negotiating mission to Cuba in 1944. With Ball's background in foreign national economies and experience with AAF evaluation projects, Perera and D'Olier considered him an ideal candidate to head the Survey's Transportation Division.[52] Ball accepted and joined the Survey in early November. Duty with the Survey, like his assignment with the Lend-Lease program, provided Ball with a sense of national service and, as he later confided, put him "where the action was."[53]

Another friend of Perera that he and D'Olier wanted as a Survey director was Paul Nitze. Educated at Hotchkiss and then Harvard in economics and sociology, Nitze was part of the elite East Coast patrician class that would eventually supply many of the Survey's directors. Before the war Nitze had been a member of the New York investment firm of Dillon, Read and Company, responsible for some of the company's investments in American electrical power industries. Prior to joining that company, Nitze had worked as an economist for an investment firm in Chicago. Anticipating the work he would later do for the Survey, Nitze in 1929 wrote a report for the firm analyzing the problems with the German economy. By 1944, Nitze had served in various governmental agencies that addressed economic problems created by the war. In October, he accepted the post as director of the Survey's Equipment and Utilities Division.[54]

Perera and D'Olier wanted a talented economist to head the division that would assess the overall effects of strategic bombing on the German economy. After considering a number of names during November and December, on a recommendation from Paul Nitze they decided on economist John Kenneth Galbraith.[55] Prior to joining the Survey in February 1945, Galbraith had served as an economic advisor to the National Defense Advisory Commission and as a director for the Price Division of the Office of Price Administration. Like his fellow directors, Galbraith would bring to his work with the Survey in Europe a "sense of discovery and excitement."[56]

Serving as the Survey's Military Analysis Division director, Major General Orvil Arson Anderson of the AAF saw in the Survey more than just discovery and excitement. Anderson appreciated the opportunity that the Survey provided for laying the groundwork for "the proper development of the future of the Army Air Force," in which he had an "abiding faith" and for which he felt a "consuming ambition."[57] Perera and D'Olier had determined that a high-ranking military officer would be able not only to evaluate the operational aspects of the AAF but to provide instruction to Survey members on the theory and practice of strategic bombing.[58] Anderson had set an altitude record in a balloon in the 1930s, served on the air planning staff with Haywood Hansell in 1941, and flown combat missions as a command pilot over Germany in 1943. Appointed a Survey director in November 1944, Anderson would make a name for himself not so much for his division's published report as for the strong and at times "heavy-handed" influence he would exert on Survey conclusions. The Survey, declared Anderson, should produce not a bunch of "historical examples," but rather conclusions based on an "impartial" study of the facts and looking toward the future of the air force rather than the past.[59]

For the other Survey divisions, Perera and D'Olier selected prominent American industrialists and specialists. Professor Harry F. Bowman of the Drexel Institute of Philadelphia would lead the Physical Damage Division. Psychologist Rensis Likert of the Department of Agriculture would head the Morale Division. An active participant in civil defense issues, Colonel Frank McNamee, Jr., was selected to head the Civil Defense Division. The director of the Aircraft Division would be Theodore P. Wright, vice-president of the Curtiss Wright Aircraft Corporation. The position of Survey secretariat would go to Charles C. Cabot, justice of the Superior Court of Massachusetts.[60]

By mid-November 1944, Perera and D'Olier had brought together an extremely talented group of civilian experts that Orvil Anderson remembered as a "good echelon of men," with a "low order of prejudice," but more important for the general, without "Army ego."[61] The challenge that lay ahead during the remaining two months of 1944 would be to refine the organizational framework that the AAF had established and teach the Survey's hundreds of experts the American way of strategic bombing.

VI

Paul Nitze commented in his memoirs that when he joined the Survey in October 1944, "it was still little more than an organization on paper."[62] Implicit in Nitze's remembrance was that he and the other civilian directors built the Survey from scratch and carried out the purported "impartial" and "unbiased" evaluation of strategic bombing. But the record demonstrates that the Survey was anything but a "paper" organization in October 1944. Senior air officers had spent the preceding seven months establishing the Survey's scope, framing its questions, and building an organizational framework that reflected the AAF's conceptual approach to strategic bombing. Arguing that the Survey was simply an organization on paper trivializes the extensive effort put forth by the AAF to shape the Survey's evaluation.

During the months of November and December 1944, Alexander, Nitze, D'Olier, and Perera met with senior AAF officers to discuss the scope and direction of the Survey's evaluation and learn firsthand the approach that the AAF was taking toward strategic bombing. These meetings produced no radical change from the so-called paper organization that the AAF had already established. In fact, the meetings reinforced the overall approach that the Survey would take toward evaluating the effects of strategic bombing on Germany.

Perera and D'Olier met with General Muir Fairchild on 28 October to discuss the Survey. Since his days teaching strategic bombing courses at ACTS, General Fairchild had become the head of the Joint Strategic Survey Committee, a very respected agency that made broad planning and policy recommendations to the Joint Chiefs of Staff. General Fairchild lectured Perera and D'Olier on the general theory of air power, the evolution of American strategic bombing, and the differences between RAF area attacks and AAF precision bombing. Fairchild declared that the Survey would have to address the effects of strategic bombing on "vital and essential industries; the enemy economy generally; enemy morale; [and] the decision of the German High Command." The Survey's results "might" be of use for the AAF's bombardment of Japan, but its conclusions certainly "would furnish a direct guide to the post-war military organization of the United States," which for Fairchild embraced an independent air force.[63]

About a month after talking with Perera and D'Olier, Fairchild met with Alexander and Nitze. Fairchild explained that he agreed with the two men's plan for the conduct of the Survey. He considered their plan to be "excellent" because it demonstrated a lot of careful thought on their part toward solving the problems that were confronting the Survey. In fact, the general was so pleased with Nitze and Alexander's plan for the Survey that he had "very little in the way of constructive suggestions to offer." Fairchild found little to criticize because Nitze and Alexander had built on the plan the AAF had established prior to November 1944 when the civilian heads joined the Survey. Like the organization "on paper," Nitze and Alexander's Survey would consist of a number of divisions that would analyze the effects of strategic bombing on certain war-time industries and the overall economy and morale, and would determine the value of area versus precision bombing. General Fairchild confirmed that the critical objective of the Survey would be to evaluate the effects of strategic bombing on "industrial structures in general," with the end result being an assessment of "how good" the overall strategic bombing offensive worked against Germany.[64] It was within this conceptual framework that sought to evaluate the relative effectiveness of strategic bombing that Nitze, Alexander, and the others would conduct their evaluation.

While shuttling between Washington, D.C., and London trying to get the Survey under way, Paul Nitze spent a week with Colonel Fred Castle, a wing commander in the Eighth Air Force, learning the concept of strategic bombing as the Americans were practicing it. Nitze had great respect for this combat leader who would eventually lose his life on a bombing mission over Germany. Nitze remembered that Castle enjoyed "educating me on all the manifold problems of his command and also speculating on those of the postwar world, and how the United States might best go about dealing with them." Castle provided Nitze with an essay that he had written, "Airpower in This War and the Following Peace." In the essay, Castle argued that during World War II American air power was being used for "economic-strategic warfare against the heart of the Nazi military system." Castle warned that the United States must not wait too long in drawing conclusions about air power's use in war because it would prove to be "the most important implement of national policy of the future." Castle deeply impressed Nitze with his courage and intellectual capacity.[65] Nitze would take Castle's recommendation to heart; his work with the Survey would be guided by the belief that it would lay the theoretical groundwork for American air power in the future. Nitze later noted in a letter to John Kenneth Galbraith that "almost all discussion on the concepts of the role of air power in general and strategic bombing in particular . . . takes off from the Survey's reports as the one body of authoritative and impartial data and analysis on the subject."[66]

Lectures given to Survey members in London in December 1944 expressed the same notion that the Survey would lay the theoretical groundwork for postwar air power. Hamilton Dearborn, who was a member of the Economic Division's training branch, told new Survey analysts that

> the fundamental, and the most interesting, task of the Strategic Bombing Survey is to lay the foundations for a broad theory of air strategy—to produce the equivalent of Clausewitz on ground warfare, or Mahan on naval warfare. No such theory exists today, and none could be built up without the material which it is the function of the Survey to gather.[67]

Other lectures stressed the importance of understanding the effects of strategic bombing on the industrial capacity of Germany. Major Walter W. Rostow, a Rhodes Scholar and a member of the EOU who would later rise to prominence in various government positions, discussed the history of the AAF in Europe, emphasizing the nature of selecting critical economic target systems for attack.[68]

During these training lectures, Survey instructors emphasized that the Survey would analyze urban area attacks in terms of their effects on the war-making capacity of Germany. Rostow, in the same lecture, posited that an area raid was "a raid in which you set yourself to do a maximum of physical damage of all sorts . . . an area raid is designed to destroy general enemy resources to the maximum extent, and it is for this reason that the center part [of the city] chosen is somewhere where fire will take hold and burn of itself." Another lecturer argued that "the main physical effect of area bombing is the destruction of dwellings, but there is also an economic effect because the workers in these dwellings will be kept away from work in factories because they have to settle somewhere else."[69]

Believing in the American approach toward strategic bombing and prepared to carry out their evaluation within that conceptual framework, Survey analysts were ready to begin the work that would lay the theoretical groundwork for air power. From March to November 1944, the AAF had played an important part in establishing the parameters within which the Survey would conduct its evaluation. The AAF had taken great steps to insure that the Survey's conclusions would be "sound and substantiated" and support the future independence of the air service.[70]

CHAPTER 3

The Evaluation of Strategic Bombing against Germany

> Hamburg had put the fear of God in me.
>
> ALBERT SPEER, 1970

> That is why I stress and will continue to stress in this Survey that you have got to know what you are looking for, then seek to confirm it.
>
> ORVIL ARSON ANDERSON, 1945

At a Survey directors' meeting on 1 April 1945, Franklin D'Olier expressed his amazement that the "Air Corps should have given us this job with no qualifications . . . at no time has there been the slightest inclination to interfere with us. They want us to find out what the facts are from an absolutely impartial civilian point of view."[1] D'Olier was naively correct. The Survey did conduct an "impartial" civilian-led evaluation of strategic bombing, but that evaluation was shaped by the AAF during the year prior to D'Olier's conference with his civilian directors.

Between January and March 1945, the Survey had grown into an organization of approximately three hundred civilian and eight hundred military analysts and support personnel. When Germany surrendered in May 1945, Survey field teams were inspecting bombed targets in France and Germany and gathering extensive data on the German wartime economy. Survey analysts came to realize, though, that statistical data told only part of the story. They turned to interrogations of important German officials to fill in the gaps. By August 1945, John Kenneth Galbraith, George Ball, Paul Nitze, and the other directors had moved back to Washington, D.C., to craft their final division reports. Some of them were also preparing to continue their work in the Pacific.[2]

To write those final reports they had to develop an evaluation methodology to gauge the impact of strategic bombing on German war-making capacity. If the Survey's mandate had been only to assess the amount of physical destruction caused by strategic bombing, the task would have been straightforward and relatively easy.[3] But they needed a method that would enable them to explore the relationship between discrete industries and the entire war economy, and the effects of strategic bombing thereon. If the selection of strategic bombing targets was a complex affair, the evaluation of strategic bombing would be equally as demanding.

The more than two hundred published reports and studies from the European Survey, completed by late 1945, attest to the staggering amount of research and statistical data that Survey members collected and analyzed.[4] The published reports seem to contain collectively, and at times individually, competing conclusions and contradictions. Yet the discursive nature of the Survey's published reports conforms to a logical pattern when understood within the framework of the American conceptual approach to strategic bombing.

For example, The European Survey's Morale Division and Area Studies Division concluded that strategic bombing did not lower German morale enough to force Germany to surrender, and that RAF area attacks against German cities were largely ineffective in reducing German war production.[5] But the chairman's *Over-all Report,* which summarized the findings of the division studies, argued that air power, when applied against appropriate target systems, was "decisive in the war in Western Europe."[6] How could strategic bombing on one hand be indecisive against German morale and German cities, yet on the other still claim to be decisive in the war against Germany? Considering the American strategic bombing concept, the most effective way to break the enemy's will to resist was not to attack morale directly by killing people but instead to break the enemy's capacity to resist by damaging the "basic industries" of its war economy. The Survey's analysis flowed from the logic of that conception. The apparent contradictions and competing conclusions of the Survey's published reports thus fade away when framed by the American concept.

Strong disagreements between members of the European Survey did occur concerning the degree of effectiveness with which certain target systems were bombed. But those disagreements never challenged the relevance of American air power.

I

The first task that Survey analysts faced when they began their evaluation was to collect the evidence on the effects of strategic bombing. Small Survey "field teams" inspected locations in the European theater that had been subjected to Allied bombing. At the inspection site, the teams assessed the level of physical destruction of the target, collected production records and other related data, and interrogated, when possible, plant managers, workers, and other individuals with knowledge about the bombed target. After each inspection, the teams wrote up a standardized "form and content plant report" that consolidated the information they had gathered.[7]

The division directors took their field teams' data, analyzed them, and wrote reports that attempted to answer the questions given to them by the AAF. The Equipment Division, for example, conducted "a study of the total production loss to the enemy" in certain manufacturing industries and the "effects of that loss on the output of finished munitions." Galbraith's Economic Division made "a study of the total economic effects of strategic bombing on Germany." The Area Studies Division, under the directorship of George Ball, wrote a final report that evaluated the "specific economic consequences of area bombing in Germany."[8] Concerned about the potential for disparities among the division studies, Henry Alexander issued a standard outline for the divisions to follow when they crafted their final reports.[9]

The divisions submitted their completed studies to the Survey chairman.[10] The chairman based his *Over-all Report* on the analysis provided by the individual divisions. One of the primary objectives for the chairman's office was to synthesize the division studies into a concise and literate report that could be understood, as D'Olier emphasized, by "the man in the street," with some clearly "defined principles to adopt in respect to the use of bombers."[11]

But the most significant challenge faced by Survey directors was to devise a method of evaluation that enabled them to understand the huge mass of data that the field teams collected. In simple terms their methodology was to take the data collected by the field teams on selected targets—for example, the ball-bearing plants at Schweinfurt, Germany, that the AAF bombed heavily in 1943—and determine what impact strategic bombing had on those plants. They would then use the discrete findings from the Schweinfurt plants to evaluate the effects of strategic bombing on the entire German ball-bearing industry and then on the whole war economy. It was important for all Survey analysts to understand how their own discrete field of study related to the general work of the Survey. According to an Economic Division analyst, it made little sense "to study industries one by one without considering their relations to each other and the total war economy." Survey analysts needed to appreciate, therefore, "the interdependence of industry" so that they did not overlook "important data" in the course of their work.[12]

Because of the complexity of their economic-based evaluation, counterfactual speculation became an important part of Survey analysts' methodology. To determine the effects of strategic bombing on a given industry, or the overall economy for that matter, they estimated what the production level of that industry would have been if strategic bombing attacks had not taken place.[13] The difference between estimated production and actual production would give them a good idea of the effectiveness of strategic bombing.

The chairman's office made this point clearly in late January

1945 as the early work of the field teams began to produce data for division analysis: "To estimate the total economic effect, we have to compare Germany's total output and available manpower with what they would have been in the absence of our bomber offensive." As a guide to the field teams conducting data collection, the chairman's office emphasized that "to determine what production would have been in the absence of bombing, we must start out by examining the German plans for production." It cautioned, however, that "subtracting actual from planned output . . . will by no means yield the loss due to bombing." Realizing the German penchant for meticulous record keeping, the chairman's office admitted that "the production plans of the Germans still remain the most practical starting point for determining what production would have been *if* bombardment had not interfered with their production programs."[14] The Pacific phase of the Survey also featured counterfactual arguments over the AAF's role in ending the war against Japan.[15] Speculations on events that might have happened in the past, and predictions of future events, were embedded in the American conceptual approach to strategic bombing, and the United States Strategic Bombing Survey had its evaluation methodology and conclusions shaped by that conception.

Germany's surrender in May allowed Survey field teams to move freely within the Allied occupation zone.[16] Consequently, more and more evidence piled up on the desks of the division directors, who started to feel pressure from the chairman's office to produce tentative conclusions on the effects of strategic bombing.[17] The directors had come to realize that to analyze the data and produce conclusions the Survey could not only rely on statistical evidence.[18] Interrogations of key German officials, therefore, became a crucial element in the European Survey's methodology.

Undoubtedly, the most important German official interrogated during the European Survey was Albert Speer, Hitler's wartime economic minister. The Survey questioned him at Flensburg, Germany, at the end of May, shortly after the collapse of the Doenitz government. George Ball recalled that Speer gave the Survey "detailed information for which our field teams had been searching and which our analysts had been painfully trying to piece together out of bits and pieces of fact, gossip, and rumor." After the Survey had spent months sifting through production records and other related documents, Speer's testimony, according to Ball, "was like stumbling on the page of answers after one had worked on a puzzle for months."[19] Following the six-day interrogation of Speer in late May, Galbraith drafted a précis of his Economic Division's findings. The evidence that Galbraith drew on for his conclusions relied heavily, as he put it, "on the judgment of German officials" like Albert Speer.[20] Paul Nitze also emphasized the crucial role that Speer's testimony played in the formulation of Survey conclusions. Nitze reasoned that without Speer's "help it never would have been possible to secure the complete and well documented picture which we have now obtained."[21]

One historian has argued that there was a fundamental difference in methodology between the European and Pacific portions of the Survey. Because there was a dearth of production records in Japan (as compared with Germany), Survey analysts in the Pacific had to rely heavily on interrogations of Japanese officials for their evidence, according to this historian.[22] Yet the record shows that interrogations of important government officials were nearly as important for the European Survey. Relying on interrogations and constructing counterfactuals, therefore, were a part of Survey methodology in Europe and would remain so once the Survey began its evaluation in the Pacific.

II

Albert Speer, during his weeklong interrogation with the Survey, told Directors Ball, Galbraith, and Nitze that the RAF's area raids on the German city of Hamburg in the summer of 1943 had a powerful effect on the morale of the city's population. According to Ball's translation of Speer's remarks, "the losses in Hamburg were great, the greatest we had suffered in any raid, particularly from burning houses. And the depression among the population was extraordinary." Speer stated to Ball that shortly after the raid he informed Hitler that if Germany "underwent 6–8 more such raids on big cities," they would produce "a huge shock" on armament production and, more important, on the morale of the German people.[23] According to Ball, Speer said that if the Allies had "continued those attacks, knocking Hamburg completely out of the war, German morale . . . would have suffered a critical blow."[24] Ruminating years later on the interrogation, Ball considered Speer's "insights" on the potential decisiveness of area attacks on morale to be "curious [and] fascinating."[25]

The implications of Speer's testimony about Hamburg were in fact quite profound. Military strategist Bernard Brodie argued in a postwar analysis of strategic bombing that "the terrible shock given to the entire German state by the series of extremely heavy attacks directed at Hamburg at the end of July and the beginning of August 1943 suggests what might have happened if attacks of comparable intensity could have been directed also against a substantial number of other German cities at about the same time and in rapid succession."[26] But George Ball did not grasp the potential decisiveness of area raids that Speer's testimony suggested and Brodie's analysis stated forthrightly. Instead, Speer's testimony on the Hamburg raids seemed "curious" to Ball. The testimony seemed curious because Ball and his fellow Survey analysts directed their analysis toward the effects of area raids on German war production, not morale.

It was also possible that Ball and other Survey analysts did not explore the potential effect of area attacks on morale (suggested by the Speer testimony) because of their moral uneasiness over killing large numbers of enemy civilians. The Survey knew that their findings would have some effect on the conduct of the AAF's aerial war against Japanese cities.[27] Perhaps Ball and some of the others felt that a strong emphasis on the potential decisiveness of area raids—with morale as the objective—might increase the AAF's area raids on Japanese cities. Paul Baran, a friend of Ball and an important analyst in the Economic Division, told Galbraith that he (Baran) was an "outspoken enemy of area bombardment," and implicitly its immorality.[28] Galbraith expressed a loathing in his memoirs for the fire raids against Japanese cities and referred to them as "an appalling business."[29] One can assume that he felt the same way about the RAF's area raids against German cities.

The Survey, in its formal evaluation in Europe and the Pacific, never addressed the morality of strategic bombing in general, and more specifically the morality of the area bombing of German and Japanese cities.[30] However, the postwar accounts by Survey directors, a few snippets of contemporaneous documents, and the dismissal of Speer's testimony concerning the Hamburg raids suggest that ethical considerations were on the minds of at least some Survey members.

The purpose of psychologist Rensis Likert's Morale Division was certainly not to explore the morality and ethics of strategic bombing but to "submit a report [that] evaluated the effects of bombing upon enemy morale."[31] Paul Nitze told Likert and other Survey directors that it would be "necessary for the Economic and the Morale Divisions to work together, as closely as possible."[32] Nitze's guidance to the Survey directors revealed the importance the Survey placed on the link between morale and the entire war economy. For Survey analysts, morale was an important factor to study mainly as it affected the German worker's willingness and ability to support war production. The Morale Division stated: "The crucial spot in which to examine the effects of lowered morale upon the German war effort lies in war production." The division then followed this statement with a question that got at their fundamental reason for studying the effects of strategic bombing on enemy morale: "Did depression in general, and defeatism and disaffection from the Nazi regime in particular, show themselves in lowered industrial production?"[33]

The Morale Division's methodology for evaluation was somewhat different from that of the rest of the Survey. Because the focus of the division's study was on the morale of the German civilian, the data they collected were made up of interviews, German wartime documents concerning morale, and civilian mail captured during the war.[34] Still, in evaluating these sources, the Morale Division reflected the Survey's reliance on statistical evidence and its quantitative approach toward studying the effects of strategic bombing. In the captured mail and interviews, division analysts would look for key words or phrases that demonstrated direct or indirect "spontaneous expression[s] of lowered morale." For example, if a civilian explicitly mentioned the word "bombing" with regard to lowered morale, that would weigh more heavily in their assessment than an implicit statement. It was significant, according to the division, that 14 percent of captured German civilian mail contained "direct expressions of lowered morale."[35] Being able to quantify strategic bombing's effect on German morale fit comfortably with the notion that the Survey was a "scientific" study.

The Morale Division's field teams followed closely behind the advancing Allied armies into Germany, interviewing civilians who had experienced firsthand the effects of strategic bombing. In order to draw out as much information as possible, division analysts used drugs to relax their interviewees. By 1944, it had become common practice in the army's medical service to treat soldiers with "battle fatigue" or "exhaustion" with sedatives like pentathol or morphine to dampen their painful combat memories, thereby allowing them to talk about their experiences with a psychiatrist.[36] Some of the Morale Division's medical officers were naturally drawn from the army medical service. According to one Survey medical officer, the division initially used "morphine" to "render people comatose," but the morphine had the disadvantage of being insoluble in "cocktails." Apparently desiring a drug that the civilian interviewees would not notice in the "cocktails," the division made a request to a physician in the United States to send them a "a quick acting sedative which [was] readily soluble in alcohol."[37]

One reason for focusing their analysis on the morale of the individual German rather than on the collective will to resist of the German people was the belief of Survey analysts and the AAF that the Nazi "police state" maintained unbreakable control over the nation.[38] The Morale Division's published report, *The Effects of Strategic Bombing on German Morale*, argued that "German controls, particularly terror and propaganda, helped to prevent depressed morale from being translated into subversive activity seriously detrimental to the war effort."[39] Many AAF leaders also had strong reservations about morale as the primary objective for strategic bombers because of what they believed to be the power and influence of the Nazis over the civilian population. An after-action review of Operation Clarion (a late-February 1945 operation conducted by the AAF to disrupt German transportation facilities and oil supplies and possibly precipitate a "crisis" among railway workers) cautioned that there was no evidence "that the attacks broke the morale and economy. The German people are too stringently regimented for an operation of this type to have such far reaching consequences."[40]

The Morale Division's report stated forthrightly that strategic bombing attacks (like Clarion) "seriously depressed the morale of German civilians." And bombing did not, according to the report, "stiffen morale." But, more important, the division report argued, strategic bombing did not decisively affect the behavior—or the capacity—of the German people to support the war effort: "Lowered civilian morale expressed itself in somewhat diminished industrial productivity [but] German controls were fairly successful in keeping traditionally obedient and industrious workers at a routine level of performance. . . ."[41] For lowered morale to be decisive, therefore, it needed to affect individual German behavior to a point where the workers were kept from "performing" their part in war production. The division report concluded that strategic bombing did not accomplish this objective and was therefore not decisive against German morale. "Discouraged workers," argued the division, were "not necessarily unproductive workers, and German production kept up amazingly."[42]

The AAF did its part to ensure that Survey members understood the primary purpose of American strategic bombing to be the destruction of the enemy's war-making capacity, not morale. A May

1945 memorandum prepared by the intelligence officer of the Eighth Air Force for the Strategic Bombing Survey explained the AAF's conceptual approach to strategic bombing. Quoting from the Casablanca directive of 1943, which stated the Allied grand strategy for the defeat of Germany, the report argued: "In the historic words of the 'Casablanca' directive, it was the progressive destruction and dislocation of the German military, industrial and economic system . . . to a point where . . . capacity for armed resistance is fatally weakened." This, according to the report, was "the underlying concept on which all strategic operations of this Air Force have been carried out."[43] But the report omitted an important clause from the Casablanca directive, according to which the ultimate objective for the Combined Bomber Offensive was "The progressive destruction and dislocation of the German military, industrial and economic system, *and the undermining of the morale of the German people* to a point where their capacity for armed resistance is fatally weakened."[44] The Eighth Air Force memorandum omitted the clause that made morale an objective probably because it wanted to confirm in the minds of Survey analysts who read the report the AAF's approach to strategic bombing, which was subtly different from that stated in the Casablanca directive.[45] Survey analysts, however, fully accepted the notion that the purpose of American strategic bombing was to attack the war-making capacity of the enemy, and they conducted their evaluation with that conception in mind.

III

A troubling tendency in post-1945 writings on strategic bombing in World War II has been the conflation of the term area bombing (or area attacks, area raids, fire bombing, fire raids) with the term morale bombing (or terror bombing, terror attacks, morale attacks). According to this line of thinking, when American bombers conducted an area raid against a German or Japanese city, it was necessarily morale bombing—with the morale of the enemy being the objective of the attack. The two terms are treated synonymously because the results of area bombing apparently confirmed the notion that the enemy's morale was the objective: Area bombing did cause indiscriminate destruction within a designated aiming area in German and Japanese cities, and area bombing did cause massive terror and suffering to the enemy population. Hence, in this formulation, when the AAF carried out limited area bombing against German cities and extensive area bombing against Japanese cities, the objective of those attacks automatically became morale.

Historian Ronald Schaffer, in his important 1985 book *Wings of Judgment*, treats area and morale bombing as one and the same. Shaffer argues that the AAF was able to conduct Operation Clarion in February 1945 "because the people who strongly opposed *morale and area bombing* lacked the power to impose their views." Or in another passage, Schaffer notes that the great number of American bombers and crews "toward the end of the war also contributed to U.S. *terror and area attacks*."[46] It is arguable whether the AAF, especially by the closing months of the Pacific war and the torching of Japanese cities, considered morale to be the primary objective for area bombing.[47] But it is certain that AAF planners, operators, and evaluators thought of area bombing as a method of dropping bombs on strategic targets in enemy cities. It was completely possible, in their minds, to conduct an area attack against the enemy's war-making capacity. Area bombing, therefore, was not always synonymous with attacking morale.

George Ball's Area Studies Division noted that there was a "mode" (method) and "objective" for area attacks on cities. The difference between the methods of area and precision bombing, according to the Area Studies Division, was "in the size and character of the bomb pattern." The objective of precision raids was the systematic attack on "selected classes of installations" (e.g., oil plants, aircraft plants, marshaling yards, etc.). In contrast, the objective of area raids was "urban centers containing various classes of installation, civilian, military, and industrial."[48] Area raids meant the general destruction of the city's war industry, while precision bombing attacked specific industries. The overall objective of both area and precision bombing, though, was still the enemy's war-making capacity.

There were a number of key factors that the Area Studies Division believed led to a reduced capacity to produce war materiel: "absenteeism; direct damage to plants; destruction of inventories; disruption of facilities; disruption of transportation; diversion of resources to repair and replacement; casualties; dispersal of industries; [and] evacuation of [the] civilian population." By using these factors, the analysts could then "compare variances between planned and actual production of plants in raided areas with like variances of undamaged plants in non-raided areas," thus providing a reasonable indication of the overall "production loss caused by the area raid."[49]

Note that analysts took account of worker absenteeism from factories and casualties, suggesting that they were interested in the effects of area raids on the morale of workers. But the Area Division used worker absenteeism and casualties as analytical categories to determine how area raids affected the ability of workers to contribute to war production. Damage caused to workers' homes from area attacks would usually force those workers to be absent from the factories to repair their homes or move to new ones, thus lowering the output of factories. The term "casualties" to the Area Division meant the number of civilian workers killed or wounded by area attacks. Like worker absenteeism, casualties caused by area raids would affect the war-making capacity of the city by preventing people from going to work in the factories.[50]

The Survey, because of its focus on Germany's war-making capacity, never addressed the large issues of mass killing and mass casualties from bombing. The focus was always far more narrow: Did the casualties and death disrupt and cut production? Thus, the killing or injuring of children or those too old to work, or workers' unemployed spouses, was important only for its *indirect* effect on production.[51]

The Area Division investigated a number of German cities subjected to area attacks to "determine the economic effects of the area raids." The division's Hamburg study argued that "concentrated attacks [precision bombing] on limited targets were more effective in disrupting vital production than were the area raids on workers' quarters throughout the city."[52] The study went on to conclude that although area attacks on Hamburg did lower the overall war production of the city, they were not "as effective in disrupting the enemy's ability to wage war as the destruction of transportation facilities in general throughout the industrial regions of the country."[53]

Building on the findings of the Hamburg study, the published *Area Studies Division Report* was more direct in pointing out the indecisive nature of area attacks on German war-making capacity. Because area raids generally damaged "sectors of the German economy not essential to war production," the raids, according to the report, "did not have a decisive effect upon the ability of the German nation to produce war material."[54] According to the report, a city attacked by an area raid would experience an immediate decline in the labor force due to the deaths of workers or absenteeism, but the city would be able to quickly recover most of its industrial labor force within two to three months following the raid.[55]

IV

In the summer of 1940, when he helped write AWPD/1, Haywood Hansell believed that the AAF should use its strategic bombers to attack critical target systems that linked together the enemy's war economy.[56] AWPD/1 ended up selecting German transportation and electric power as two high-priority targets for the AAF to bomb.[57] In his 1986 memoirs, Hansell used Survey conclusions to argue that the AAF's strategic bombing campaign against Germany had vindicated AWPD/1's choice of target systems.[58] The European Survey's *Summary Report*, which Hansell cited in his memoirs, argued that attacks against German transportation (inland waterways, railroad tracks, and marshaling yards) "was the decisive blow that completely disorganized the German economy."[59] The *Summary Report* went on to state, counterfactually, that if "electric generating plants and substations had been made primary targets . . . the evidence indicates that their destruction would have had serious effects on Germany's war production."[60]

It is interesting to note that neither AWPD/1 nor Hansell's memoirs addressed the physical damage to targets caused by strategic bombing. Instead, they both focused on the impact that strategic bombing would make, or had made, on the critical target systems of the German war economy. Like AWPD/1 and Hansell's memoirs, the Survey, by the spring of 1945, placed little importance on studying the way strategic bombing damaged buildings and structures. John Kenneth Galbraith noted that examining physical damage to industrial plants "became little more than an exercise in viewing rubble."[61]

Paul Nitze agreed with Galbraith about the decreased importance of studying the amount of physical damage caused by strategic bombing. He recommended to D'Olier that the Survey reduce the size of the Physical Damage Division and direct its energy instead toward evaluating the effects of strategic bombing on the German war economy. As a result the Survey transferred most of the analysts from the Physical Damage Division, under the directorship of Harry Bowman, to other divisions. These transfers apparently upset one of Bowman's assistants, Lieutenant Colonel John Bereta. Bereta sent a long letter to Bowman (who was in Washington, D.C., at the time) complaining about Nitze's desire to discredit the work of the division and remove most of its personnel. Bereta fumed that because Nitze was a trained economist, he seemed to believe "that weapons effectiveness can in some manner be ascertained from statistical, economic and industrial data." He noticed that Nitze was becoming impatient and annoyed with the division's persistence in studying the physical destructiveness of strategic bombing. Bereta was sure that this was due to Nitze's "not being a technical man . . . his life work has been economic in nature, beginning with a Harvard education." In the closing remarks of the letter, Bereta complained that he was "at a loss to express an opinion as to why the economic, industrial, and statistical phases of the Survey [were] being accented more than the physical damage phase."[62]

Part of the problem that Bereta and his division faced was the growing influence Nitze wielded among Survey members, especially Franklin D'Olier. When the Survey conducted its field operations in France and Germany from January to July 1945, Vice-Chairman Alexander and Chairman D'Olier worked out of the Survey's London headquarters and made frequent trips back to the United States. In their absence, Nitze acted as Survey chairman. Not surprisingly, D'Olier had come to rely "very heavily on him" because of his ability and expertise. Bereta noted that "many of the policies of the Survey are definitely set by Mr. Nitze due to the confidence that higher authority has in him."[63]

By June 1945, Nitze, Ball, and Galbraith were beginning to formulate initial conclusions about the effects of strategic bombing. They believed that the AAF had been most effective when it directed its bombers against basic industries such as electric power, transportation, and oil production.[64] Based on the evidence that their divisions had collected and analyzed, especially Albert Speer's testimony, Nitze recalled that unlike factories producing finished products such as ball bearings or airframes, the basic industries "once severely damaged, could not be quickly restored to full production nor could stocks be readily replaced." It was the basic industries linking together the entire German war economy that proved to be the most valuable target systems for American strategic bombers to attack, argued Nitze.[65]

With the war in Germany over, the United States concentrated its effort on the Pacific. Wanting to explore the lessons learned from the European theater for possible use against Japan, the AAF asked Survey directors to summarize their findings. Survey analysts had honed in on two basic industries or target systems that, according to them, either would have been decisive or were decisive in the war against Germany.

The Combined Bomber Offensive had removed electric power as a priority target for strategic bombers. The airmen believed that the German electric power system was too decentralized and could easily recover from strategic bombing attacks.[66] Yet analysts from the Survey's Utilities Division argued that based on their interrogations of "German power plant and systems operators . . . the bombing of power plants and primary sub-stations would have been the quickest and most effective way to have destroyed Germany's war economy."[67] Even though German electric power was not directly targeted by the AAF, the cumulative effect of ground operations and strategic bombing attacks on other basic industries placed a serious strain on electric power. The division's published study, *German Electric Utilities Industry Report*, argued that had the AAF made power plants "primary targets as soon as they could have been brought within the range of Allied strategic bombing attacks, all evidence indicates that the destruction of such installations would have had a catastrophic effect on Germany's war economy."[68]

If the AAF did not direct its strategic bombing campaign against German electric power, it did, by the closing months of the war in Europe, heavily attack German transportation and oil production. General Spaatz, on orders from Supreme Allied Commander General Dwight D. Eisenhower, reluctantly diverted his bombers from strategic attacks on the German war economy to tactical bombing against local railroad facilities in France to support the Normandy landings. Once the Allied forces had established themselves on the continent, the AAF again concentrated its strategic bombers against Germany. But having seen the value of using its bombers to attack railroads in France as a part of the Normandy invasion, the AAF decided to make similar strategic attacks against transportation targets inside of Germany.[69]

Survey analysts accepted the notion that strategic bombers should attack basic industries that linked together the enemy's war economy. Moreover, it was logical for them to conclude that the AAF's attacks on German transportation and oil production "brought about a total disintegration of the German economy."[70]

Nitze, working together with Ball and other key directors, had determined that there was no doubt about "the vulnerability of the German [war production] system to air attack." It was simply a matter of selecting the right "vital factor" for destruction, and then keeping it destroyed by continuous air attack: "The German experience strongly supports the position that one objective be selected as the basic target system. . . ." Transportation, according to Nitze, was one of those "vital factors." He posited that the "lateness" of the AAF's attack on transportation "prevented a clear-cut demonstration of its effectiveness as a means of attacking the enemy's basic economy." But even though the attacks on German transportation began later in the war, as he put it, they "preceded the final collapse of the enemy . . . in a most significant way."[71]

The Transportation Division, which was under the directorship of George Ball, published its final report, *The Effects of Strategic Bombing on German Transportation*, in September 1945. That report reiterated the conclusions that Nitze and Ball had presented to AAF leaders in June and July. The report lamented the fact that the AAF did not apply the full weight of strategic bombers against German transportation until after the Normandy invasion, but it had still "so paralyzed the German industrial economy as to render all further heavy war production virtually impossible."[72] Looking around from the inside at the effects of strategic bombing on Germany, Survey analysts comfortably accepted the conclusion that transportation, oil production, and electric power were critical industries for the German war economy.

V

The analytical divisions of the Survey had completed their final reports by August 1945 and forwarded them to the chairman's office to write the important *Over-all Report*.[73] When John Kenneth Galbraith and the other directors arrived back in Washington, D.C., in September they discovered, according to Galbraith, that the Survey secretariat, Judge Charles Cabot, had prepared an "unsatisfactory" draft of the chairman's *Over-all Report* that gave unwarranted praise to the AAF's wartime accomplishments while dismissing its failures.[74] The directors had understood from the beginning that the chairman's office would produce a final report that summarized the findings of their respective divisions.[75] Since Cabot's draft would be published as the chairman's *Over-all Report*, Galbraith decided that it must represent accurately the Survey's findings. He and Ball recommended to Alexander that Cabot's draft report be rewritten. A heated debate followed over the draft report, with Galbraith and Ball on one side and Cabot, Colonel Guido Perera, and General Orvil Anderson on the other.[76]

Lurking beneath the dispute over Cabot's draft were the conclusions that Galbraith's influential Economic Division had reached on the overall effects of strategic bombing on the German war economy.[77] The division's findings demonstrated that the German war economy was not stretched to the limit, as was popularly believed, but in fact had a "substantial cushion of potential production, so that in the later stages of the war the economy was able to be expanded substantially."[78] Drawing on the findings from the other divisions, Galbraith argued that the most effective strategic bombing attacks were those directed against transportation and electric power. The AAF's attacks on airframe and ball-bearing production, argued Galbraith's division, proved to be "disappointing."[79]

The division's published report, *The Effects of Strategic Bombing on the German War Economy,* made the same basic arguments as the earlier précis. Galbraith, in his memoirs, incorrectly implied that his division's published report spelled out "the disastrous failure of strategic bombing."[80] Although Galbraith's Survey report did emphasize the failures of certain strategic bombing targets and policies, it never came close to stating what his later memoirs termed a "disastrous failure." Still, his published report focused on the inability of the AAF, especially prior to the fall of 1944, to substantially affect Germany's war production. Not until late in the war, according to the Economic Division's report, when the AAF began to concentrate heavily on oil and transportation, did Germany begin to feel the full weight of the air attack.[81]

The most disturbing conclusion brought out in Galbraith's published report was that strategic bombing, during 1943 and into early 1944, might have helped streamline, rather than injure, the German war economy. When discussing the measures that Albert Speer took to increase production, the Economic Division's report argued:

> [Speer's] effort was also helped by the air attacks. The stress of the air raids permitted him to mobilize the energies of the population just as the growing seriousness of the war permitted him to break the inertia of Germany's governmental and industrial bureaucracy and to induce it to accept procedures which hitherto were sternly rejected.[82]

This passage does not claim that strategic bombing assisted Germany after the full weight of the air campaign began in the months leading to D-Day. Nor does it suggest that bombing improved the morale of the German civilian population. But, certainly, the contention that the AAF's limited bombing campaign indirectly helped, rather than weakened, the German economy was difficult for Perera, Cabot, and Anderson to accept.[83]

Guido Perera's concern was clearly with the emphasis that Galbraith's report placed on the effective use of American strategic bombers to attack German transportation and electric power.[84] Equally troubling to Perera was the conclusion that strategic bombing attacks against German airframe and ball-bearing production were ineffective in seriously damaging the German war economy.[85] As an original member of the COA, Perera was heavily involved with the selection of strategic targets for the AAF's air campaign against Germany. Although AWPD/1 had placed German transportation as a primary target for American bombers, Perera and his fellow COA analysts removed it in early 1944 from their primary target list. Instead, the COA recommended to the AAF that German airframe and ball-bearing production be the primary targets for strategic bombers.[86] The AAF bombed airframe and ball-bearing factories until shortly after the Normandy invasion and then made German transportation and oil production their primary strategic targets. Galbraith's analysis (based on other division findings) implicitly emphasized that the AAF had the most success attacking targets that Perera and the COA did not recommend.[87]

Ironically, Galbraith's Economic Division report vindicated the airmen's theory of air power. Even though Galbraith argued that AAF attacks against targets like capital equipment and ball-bearing plants were largely ineffective, his report noted that aerial attacks against German transportation were decisive. By early 1945, "in cooperation with other causes," they led to the complete breakdown of the German war economy, Galbraith's report argued.[88] Back in 1939 at ACTS, Muir Fairchild believed that for strategic bombing to be decisive, air leaders would have to determine the correct "vital" targets to bomb in the enemy's war economy. By acknowledging that there were "vital" target systems in Germany, and that those "vitals" were vulnerable to strategic air attack, Galbraith subtly, but profoundly, vindicated the American conceptual approach to strategic bombing. This subtle endorsement was no salve to Guido Perera, however.

In his memoirs, Perera repeatedly argued that the failures and successes of strategic bombing during World War II should be interpreted in light of the AAF's *objective* in the European theater: to prepare the way for a ground invasion of the continent, and not to destroy German industry. With this premise, Perera then discredited Galbraith's conclusions and resurrected the validity of his COA targeting recommendations for the AAF. Since, according to Perera, German frontline military strength—not the destruction of German industry—was the objective for the AAF, the attacks on ball-bearing and airframe production were effective because they reduced the capacity of the German army to resist invasion.[89] But Perera's memoirs allowed the present to cloud the reality of the past. In December 1944, as the Survey was preparing to conduct its evaluation, Perera lectured new Survey analysts on the purpose of American strategic bombing. According to Perera, American air power intended to strike a blow "directly against the industrial heart of the enemy [Germany], the mainsprings upon which its armies depend."[90] The "mainspring" Perera referred to was, naturally, German war-making capacity.

Judge Cabot's interest in the chairman's final report rested on his desire, as George Ball recalled in a letter to Arthur Schlesinger, Jr., "to advocate drafting the survey report as a public relations effort for the birdmen." Cabot, as the Survey's Secretariat, Ball charged, "rarely stirred out of London, and read little of the material turned up by the Survey. . . . [He] was indubitably a barnacle on the rear end of objectivity."[91] Ball asserted that Cabot's draft report proved to be "wholly inadequate. It was confused, diffuse and technically unacceptable. Its conclusions repeated the conclusions of individuals attached to the Survey who, because of their previous work with the Air Force, had a vested interest in the vindication of certain aspects of the air offensive."[92] The "individuals" with "vested" interests, according to Ball, were, among others, Guido Perera who was defending his work with the COA.

Air power champion General Orvil Arson Anderson wanted the Survey chairman's report to endorse the future of air power as an independent military force.[93] In an interview conducted by the United States Strategic Air Forces (USSTAF) historical section on 22 August 1945, just a few weeks before the controversy over the chairman's report, General Anderson emphasized the Survey's role in shaping the future of the air force. When asked by the interviewer about using Survey studies to determine whether or not the AAF should have switched from day to night attacks in the European war, and the implications for the future, Anderson responded: "You can never solve a war by past historic examples." The general believed that the traditional use of "historical examples" by the army and navy to plan and fight present and future wars had kept air power from achieving its full, independent potential. The Survey should prevent the other services from pulling air power as a "three dimensional force back into a two-dimensional employment, . . . making it an ancillary weapon to surface forces, restricting its freedom to fight a three-dimensional war." Such an arrangement was "hinged to our past thinking." The Survey should write its reports, believed Anderson, with a clear eye to the future, not the past.[94]

Anderson was much less worried than Perera about certain Survey conclusions concerning AAF targeting choices that would make their way into the chairman's final report. In fact Anderson sidestepped the Survey's critique of the bombing of airframe production by arguing that the AAF still achieved its objective of gaining command of the air by defeating the German Luftwaffe in aerial battle. This, according to Anderson in classic Douhet fashion, allowed the AAF "to exploit that air freedom for further attacks against the over-all enemy war machine."[95]

Anderson confirmed that destroying Germany's war-making capacity was the primary objective of the AAF. That "war machine," argued Anderson,

> represents the entire enemy nation, its overall economy. It is rather fallacious for us to reason that the economy divides itself into a war economy and a sustaining civil economy, because in a three-dimensional war that is not sound. It is all war economy. . . . Therefore you attack the enemy war machine when you attack any of its structure, because it is all military.

The general's interviewer then posited that certain attacks were more effective than others in damaging Germany's war economy and asked what conclusions the Survey had reached in that regard. Anderson explained that when attacking a "worthy" opponent's war-making capacity, "you go as far back toward his basic industries as your capabilities will carry you to get to the big heavy, meaty, war targets." Cautioning against relying on historical examples too much, Anderson said that there was no set pattern to follow when attacking the enemy's basic industries. But the Survey had concluded correctly, according to the general, "that the attack of basic industries against a worthy foe would appear to be the quickest and most effective way generally of defeating an enemy nation."[96]

Although it critiqued certain target choices that the AAF had made during the war, the Survey still concluded that the use of air power to attack basic industries like transportation proved to be a critical factor in defeating the German war economy.[97] This was exactly the kind of conclusion that General Anderson wanted from the Survey because it confirmed the soundness of the American conceptual approach to strategic bombing.

The chairman's *Summary Report* and *Over-all Report* that emerged out of the early September controversy largely from the pen of Galbraith, did not change this confirmation.[98] In fact, the three studies that the chairman's office came to publish, the *Summary Report*, the *Over-all Report*, and Galbraith's *The Effects of Strategic Bombing on the German War Economy,* were strikingly similar in their major conclusions about the effectiveness of strategic bombing in the European theater (although the tone of Galbraith's report tended to be more critical).[99] First, all three reports argued that the German economy was not efficiently run; it never achieved its full war potential, mostly because of poor strategic planning and inept economic management by Adolph Hitler and his staff. Second, attacks on urban areas were not effective in seriously reducing or breaking German war production. Finally, the AAF achieved its most decisive results by attacking German transportation, and should have devoted a greater effort to bombing German electric power.[100]

The real difference between Galbraith's Economic Division report and the other two had identical concluding sections commenting on "some signposts" for "the future." In a frequently quoted passage, the *Over-all Report* and *Summary Report* state in identical words:

> The foregoing pages tell of the results achieved by Allied air power, in each of its several roles in the war in Europe. It remains to look at the results as a whole and to seek such signposts as may be of guidance to the future. . . . Allied air power was decisive in the war in Western Europe. Hindsight inevitably suggests that it might have been employed differently or better in some respects. Nevertheless, it was decisive.[101]

Evidently General Anderson's "controversialist" stance during the debate over Cabot's draft ensured that the *Summary Report* and

Over-all Report would include favorable remarks on the "decisiveness" of strategic bombing in the European war and some comments on the future of air power.[102] His desire was fulfilled, at least for the time being.

Although other senior AAF leaders did not make official comments on the European Survey reports that were published in the fall of 1945, many of those leaders did rely heavily on the them in the postwar debates over the unification of the armed services and the independent status of the air force.[103] General Spaatz's biographer, historian David Mets, tells us that Spaatz claimed to have never read the Survey and "displayed limited enthusiasm" for it. But Mets acknowledges in his biography what the general most likely believed:

> the Survey's evaluation of [Spaatz's] work was in the main favorable. . . . It explicitly favored precision bombing. . . . It claimed that airpower had been a decisive factor in the war against Hitler. . . . The conclusions of the USSBS on the correctness of precision bombing theory matched those of Spaatz. . . .[104]

The Survey in its evaluation of Allied air power against Germany confirmed the soundness of the American concept of strategic bombing, just what the airmen had intended it to do.

CHAPTER 4

✦ ✦ ✦ ✦ ✦ ✦ ✦ ✦ ✦ ✦ ✦

The Survey Presents Its Findings from Europe and Develops an Alternate Strategic Bombing Plan for Japan

General Norstad: Under the Circumstances that existed in Germany, the enemy's capacity to resist would have been weakened by oil alone or transportation or by the combination of both to a point where he had to quit?

Mr. Alexander: Of course when you say "have to quit[,]" decisive doesn't mean that completely. There were still men standing in bushes with rifles that had to be disposed of. . . . It does not necessarily mean that every soldier would have to put down his gun and go home.

Conference between Members of
the Joint Target Group (JTG) and
the Strategic Bombing Survey,
9 June 1945

Following the publication of the chairman's European *Summary Report* and *Overall Report*, Henry Alexander held a press conference at the Pentagon on 24 October 1945 to pass out copies of both studies and to answer questions from newspaper reporters about the Survey. During the conference Alexander fielded a question on the "relative effectiveness of saturation; i.e. area bombing as against more accurate [precision] bombing." Alexander, restating the Survey's conclusions concerning area attacks against German cities, responded that the most effective method for destroying the productive capacity of Germany was the effort directed "toward the industry rather than toward the community." Most of the industry, as he put it, was located on the perimeter of German cities. Area attacks, argued Alexander, which had as their aiming point the center of the city, were ineffective in damaging the city's war economy.[1]

In June 1945, four months prior to his press conference in October, Alexander was involved in another conference on the effects of strategic bombing against Germany, but this time with members of the Joint Target Group (JTG), the agency formed by the Joint Chiefs of Staff to provide centralized target planning for the Pacific bombing campaign. In fact during the month of June, Alexander, along with D'Olier, Ball, Nitze, and other Survey directors, held a series of meetings in Washington, D.C., with key political and military leaders.[2] Planning for the land invasion of Japan fostered an interest among American leaders and agencies like the JTG in hearing the Survey's findings for possible application in the Pacific.

The JTG, and its predecessor, the Committee of Operations Analysts (COA), had been analyzing the vulnerability of Japanese cities to strategic bombing as early as the fall of 1943. Both agencies had refined their thinking on the most effective bombing methods and objectives for the AAF in its strategic air campaign against Japan. Survey directors, too, based on their findings from Europe, believed that they had determined the proper methods and objectives for strategic bombers. There were competing beliefs, therefore, about the best methods for using air power against Japan. The question of whether or not American strategic bombing combined with a naval blockade could force Japan to surrender without a land invasion shaped these competing visions.

During their visit to Washington, D.C., in June, the Survey directors demonstrated to senior military and political leaders a sophisticated understanding of the effects of strategic bombing on Germany, and, in general, of air power theory and practice. As a result, the Survey was directed to write its own alternate bombardment plan for the defeat of Japan. Paul Nitze completed the plan in July 1945. General Spaatz, the newly designated commander of the United States Army Strategic Air Forces and a devout advocate of precision bombing, took that plan to the Pacific with him in late July. He intended to implement it.

I

The COA had submitted an initial report back in the fall of 1943 on the most effective method for American strategic bombers to damage Japanese war production.[3] That preliminary study recommended that the AAF bomb Japanese merchant shipping and coke production. Because the Japanese economy was different from Germany's in that Japan's represented "an island industrial core which derive[d] its material largely from overseas," an attack against shipping and coke for steel production would have a powerful effect on "the entire structure of Japanese industry."[4] This early COA report did not recommend using incendiary attacks against Japanese cities to destroy war industry.

But the vulnerability of Japanese cities, constructed largely out of wood, to fire was widely understood. As early as 1939, the Air Corps Tactical School had informed its students about the combustible nature of Japan's major industrial cities. In February 1942, General Arnold had his staff prepare target analyses that highlighted the vulnerability of Japanese cities to fire. Always looking for new ways to use strategic bombers, General Arnold considered the possibility of fire raids to destroy Japanese industry.[5] As a result of the general's interest, the military chairman of the COA, Brigadier General Byron Gates, asked the head of the Office of Scientific Research and Development (OSRD), Vannevar Bush, to provide the COA with personnel to form a subcommittee to analyze "the susceptibility to area attack of Japanese cities and industries located therein." Gates recommended that one of Bush's OSRD experts on incendiary weapons, Dr. Raymond H. Ewell, be involved in the study.[6]

The COA submitted its study in November 1943 to General Arnold. The study noted that area attacks on Japanese cities would cause production loss from "direct damage to industrial facilities and housing [and] the diversion of Japanese industry from its normal activities to the repair and replacement of this damage." The study cautioned that the potential effectiveness of incendiary raids required further analysis. It did conclude forthrightly that "incendiary attacks on urban areas will produce great economic loss . . . but because of the wide diffusion of this loss over many industries it is unlikely that output in any one important category" would substantially reduce the Japanese military's frontline strength. The COA's subcommittee concluded that precision attacks, rather than incendiary raids, would be more effective in reducing Japan's critical war industries than incendiary raids.[7]

But other COA studies emphasized the potential of incendiary raids on Japanese cities. The COA analyzed the effects of the RAF's area raids against German cities to use in their planning for Japan. One such study, "The Economic Effect of Attacks in Force on German Urban Areas," admitted that "a straight incendiary attack against congested residential areas in Japanese cities is the *method* most frequently considered for the Far East." But for the attacks to be successful, according to the committee, they would ultimately have to "demoralize war production." According to the COA, incendiary attacks needed to do more than just attack civilian morale "to be successful," they had to ultimately affect war production to be of value as a method of strategic bombing.[8]

The great fire caused by the Tokyo earthquake of 1923 provided the COA with information on the flammable nature of Japanese cities. The COA noted that the "frame-built cities of Japan are highly combustible and can be more readily destroyed than the massive-built cities of Germany." The committee's only question was "how much more readily" they could be destroyed. Their answer was to choose the most effective bombs and "modes" of delivering those bombs.[9] Another analysis by the committee provided further information on the potential of fire raids by emphasizing that the "sustaining sources of Japanese military strength" could best be damaged by strategic bombing operations against aircraft production, coke factories, petroleum, radios and radar, ball bearings, and "urban industrial areas." The report argued that "urban industrial areas" as an objective were vulnerable to the area bombing "technique" and night attack.[10]

The COA often drew on the expertise of individuals outside the War Department. For example, upon request, Horatio Bond, the chief engineer of the National Fire Protection Association (International), enthusiastically offered technical assistance to Guido Perera and other members of the COA. Bond sent a letter to Perera in March 1944 explaining his analysis of the susceptibility of certain American industries to fire, with possible application to Japan. The letter presents a fascinating glimpse at the contradictions of a total war that brought together civilian experts and the military. Bond's letter is written on the National Fire Protection Association's official stationary. At the very top of the letter appears the association's statement of purpose:

> To promote the science and improve the methods of fire protection and prevention: to obtain and circulate information on those subjects and to secure the co-operation of its members in establishing proper safeguards against loss of life and property by fire.[11]

In the ensuing text of the letter, Bond, the civilian expert on fire protection, was of course recommending to the COA not methods to save lives and property in Japan, but methods to destroy buildings and kill people. It is doubtful whether Bond, Perera, or other members of the COA ever noticed this striking juxtaposition in what was judged a just war against a hated enemy.

In one of their final reports to General Arnold, the COA submitted in October 1944 an air plan to defeat Japan by "aerial and naval blockade and bombardment from present and future bases." The COA based its recommendations on the assumption that Japan could be defeated without a land invasion. The plan listed aircraft production, urban industrial areas, and Japanese shipping as the most promising targets. Japanese "urban areas," argued the committee, should be bombed for "overall economic results." A supporting study to the committee's report pointed out that "area incendiary raids" would "produce great economic loss, measured in man months of industrial labor. . . . The direct loss they impose on war production is not inconsiderable." Once the attacks on urban industrial areas had been completed, the committee suggested that the AAF consider "comprehensive attacks designed to reduce food supplies" as a means "of weakening the Japanese will to resist."[12]

The COA ended its work as a target selection and evaluation agency in October 1944. The AAF had established operations analyst sections in the major American bomber commands in Europe, and the final air strategy for Europe had been set, which meant that the services of the COA were no longer required.[13] But the Joint Chiefs of Staff determined that they needed another target agency for the air campaign in the Pacific. The problem for the Chiefs was that were at least six agencies that made contributions to target analysis, with no centralized control. The result was a lack of coordination between these agencies over Far Eastern target selection.

The Joint Target Group (JTG) was established by the Joint Chiefs in the fall of 1944. The JTG relieved other agencies like the COA "of target analysis functions as it absorbe[d] personnel from them." The JTG would be responsible for target analysis in the Pacific theater and would also provide information to the operating commands. The Chiefs instructed the JTG to use the "European experience" in strategic bombing to revise the bombing strategy for the Pacific, emphasizing "the development of new techniques of air attack."[14]

As a target analysis agency directly responsible to the Joint Chiefs, it was natural for the JTG to support the Chiefs' plan for American air power to attack the war-making capacity of Japan in order to make possible a successful land invasion.[15] In their first estimate on air power in the Pacific war, the JTG pointed out that "the strategic air mission can only be the rapid elimination of Japanese capacity to defend the homeland against invasion." Written by the group's director, Brigadier General John A. Samford, the estimate considered it essential that the AAF use strategic bombing operations to limit "replacements in certain weapons and materials of war essential to the defense of the Japanese homeland." General Samford noted that the "dispersal of small industry throughout congested urban industrial areas [was] of such a high order that this dispersed industry alone, if undeterred, could provide an increasingly significant volume of defense material." These industrial areas were "highly vulnerable to incendiary attacks." The estimate also recommended that the AAF use precision attacks to destroy aircraft engine factories, weapons and ammunition arsenals, electronic plants, and thermal electric power facilities on Kyushu. The intended purpose for these different methods of attack was to lessen the Japanese ability to defend the home islands against an American land invasion.[16]

A February 1945 general analysis by the JTG stated its "concept of area attacks":

> Area attacks, interpreted as attacks directed at concentrations of diversified industrial/military facilities and/or housing, are effective primarily in terms of the relatively large amount of physical damage and production loss which they impose. Maximum loss will result from \successful attacks against target areas which combine high physical vulnerability and important industrial facilities.[17]

The objective for area attacks, according to the group, was "industrial concentration[s] in principal urban areas." Within those "urban areas" were specific war industries like aircraft production, steel factories, and ammunition plants. The targets contained in the "industrial concentrations" could be attacked with incendiary or precision bombing, depending on operational and target factors. Area attacks, therefore, were a method, like precision bombing, to destroy the war industry in Japan's largest cities. The JTG realized that area attacks would kill "workers." But causing terror was not the primary purpose of area attacks, according to the JTG. Instead area attacks would produce industrial loss consisting "of direct damage to factories and their equipment . . . and of time lost by workers through the disorganizing effects of de-housing, casualties, disruption of utilities services, and general administrative disorganization."[18]

A major recipient of the JTG's analyses was Brigadier General Haywood Hansell's XXI Bomber Command. The Twenty-first had been flying bombing missions against Japan out of Tinian Island, in the Mariana chain, since November 1944. Hansell's command conducted mostly precision bombing missions against specific Japanese industrial targets. As a former instructor at the Air Corps Tactical School and an architect of precision bombing doctrine, Hansell felt that he could effectively attack Japanese war-making capacity using precision bombing methods.[19]

Owing to numerous operational problems and difficult flying weather over Japan, Hansell was never able to achieve much success with precision methods. As a result, General Arnold replaced Hansell on 20 January 1945 with Major General Curtis E. LeMay. Historian Conrad Crane notes that LeMay was probably "the most innovative air commander of World War II." It was LeMay's operational boldness that led to his decision in March 1945 to switch from precision attacks on specific Japanese industries to firebombing Japanese cities. This shift was not a result of pressure placed on LeMay from Arnold in Washington, D.C. Instead, LeMay made the change on his own owing to a number of factors that made it difficult to fly high-altitude precision bombing during the day against the fortress of Japan, as Hansell had unsuccessfully tried to do.[20] LeMay's first major area attack using incendiary bombs occurred on the night of 9 March 1945 against Tokyo. The attack killed at least seventy thousand civilians and burned major portions of Tokyo's industrial and residential sectors.

Using the results of LeMay's fire raids and intelligence on Japanese industry, the JTG put together "target information sheets" that contained data on concentrated industrial areas located in the largest Japanese cities. A late-March JTG summary listing the major Japanese industrial cities noted that the city of Nagasaki contained "industry including both plants of the Mitsubishi Steel and Arms Works, the Akunoura Engine Works, Mitsubishi Electric, several other small factories and most of the ports storage and trans-shipment facilities."[21] The Nagasaki target sheet pointed out that a "successful area attack against Nagasaki will damage or destroy factories and a large proportion of the housing in the city."[22] Neither the city summary nor the Nagasaki target sheet listed the morale of the civilian population as an objective for strategic bombers. The JTG knew that the AAF would kill large numbers of civilians with their fire raids, but the objective was to reduce the productive level of the city. Killing and injuring civilian "workers" would help lower the output of factories due to "losses in labor."[23]

The JTG prepared an air bombardment plan in June 1945 to support Operation Olympic (the code name for the planned ground invasion of Kyushu). There were two phases to the plan. The first phase would attack "production and storage capacities," while phase 2 attacked "transportation and other targets in direct support of an invasion." Both phases were designed to "reduce the present industrial output of all military products by more than 50%, to destroy 70% of central ammunition stocks in Japan proper, to reduce production capacity of ground forces ordnance and munitions by 75%, and to interdict rail and coast-wide shipping during any selected period."[24] Clearly the JTG wanted the AAF to bomb the Japanese home islands with the intent of taking war material like ammunition, rifles, aircraft, etc., out of the hands of the Japanese soldiers who would defend their country against the American invasion. The JTG's emphasis on reducing the "end products" of Japanese war industry was markedly different from the Strategic Bombing Survey's belief that the most successful strategic bombing attacks in the European theater were against "basic industries" like electric power, oil, and transportation.

Because of the perceived Japanese ability to shift their war industries to different areas within a given "urban concentration," the JTG argued that "strong air forces can be exploited better against broad objectives than against narrow ones regardless of their calculated significance." For the JTG "broad objectives" meant "urban concentrations" of factories that produced war material. And by June of 1945, based on the results of the XXI Bomber Command's fire raids against Japanese cities, the JTG believed that an effective method against "urban concentrations" of industry was area attacks. The group noted that certain targets were "nominated for high level attack; others for low level attack."[25] In the vernacular of the AAF in the closing months of World War II in the Pacific, low-level attacks came to mean area or fire raids against "urban concentrations" of industries, while high-level attacks meant precision bombing of specific industries. But both were methods, according to the JTG, to attack the ability of Japan to resist an American land invasion.

II

The directors of the Strategic Bombing Survey agreed that both area and precision attacks were methods to destroy the enemy's war-making capacity. But based on their findings in Europe, Survey directors concluded that the decisive targets were basic industries like oil, electric power, and transportation. The JTG, however, believed that the final goods produced by the war-making capacity—ammunition, aircraft, naval ships, etc.—should be the primary targets for the AAF.

Survey directors and JTG members had an opportunity to discuss their differences during a series of meetings in June 1945. On a trip back to Washington, D.C., in late May, Franklin D'Olier was summoned by General Arnold to report on the Survey's findings. Immediately following the meeting with Arnold on 6 June, D'Olier got on the phone with his directors in Europe. He informed Henry Alexander that General Arnold wanted the Survey to present its findings to the JTG and other military leaders in Washington and ultimately to use the Survey's findings "to make a very important contribution to the situation in Japan." D'Olier instructed Alexander, Nitze, Ball, and General Anderson to leave as soon as possible, and he guaranteed them that once they arrived in Washington they would "have a very, very interesting time."[26]

On 9 June, they held their first meeting with members of the Joint Target Group. Representing the JTG was its director, Brigadier General Samford. Also attending the conference was Major General Lauris Norstad, the assistant chief of air staff, and Colonel George Brownell, who was Robert A. Lovett's (the assistant secretary of war for air) military executive. The purpose of the meeting, stated Norstad at the beginning of the conference, was "to find out in general terms what [the Survey had] found in Europe" and to provide General Arnold (who had just departed for a visit with the operating commands in the Pacific) with "some broad statements and conclusions that you people have reached." Setting the tone of the conference, D'Olier noted that he "was already impressed with what bombing had done to the economy of Germany in completely breaking their capacity to resist." The conference began in the morning and did not conclude until late in the afternoon.[27]

The Joint Target Group had prepared a list of questions for the Survey to answer and for discussion among the conference attendees. The questions reflected the emphasis that the JTG placed on the need for the AAF to destroy the end products of Japanese war industry. The first question to the Survey was whether "the productive capacity of a modern enemy is the factor which is most likely to be decisive in avoiding defeat." General Samford of the JTG qualified the question further: "We do refer in this question to the exploitation, that is the productive capacity that is being exploited, and then we treat with sustained war action rather than to bring us back to a specific battle."[28] Here Samford was cryptically hinting at the JTG's belief that the most effective way to prepare for a land invasion of Japan was to destroy its finished war products and not to attack the basic industries of its war economy. General Anderson of the Survey countered by arguing that their findings in Europe had showed that "cutting the pipeline or productive resources is the most effective way of insuring defeat of that nation or that force. . . ."[29] Anticipating the same remarks he would make to an AAF interviewer in August, Anderson's "pipeline or productive resources" were the basic industries like electric power and transportation.

Alexander followed by succinctly summing up the Survey's position: "The indications are that the bombing of a number of end-products was far less effective than the bombing of the more basic items or basic services."[30]

Disagreement between Survey directors and JTG members during the conference over strategic bombing objectives produced differences over the most effective bombing methods. General Norstad read a question posed by the JTG: "What aspects of the [European] bombing program had little, if any, military consequences, and what was their other value, if any?"[31] Drawing on the testimony of Albert Speer, Alexander pointed out that "Speer and his colleagues expressed the view that the area bombing had no military effect."[32] Norstad asked whether or not it was better for strategic bombers to attack "narrow" or "broad" segments of the enemy's "productive capabilities." General Samford insisted that it was the JTG's belief that if the AAF used precision attacks against a "narrow segment" like ball bearings, the enemy "could probably escape and survive. . . ." But using strategic bombers to attack a wide area of the enemy's war capacity like "ball-bearings, transportation, oil, end-products, basic equipment, basic processing industries, and raw materials" would give the enemy "no possibility of escape." Nitze then restated the Survey's position by pointing out to Samford that the testimony of Speer and the other German officials was in "direct opposition" to the JTG's "principle."[33] For Nitze and his fellow Survey directors, the decisive method and objective for strategic bombers were precision attacks against the "basic segments" of the enemy's war-making capacity.

Paul Nitze, during the 9 June conference with the JTG, displayed his penchant for counterfactual speculation when evaluating the effects of strategic bombing. Trying to understand the relationship between discrete industries in the overall German war economy, the JTG asked if the "rates of recovery of particular industries [were] importantly affected by attack[s] on other target categories." The question allowed Nitze to demonstrate, counterfactually, the Survey's belief that a strategic bombing attack on the German electric power system would have had a crippling effect on the overall German war economy. Nitze stated that "if there was a target system which we had not attacked on a concentrated systematic basis which might have been decisive, the Germans . . . come out with the answer that power would have done it." Germany, argued Nitze, would not have been able to prevent "a complete breakdown of their distribution system" if the AAF had knocked out twenty key power plants in the German system. Nitze emphasized to Samford: "If you had gone after heavy generating equipment with big bombs they couldn't have rebuilt in less than two or three years the equipment necessary to put them back into operation."[34]

If one could remove the titles of rank of conference participants like General Anderson and General Samford, and if one could remove the explicit references to strategic bombing in the discourse, the discussions between the JTG and the Survey would seem like an economic conference about Germany's gross national output. Guilio Douhet emphasized in 1921 that the essence of air strategy was selecting the appropriate targets for strategic bombers. And as the American conceptual approach to strategic bombing developed in the 1930s, those targets became essentially economic in nature. Therefore, the most qualified individuals to formulate air power strategy (as opposed to tactics and operations) were civilian industrial and economic experts, not airmen.[35]

But General Anderson, during the conference, tried to place what was essentially an economic analysis by the JTG and Survey directors into a military context, with Anderson himself being the foremost expert. At one point George Ball, Paul Nitze, and Robert Russell (Survey director of the Oil Division) were explaining to General Norstad the importance of oil for Germany's war economy. Nitze stated that the AAF was most successful when it went after critical industries "like oil." Ball agreed and told Nitze that he was "absolutely right." Anderson then referred to the AAF's early attacks on oil and other targets in 1942 and 1943. He posited that "they were largely a mistake, and from a point of view of the economic system the dividends were quite low."[36] From a military standpoint, though, where he saw himself as the expert, the mistakes in fact had a positive aspect. Anderson boasted:

> we certainly created the impression that we lacked a system and the ability to think. They thought we were vicious piece-mealers and it made our air war much simpler. We didn't show system. We grabbed a marshaling yard and we grabbed a [submarine] pen. I think they never gave us credit for a system, and Speer said he didn't sense that we were going after his economic system until late in 1943. If we had shown our system it would probably have been three or four times harder to destroy it.[37]

In the above passage Anderson was not talking about air power strategy or target selection but emphasizing instead the operational ability of the AAF to deceive Speer and the Germans as to which "target system" they were attacking. When he said the AAF "grabbed" a railroad marshaling yard or submarine pen, he was referring to their operational ability to bomb those targets. The difference is subtle but important. While Anderson was an expert at the operational aspects of air war, such as deception and putting bombs on target, he was not the expert at determining which industries, both basic and productive, were the most critical for an enemy's war economy. Nitze the Wall Street industrialist, Russell the executive vice-president of Standard Oil, and Ball the corporate lawyer were the experts in the field of air power strategy.

And those civilian experts were most comfortable with evaluating the economic effects of strategic bombing on Germany during the war. General Anderson brought up again the effectiveness of the RAF's area raids against German cities. George Ball, referring to Speer's testimony, pointed out that "the Hamburg raid in 1943 scared them to death." Colonel Brownell, who had been quiet up to then, perceptively noted that Ball's statement placed "some doubt on what [Ball] said earlier about the effectiveness of area raids." Ball retorted: "What Speer said was that he was terribly worried at the time. He thought if those raids were continued that the war was lost, but he later realized he had been wrong, as other people in

Germany realized." Anderson told Brownell that Germany could materially "recover faster than they expected," hence the lack of effectiveness of area raids against German cities. But General Norstad probed at the profound implications of Speer's testimony: the potential effects of area bombing on German morale. Norstad suggested to Anderson and Ball that "there was probably a certain amount of hysteria connected with [the area raids]."[38] "Hysteria" for Norstad clearly meant the ability of the RAF's area raids on cities like Hamburg to cause terror among the civilian population. But because Ball framed his analysis of area attacks in terms of German war-making capacity and not morale, he easily moved the discussion back to the economic effects of area bombing and Hamburg's "surprisingly fast recuperation."[39]

Although morale as an objective had been a key topic of discussion for the Committee of Historians back in 1943, it was simply not an important topic for discussion during the daylong conference between the JTG and Survey directors in June 1945. Some historians have either misread the entire transcript for the 9 June conference or failed to read it at all. The conference has been portrayed, incorrectly, as a debate between the JTG's purported emphasis on using the XXI Bomber Command's fire raids to attack Japanese morale and the Survey's purported attempt to have the AAF halt the fire raids, stop attacking morale, and bomb "basic industries" like electric power and transportation.[40] But if the central issue of the debate between the JTG and Survey members was over the effects of strategic bombing on morale, then one would have expected it to take up much more time at the conference. The conferees spent the entire day on 9 June discussing the effects of strategic bombing, resulting in a seventy-five-page typed transcript of the meeting. Out of those seventy-five pages only about one page reflected discussions over morale.[41] George Ball insisted that he did not "think that the question of morale in and of itself [was] important. It doesn't mean anything unless it is translated into political action or a decrease in production."[42] The Survey's Morale Division director, Rensis Likert, was left back in Germany and did not attend the conference.

The European Survey did not evaluate the effects of strategic bombing on Germany's political decisions during the war. Instead, Survey members directed their analysis toward the effects of strategic bombing on the German war economy. They believed that a strategic bombing campaign directed against the "basic industries" of the enemy's war-making capacity could be decisive, but only in terms of that war-making capacity, not the civilian population's morale or the political will to resist.

The European Survey's *Summary Report* argued that "Allied air power was decisive in the war in Western Europe. Hindsight inevitably suggests that it might have been employed differently or better in some respects. Nevertheless, it was decisive."[43] But that published report never defined the word *decisive*. Implicit in the Survey's use of the word *decisive*, of course, was the notion that something was decided. But who were the agents of that decision? The European *Summary Report* did not argue that strategic bombing forced Adolph Hitler to "decide" to end the war. What the report did argue was that Allied strategic bombing broke Germany's capacity to resist, and in this sense, according to the Survey, it "was decisive."

Survey members themselves disagreed on how and why strategic bombing was "decisive" and indeed often on what they meant. During the 9 June meeting with the Joint Target Group, Henry Alexander told Norstad he thought that "the oil system was decisive. I think the decisiveness was aided and speeded by the attack on transportation as well." Then Ball interjected: "I think the transportation would have been decisive without the oil." Seeking clarification, General Norstad inquired if "the enemy's capacity to resist would have been weakened by oil alone or transportation or by the combination of both to a point where he had to quit?" Shrewdly, Alexander hedged his response to the general:

> Of course when you say "have to quit[,]" decisive doesn't mean that completely. There were still men standing in bushes with rifles that had to be disposed of. Of course, he couldn't make any effective defense or

> any appreciable defense for any length of time with those two factors as they were reduced. [Decisive] does not necessarily mean that every soldier would have to put down his gun and go home.

General Samford of the JTG wondered whether "it could be said that in this condition, that had there been just the attack on transportation and oil, even had they been implemented further, that all of the rest which was done was unnecessary."[44] Here Samford was asking the Survey directors to state forthrightly that strategic bombing against two "basic industries" like transportation and oil was crucial, and that "all of the rest" had been a mistake.

Orvil Anderson said "no, but it can be stated that it was almost unnecessary." He went on to admit that strategic bombing could reduce a given target "system" to a point where the law of "diminishing returns" dictated that there was "something of more immediate value and greater value, whether that be 5% of [Germany's] remaining production or 7% would have to be determined, but we all approach a law of diminishing returns that drives us from a target. The last 10% might be vital."[45] Anderson's rambling language, laden with economic jargon, hid a deeper ambivalence about the decisiveness of strategic air power. Like Alexander, Anderson could comfortably state that a properly planned and executed strategic bombing campaign directed at basic industries would break an enemy's capacity to resist, and in this sense, be decisive. But to take the next step and argue, in the case of Germany, that it made "all of the rest" unnecessary was more than he or Alexander was willing to claim. Such a step would have required a counterfactual argument stating that the land invasion of Europe was unnecessary to defeat Germany.

III

The JTG considered the information that the Survey had presented to them, yet because the JTG was committed to planning for the use of air power to support a successful ground invasion of Japan, they did not place top priority on attacking "basic industries" like transportation with precision bombing methods, as the Survey's European analysis suggested. Instead the JTG recommended the XXI Bomber Command continue its fire raids on Japanese urban areas, with some modifications, to destroy large quantities of war material that the Japanese would use to resist the American ground invasion of the home islands.[46]

In one of its final air estimates of the Pacific war, "Principles for the Selection of Air Target," the Joint Target Group developed a sophisticated theory of air power that manifested their belief in the necessity of invading Japan with ground troops. The estimate stated that a fundamental of modern war was to use as early as possible "long range weapons of war [strategic bombers] to create conditions under which engagements of enemy armed forces in being can be brief, decisive, and preponderantly favorable." The use of strategic bombers, argued the JTG, "can best be described as preparatory." The group's estimate cautioned, though, that "long chance objectives," like the basic industries of a war economy, have a "high probability of achieving no significant success whatsoever" in preparing for the decisive engagement of the "armed forces." The most promising objectives, therefore, would be the enemy's "reserve position," which consisted primarily of war material that the enemy's armed forces could use to fight the "decisive engagement."[47]

Brigadier General A. W. Kissner, chief of staff of Curtis LeMay's XXI Bomber Command, disagreed. In fact he stated emphatically to General Kuter that the JTG's program for the XXI Bomber Command's strategic air campaign against the Japanese home islands failed "to recognize the potency of strategic air bombardment as a decisive force by itself." Kissner did not want to split up his command's strategic bombing campaign into "'preparatory' and 'participating' phases with respect to plans for invasion by surface forces," as the JTG suggested. Instead he recommended to Kuter that the XXI Bomber Command should "proceed according to its own time table" and not be made "contingent upon, land invasion plans. It is considered that the strategic bombing effort should be planned as an end within itself rather than as a means to an end, namely, invasion."[48]

The differences between the JTG, the key leaders of the XXI Bomber Command, and Survey directors over the necessity of the ground invasion of the Japanese home islands shaped their views over strategic bombing methods and objectives. The JTG, in fact, during the "preparatory phase" of their bombardment plan, wanted Curtis LeMay's command to curtail the number of fire raids against "urban concentrations" and increase the precision raids against specific industrial targets. Area attacks should resume in full force, argued the JTG, once the preparatory phase had been completed and the ground invasion date drew nearer.[49] LeMay and Kissner, however, owing to operational considerations, wanted to continue with the firebombings of Japanese cities, which they believed would eventually force Japan to surrender without a ground invasion.[50] Survey directors like Paul Nitze agreed that a properly directed strategic bombing program could bring about a decision, and in this sense they were in line with LeMay and Kissner. But since the Survey argued that the best objectives for strategic bombers to attack were basic industries such as electric power and transportation, they therefore recommended that the AAF use, primarily, precision attacks instead of area raids.[51]

IV

The Survey directors had impressed senior AAF leaders and members of the War Department with their knowledge of air power theory and practice. After the series of meetings with the JTG, they met on 19 June with Secretary of War Henry Stimson, Assistant Secretary of War for Air Robert Lovett, and Army Chief of Staff General George C. Marshall.[52] Stimson noted in his diary that the Survey's "report was of great interest both because of the damage that it showed and the failures that it indicated. . . ." Based on the Survey's findings on the "differences between the German and Japanese industrial setup," Stimson asked them to "advise us as to any differences of *method* to be used in Japan."[53] Stimson had previously expressed his concern to General Arnold over the AAF's fire raids on Japanese cities where at least a few hundred thousand Japanese civilians were killed. Stimson may have been troubled by the moral implications of killing civilians. He was also worried the United States might be tagged with "the reputation of outdoing Hitler in atrocities."[54] The Survey's emphasis on attacking basic industries like transportation and electric power with precision bombing "methods" may have provided Stimson with a comfortable alternative to the firebombing of Japanese cities.

Paul Nitze was given the mission of fulfilling Stimson's desire for an "alternate strategy for the air attack on Japan."[55] It is unclear why Nitze got the job over the other Survey directors. Nitze's demonstrated analytical acumen in the June meetings with the JTG must have helped. Certainly Alexander and Ball, and for that matter Galbraith, were all qualified, based on their European experience, to write an alternate plan for the strategic bombardment of Japan. Galbraith did not mention in his memoirs the Survey's alternate bombardment plan. But he did provide a glimpse of the personality of Paul Nitze and a possible explanation as to why Nitze was given the job. Galbraith recalled that Nitze was a "self possessed man, [who] devoted the rest of his life to studying the theory and practice of aerial destruction, emerging in the end as a devout practitioner of the art."[56]

Nitze recalled in his memoirs that he wrote the alternate plan over the Fourth of July weekend while vacationing at a Long Island beach with family and friends. He claimed that since Japan was isolated owing to the American naval blockade around the home islands, "the only means of transportation were the rail network and intercoastal shipping. . . ." Nitze reasoned, therefore, that a "concentrated air attack on the essential lines of transportation and . . . the Kammon tunnels would isolate the Japanese home islands from one another and fragment the enemy's base of operations." Nitze said that he believed the "interdiction of the lines of transportation would be sufficiently effective so that additional bombing of urban industrial areas would not be necessary."[57]

The actual plan that Nitze wrote for the Survey in July 1945 called for top priority to be given to precision bombing attacks on Japanese transportation and "an increased emphasis on the [naval] blockade of the Japanese home islands." Next in priority would be a "concentrated attack in a short period of time" on Japanese central ammunition reserves. But the AAF should attack ammunition reserves, according to the plan, only if it had confirmed intelligence that these reserves were centralized at a few locations and that "a significant portion of them" could be destroyed. Following the attack on ammunition, the plan called for the AAF to bomb electric power and nitrogen production plants that they had not already destroyed by either "precision bombing attacks or by urban industrial concentration attacks." Nitze also recommended in 1945 that the AAF bomb rice production in Japan with chemicals, thereby starving the people and eliminating any "hope of long term resistance."[58]

Nitze gave a low priority to area attacks on industries in Japanese cities. The plan did not, however, omit this method of bombing, as Nitze implicitly suggested in his memoirs. Instead the plan recommended that the AAF bomb

> urban industrial concentrations only insofar as operating considerations make it probable that there is a relatively small chance of hitting any of the precision targets listed above, selected as priority targets, or make it probable that the most efficient method of destroying such precision targets is by area rather than precision attack.[59]

The above passage from the Survey's plan clearly demonstrates Nitze's view that area and precision attacks were different methods for the AAF to bomb Japanese war-making capacity. According to Nitze's plan, the most effective way to destroy Japanese "end products" (the JTG's primary concern) was by precision attacks against Japanese transportation that linked together the factories that produced war material. However, Nitze cautioned that for the recommended bombing program to be decisive, it would "take time."[60]

The JTG disagreed with certain parts of Nitze's plan. They placed greater emphasis on continuing the XXI Bomber Command's area attacks against Japanese cities to destroy "identified concentrations of end product industries and stores, including ammunition storage." The group believed that the targets contained in these "concentrations" were "highly vulnerable to incendiary attacks." The purpose of the raids, argued the JTG, was "to destroy by fire large quantities of war material produced and being produced . . . thereby creating expenditures over which the Japanese cannot exercise control."[61] The JTG's reliance on area raids to destroy Japanese end products reflected their belief that strategic bombing should be directed at ultimately preparing the way for a successful American land invasion of fortress Japan.

The JTG did agree, though, with the high priority the Survey plan placed on attacking Japanese transportation. In fact the group called for an "overwhelming attack upon rail transportation and coastwise shipping to disintegrate the Japanese home islands industrially; as an economic entity; and as a final defense line."[62] The Survey's alternate plan asserted that, given time, a properly designed strategic bombing campaign eliminating Japanese transportation could be "decisive on enemy military capabilities."[63] Implicit in the Survey's plan was that somehow, once the decisive attacks against transportation had broken Japan's capacity to resist, the war would end without a land invasion. Yet Nitze's alternate strategic bombing plan never explicitly promised that Japan would surrender unconditionally.

It is also worthwhile to note that neither the Survey's alternate strategic bombardment plan nor the conferences held between the Survey and the JTG in June 1945 ever mentioned specific numbers of casualties for the planned invasion of Japan. Nitze recalled in a 1994 interview that he "thought the 500,000 U.S. casualties" grossly underestimated the number of troops that would have been killed or injured in the planned invasion of the Japanese home islands.[64] However, *prior* to Hiroshima, Nitze *never* addressed the issue of American casualties in any of his work with the Survey concerning the strategic bombardment of Japan.[65]

General Spaatz had the strategic bombardment plans of the Survey and the JTG presented to him on 18 and 19 July.[66] The Survey directors who had spent the first half of the summer in Washington, D.C., sensed that the JTG had not given their ideas on strategic bombing an impartial hearing. Henry Alexander was relieved that the "judge" who would listen to "both sides of the case" that he and the other directors felt was lacking in their earlier discussions seemed "to have been found" in General Spaatz.[67] The meeting with the general went very well for the Survey and their alternate bombardment plan for the defeat of Japan. D'Olier spoke with Anderson on the phone shortly after the meeting on the eighteenth and crowed: "everything has wound up very, very satisfactorily." D'Olier claimed that they had convinced General Spaatz (and AAF Deputy Chief of Staff General Eaker, who was also at the meeting) that transportation was "absolutely the prime target." The AAF was "going at it just as soon" as possible, boasted the chairman.[68] General Eaker noted that Spaatz "was inclined to concur with the D'Olier Committee's recommendation. . . . [The] disruption of Japanese transportation is of such significant importance that an overwhelming attack on transportation may well have a direct and early effect on the other priorities."[69]

Spaatz and other airmen thought that American air power probably could end the war against Japan, thereby eliminating the need for an "other" priority—the land invasion.[70] As the newly assigned commander of the U.S. Army Strategic Air Forces in the Pacific, Spaatz, in accordance with a directive from General Arnold, intended to implement the plan.[71] As a devoted advocate of precision bombing doctrine, Spaatz certainly must have appreciated the Survey's emphasis on the precise destruction of Japanese transportation. The Survey's plan would reduce the XXI Bomber Command's fire raids that had already killed hundreds of thousands of Japanese civilians, probably easing Spaatz's moral concerns.[72] The Survey's plan also held out the possibility that air power would be an independent force in Japan's capitulation. Anything that might avoid the land invasion of the Japanese home islands and prove the decisiveness of air power must have appealed to the general.

V

But the American Joint Chiefs of Staff and President Harry S. Truman had decided at a high-level meeting on 18 June 1945 to go ahead with the plans for a massive ground invasion of Kyushu (Operation Olympic), requiring about 767,000 American troops. Olympic was set to begin on 1 November 1945. The JCS had considered the possibility that strategic bombardment, coupled with a naval blockade, against Japan might end the war. Yet as General Marshall explained to the president at the 18 June meeting, the ground invasion of Kyushu was essential, "both to tightening our stranglehold of blockade and bombardment on Japan, and to forcing capitulation by invasion of the Tokyo Plain."[73]

General Spaatz did not arrive in the Pacific until late July 1945 with the Survey's alternate strategic bombing plan. The momentum of the XXI Bomber Command's fire raids kept Spaatz from implementing his late-July directive to shift targeting priorities to precision attacks against Japanese transportation.[74] The atomic bombings of Hiroshima and Nagasaki on 6 and 9 August 1945 and the subsequent Japanese decision to surrender on 15 August made whatever intentions Spaatz had on targeting moot. The war had ended without a land invasion. But what ended the war? Was it the AAF's conventional strategic bombing campaign against Japanese cities that persuaded the Japanese leadership to surrender? Or was the threat of an American land invasion enough to convince Japanese policy makers to end the war? Did the combat use of the two atomic bombs force Japan to surrender unconditionally? If the atomic bombs had not been dropped, could the Survey's alternate bombing plan (providing Spaatz had implemented it) have ended the war without a land invasion?

After submitting their plan to General Spaatz, Franklin D'Olier and Paul Nitze returned to London in late July to complete their work on the European portion of the Survey. On 7 August, the day after Hiroshima, D'Olier telephoned Fred Searls in Washington, D.C., and commented on their excitement "about this new bomb." D'Olier then queried: "What effect, if any, do you think it is going to have on the Bombing Survey?" Searls gave no answer to D'Olier.[75] But the chairman and his directors were aware, even before President Truman issued a formal request on 15 August for the Survey to continue its work in the Pacific, that they would be evaluating the effects of strategic bombing on Japan.[76]

Paul Nitze implicitly claimed in his 1987 memoirs that he knew beforehand the answers to so many of the perplexing questions surrounding the end of the war in the Pacific. Nitze recalled that after Fred Searls had informed him about the atomic bomb in July 1945, they both "concluded that even without the atomic bomb, Japan was likely to surrender in a matter of months. My own view was that Japan would capitulate by November 1945."[77] Nitze's thinking in July 1945 undoubtedly shaped the counterfactual statement he would write in the Pacific Survey's *Summary Report* about seven months later concerning the end of the war with Japan. That report stated: "certainly prior to 31 December 1945, and in all probability prior to 1 November 1945, Japan would have surrendered even if the atomic bombs had not been dropped, even if Russia had not entered the war, and even if no invasion had been planned or contemplated."[78] Counterfactual speculation, though, was nothing new for Paul Nitze or his fellow Survey analysts.

CHAPTER 5

The Evaluation of Strategic Bombing against Japan

> We have the facts and there just can't be much argument about that. It is when we get to the conclusions that the trouble arises.
>
> PAUL NITZE, April 1946

After spending three months in Japan from October to December 1945 evaluating the effects of strategic bombing on Japan's wartime economy and its political decision to surrender, Paul Nitze briefed members of the Senate Committee on Atomic Energy about the Survey's findings from the Pacific. He told the senators that by the closing months of the Pacific war, "Japan was already defeated by air power, and that the major influence of the atomic bomb was that it made an invasion unnecessary." But this was not the conclusion that Nitze would publish six months later in the Pacific Survey's *Summary Report*. Anticipating what would become the Pacific Survey's early-surrender counterfactual, Nitze revised the conclusion he had presented to the senators. Japan, argued Nitze, "would have surrendered prior to November 1 in any case; the atomic bomb merely accelerated the date at which Japan surrendered."[1] This striking remark made by Nitze, positing that the combat use of the atomic bomb was unnecessary in forcing Japan to surrender unconditionally, raised no questions or responses from the members of the committee.

The Pacific phase of the Strategic Bombing Survey was more complicated than its European phase. When conducting their evaluation in Europe, Survey analysts followed closely behind the advancing Allied armies into Germany. Many European Survey conclusions about the effects of strategic bombing were shaped while the war was still being fought. In the Pacific, in contrast, the Survey's entire evaluation was conducted after the war had ended. And in the Pacific, unlike Europe, surrender occurred without a land invasion. Therefore, in many of the Pacific Survey's published reports, analysts like Paul Nitze felt compelled to explain the role of strategic bombing in bringing this about.

President Truman further complicated matters for the Survey when he instructed them to evaluate "all types of air attack" against Japan and to submit the reports directly to the secretary of war and the secretary of the navy.[2] In Europe the Survey was fundamentally an AAF-inspired evaluation, with the published reports going only to the secretary of war. By requiring the Survey to evaluate not only the Army Air Forces' use of air power against Japan, but also the navy's, President Truman opened the door for an intense interservice rivalry between the AAF's representative on the Survey, General Orvil Anderson, and the navy's Rear Admiral Ralph Ofstie.[3] It was a rivalry fueled by postwar budgets and defense policy, and it mentally tired out the Survey's vice-chairman, Paul Nitze, when he wrote the Pacific Survey's *Summary Report.*

I

Many of the key directors from the European Survey decided not to go to the Pacific to evaluate the effects of strategic bombing against Japan. Shortly after explaining to the press in October 1945 the Survey's results from Europe, Henry Alexander returned to his previous position with J. P. Morgan and Company. Although Alexander would continue to advise the Survey during the Pacific phase, the de facto vice-chairman for the Pacific Survey became Paul Nitze.[4] George Ball took on a new job with the government as the general counsel of the French Supply Council. John Kenneth Galbraith spent the month of

October with the Survey in Japan and attended a number of important interrogations of Japanese officials. But in early November he returned to the United States to work for the State Department, and, like Alexander, was more of an advisor than division director.[5] Milton Gilbert, chief of the National Income Unit of the Department of Commerce, took over as director of the Overall Economic Effects Division.[6] Paul Nitze lamented to his mother that the "best men" like Alexander and Galbraith "had to leave" the Survey, making his work as vice-chairman more difficult.[7] As in Europe, Franklin D'Olier remained the titular chairman of the Survey.

Drawing on the European experience, the Survey relied mostly on interrogations of key Japanese military and government officials.[8] Unlike the Germans, the Japanese leadership kept very few industrial records (many were destroyed by the Japanese prior to the American occupation of the home islands). The Urban Areas Division, for example, had to rely on the responses to questions distributed to over eight thousand Japanese industrial and civic leaders between October and November 1945. The division's experts used the statements on the completed questionnaires as their primary source of evidence for their conclusions concerning the effects of strategic bombing on the economies of Japanese cities.[9] Emphasizing the importance of the interrogations of Japanese leaders, Galbraith lectured Survey analysts in October to show more patience "with each interrogation to be sure that complete information is secured on any important points. . . ."[10]

The data collection portion of the Pacific Survey went much faster than in Europe. While it took almost eight months to collect information on the effects of strategic bombing in Germany, the Pacific Survey did it in about three months. The intensive data collection began in early October and ended when most of the Survey departed Japan on the navy ship USS *Ancon* in mid-December 1945.[11] There were three primary reasons for the speed of data collection: (1) the experience gained in Europe made Survey analysts in the Pacific much more efficient in collecting and processing information; (2) since the preponderance of data in the Pacific Survey was made up of interrogations and questionnaires, analysts did not have to spend as much time interpreting voluminous production and statistical records; (3) Pacific Survey analysts could move about freely from the very start of their evaluation owing to the American occupation of the Japanese home islands. Nitze was so impressed with the Survey's work in Japan that he called it "the fastest moving, hardest-hitting post-war organization on record."[12]

Franklin D'Olier was delighted, and perhaps smug, over the way the press and senior military leaders had praised the Survey's reports from the European theater. He listened to Survey Director Frank McNamee, who had just arrived in Tokyo from Washington, D.C., boast about how well the American press had received the Survey's European reports. McNamee told D'Olier and the other Survey directors that the reception of the Survey's reports had "been so tremendous that 8000 additional copies of the summary [report] and 3500 additional copies of the overall report have been published."[13] D'Olier and Nitze were certainly hoping that the published reports produced by the Pacific Survey would draw the same kind of favorable response.

By late November 1945, most of the division analysts believed they had accumulated enough evidence to begin writing preliminary reports. Vice-Chairman Nitze wanted the divisions to have the preliminary drafts completed prior to departing for the United States on 1 December.[14] He probably wanted the drafts in early so that he could get a head start on reviewing them for the writing of his own chairman's summary report.[15]

II

Since the collection of data had gone so much faster in the Pacific phase of the Survey, one would also have expected the writing of the Pacific Survey's published reports to take less time than for Europe. During the European phase, Survey directors like John Kenneth Galbraith began writing their final reports in July 1945 and for the most part had them completed and ready for publication by October 1945. But instead of taking four months or less, Pacific Survey analysts spent on the average of eight to nine months to complete their final reports. They began drafting the reports in late November on the eve of their departure from Tokyo and did not send the final versions to the publisher until roughly July 1946 (and in one extreme case, June 1947). Nitze complained that after establishing Survey headquarters in Washington, D.C., upon their return from the Pacific in December, many of his analysts were more concerned about returning to civilian life than doing their job. Nitze lamented in a letter to his mother: "Trying to run this Survey job in peace time, largely with Army personnel who want to get out immediately and don't propose to do much work in the meantime is enough of a struggle, particularly as many of the best men have just had to leave."[16]

Yet the fundamental cause of Nitze's distress and of the lengthy time that it took to publish many of the Pacific Survey reports was the bitter interservice rivalry between the AAF and the navy over who had played the greatest role in ending the war against Japan. Nitze said that his *Summary Report* had "assumed the nature of a 'cause celebre' with neither the Army [AAF] nor the Navy liking the present version, and a good deal of fur flying in all directions."[17] The principal "fur" flingers that Nitze referred to were Orvil Anderson and Admiral Ralph A. Ofstie, the director of the Pacific Survey's Naval Analysis Division.

Back in November 1925, about one month before the American senior military leadership court-martialed General William Mitchell for behavior that they believed violated good order and discipline (Mitchell's public advocacy of an independent air force and his statements that the navy was irrelevant for national defense), Lieutenant Ralph Ofstie told a presidential board that "air power does not exist absolutely; that it exists only in conjunction with other forces which can cooperate with or which can transport it."[18] Army Lieutenant Orvil Anderson, then a flier, had disagreed. In fact he testified in December 1925, during the Mitchell court-martial,[19] that Mitchell's call for an independent air force was correct. The navy, according to young Orvil Anderson, because it viewed air power as a supporting arm of the fleet, had a flawed conception of air power for the national defense.

The interwar years and the combat experience of World War II only reaffirmed for Anderson and Ofstie their ideas on the proper role of air power. To Anderson, World War II had demonstrated that air power "played such an outstanding role in this war that it will never again be thought of as subsidiary to ground or naval warfare. . . ."[20] Admiral Ofstie, however, held a different view. In September 1945, he stressed to members of his Naval Analysis Division that their mission was to provide a thorough study of all air operations in the Pacific that brought the United States within "striking range of the Japanese homeland, and without which there would have been no successful conclusion of the war. . . ." In Ofstie's conception, the crucial events that led to the defeat of Japan were the navy's campaigns in the Pacific that relied heavily on carrier-based air power. Anticipating the influence that the Pacific Survey's published reports would have on future defense organization and policy, Ofstie stated that the "Survey's effort . . . may well be the basis for the major decisions respecting our post-war national security."[21]

In the months immediately following the end of World War II in the Pacific, American military leaders did their best to point out that victory over Japan was a team effort and that no single service had "won the war." Lieutenant General James A. Doolittle, who had commanded the Eighth Air Force in Europe and during the closing weeks of the war in the Pacific, told members of his command that World War II in the Pacific was "won by teamwork between Land, Sea and Air. . . . No single individual, arm, [or] service won the war. It was won by the greatest civil and military team that history has ever known."[22] Yet that was the past, and the future meant something different to the general. Looking ahead, he envisioned the defense organization of the United States consisting of a "modern air-arm composed of long range bombers, long range fighters, and long range air transports *backed* by an adequate Navy and Ground Force. . . ."[23] Naval officers, however, did not want to take a "backseat" to the airmen and their concept for the American postwar military establishment.[24]

Paul Nitze, after he arrived in Washington, D.C., from Japan in December 1945 to begin writing the Pacific Survey's *Summary Report*, was, in a sense, caught in the middle of the postwar rivalry between the navy and the AAF over the role of air power in the national defense, and more important whether or not the AAF should be granted independence. General Anderson and Admiral Ofstie both knew that the Survey's explanation of the role the AAF and the navy played in "winning" the war in the Pacific would have a substantial impact on future defense organization and strategy.[25] Both officers, therefore, did their very best to shape the arguments the Survey would produce.

Ofstie and Anderson sought to shape the central arguments in the chairman's *Summary Report*. From December 1945 to June 1946 at Langley Field, Virginia (the Washington, D.C., headquarters of the Pacific Survey), Nitze complained that he "had to write every word of the damn document, and [he got] the full brunt of the pressure from all sides."[26] Yet as hard as Nitze may have tried to maintain a balance between the two services, the interests of the AAF won out over the navy in the Pacific Survey's *Summary Report*.

Nitze appears to have written his first preliminary draft of the *Summary Report* on 12 March 1946. There were probably five subsequent drafts written between 12 March and 1 July when the final *Summary Report* was published.[27] Some of the changes contained in these drafts were striking in their emphasis on the AAF's role in the war against Japan and in their advocacy of an independent air arm. Nitze's 12 March preliminary draft pointed out that high-level bombing conducted by the AAF against Japanese shipping was not productive. The draft argued that "the accuracy of high level bombing against maneuvering ships was so low as to give disappointing results with the limited forces available." Although acknowledging that the AAF was able to apply only "limited forces," the draft still emphasized that high-level bombing was ineffective.[28] The 1 July published version of the *Summary Report* omitted this criticism of the AAF.

The published *Summary Report* also deleted some favorable statements made in earlier drafts about the importance of American carrier-based aircraft. A March outline of the report argued that the United States had "underestimated the ability of carrier-based air to neutralize Japanese land based air."[29] The published *Summary Report* acknowledged that the loss of the "antiquated battleships at Pearl Harbor had little effect on the [American] Navy's combat capabilities," but it did not give credit to the navy for destroying Japan's land-based air force, as the earlier draft had done.[30]

Another draft written in March emphasized that prompt passage of a bill by Congress to reorganize and unify America's military establishment was in the "national interest." According to the draft, the lessons from World War II highlighted the need for better "coordination in planning, intelligence, research and development, and operations." But it was more important, argued the report, that America's "entire military establishment be designed to meet the new strategic and tactical problems arising from the atomic bomb and increas[ed] power and range of modern weapons than that there be an independent and coordinated role for the air forces."[31] This was not the kind of conclusion concerning the future organization of the American military that the airmen wanted to hear because it made the independence of the AAF secondary to the problems that the atomic bomb and modern weapons presented to the United States.

Wanting to reshape the conclusions in the *Summary Report*, Orvil Anderson submitted to Nitze a "Suggested Draft on Conclusions." Anderson's draft described the application of strategic air power during the Pacific war as "spectacular." The Pacific war had proved, according to Anderson, that no longer was it "necessary to defeat armies to win a war. It can be won by defeating an economy." Anderson stated that one of the most important questions that the United States faced was "whether airpower can be used as a primary weapon, with ground and sea forces in ancillary roles. . . ."

His answer to this question was clear: "Since airpower is the only force capable of being launched directly against the enemy economy, it has become the primary weapon and must dictate the future structure of our armed forces and the overall strategy of another war." Anderson's draft charged that if the nation did not heed the Survey's "recommendations" for an independent air service, the future would be "fraught with grave warning. . . ."[32]

Admiral Ralph A. Ofstie, director of the Pacific Survey's Naval Analysis Division, recalled that the Survey's secretariat, Walter Wilds (who replaced Judge Cabot in the Pacific), believed that all of the Survey directors were "convinced of the desirability of setting up a separate air establishment." Yet for his part, Ofstie "expressed difficulty in understanding how the Survey had arrived at its [impartial] conclusions relative to a separate air department particularly when it so exactly coincided with Air Force proposals."[33] Ofstie did everything he could to move Nitze and other Survey directors away from what he called the air force's "party line" and toward the postwar interests of the navy.[34] Those interests did not embrace an independent air force, because an independent air force could possibly subsume the navy's carrier-based aircraft.

Ofstie was unhappy with some of the conclusions and recommendations of an April draft of the *Summary Report* that Nitze had written. The draft pointed out in a section on "the impact of the atomic bombs on the role of airpower" that the bombs "raised the destructive power of a single bomber or guided missile" by a huge factor. Ofstie commented on the draft's margin that he had "never heard" of employing atomic bombs on "guided missiles."[35] He later recalled that exploring the potential use of "guided missiles" was not within "the purview of the Survey."[36] Ofstie made his most lacerating comments on the draft's "recommendations" for the future. The draft noted that the "Survey had been impressed with the need . . . to unify and reorganize our military establishment. . . ." But Ofstie questioned whether "all the Directors" agreed with the purported need to reorganize and unify the military establishment. Nitze's draft lamented that the "lack of complete integration" of the Pacific Command during World War II was traceable "to the basic structure of our prewar military organization." Ofstie called this "nonsense." It was obvious to him that the draft was advocating an independent air force. So "why not say so," asked the admiral. The final paragraph of the draft argued that the United States "should unify and reorganize" its military establishment, implicitly recommending an independent air service. In Ofstie's mind, however, the *Summary Report* draft had arrived at a conclusion that was "totally unsupported by the work of the Survey, and certainly not related to the [presidential] directive."[37]

Ofstie's biting marginal comments on Nitze's draft were largely unsuccessful in changing the published (1 July 1946) *Summary Report*'s recommendations and conclusions. The published report began its concluding remarks by stating that "the role of air power should be given thorough consideration by those working out the solutions to new problems arising under [future] conditions."[38] Nitze's *Summary Report* did not explicitly call for an independent air force, but he left little doubt that that was what he had in mind. The lessons learned from the war in the Pacific, according to the report, "strongly support that form of organization which . . . provides unity of command and is itself oriented toward air and new weapons[. The] Survey believes that, in addition to the Army and the Navy, there should be an equal and coordinate position for a third establishment." This "third establishment" would have to conduct not only strategic bombing but also the air defense of the United States, and have the responsibility for "guided missiles." The report emphasized that "the mission of such a new establishment would differ considerably from that of an autonomous air force . . . which would conduct strategic bombing along the lines of World War II. The "new establishment" needed to have "additional and broader experience than has heretofore been required by the Army Air Forces alone."[39]

In July 1946, shortly after the publication of the *Summary Report*, Orvil Anderson felt that he needed to clarify for the secretary of war and the commanding general of the Army Air Forces some of the *Summary Report*'s conclusions. In a lengthy memorandum Anderson considered the *Summary Report* to be "an instrument which perceives the truth but has not pointedly developed the fundamental issues as a working thesis." Regarding the report's conclusion on the need for reorganization and unification, Anderson believed that the Survey had taken an appropriate stand on that issue. Yet the *Summary Report* did not go far enough, argued the general, in spelling out the need for an independent air force that would subsume all types of air power, both naval and land based: "Within this new Department of Air, it is important that we concentrate our air strength and centralize the responsibility for development of our future air weapons."[40] General Anderson wanted to be sure that nobody misunderstood the Survey's implicit call for an independent air force.

III

But how would the atomic bomb fit into such an independent air force? Anderson was pleased by the *Summary Report*'s counterfactual conclusion concerning the end of the war with Japan, which stated that "certainly prior to 31 December 1945, and in all probability prior to 1 November 1945, Japan would have surrendered even if the atomic bombs had not been dropped, even if Russia had not entered the war, and even if no invasion had been planned or contemplated." But he was troubled that the *Summary Report* did not immediately follow up the counterfactual conclusion with a statement on the potential of atomic power.[41]

Anderson was obliquely pointing to a fundamental conflict in Nitze's *Summary Report*. While the report's concluding remarks did suggest that atomic weapons would be a decisive factor in America's postwar defense establishment, the report also argued that the atomic bombings of Hiroshima and Nagasaki were indecisive in forcing Japan to surrender.[42] Nitze, according to his biographer Strobe Talbott, wanted to demystify the power of the bomb and force America to view it not as the "absolute weapon" but as a simply more powerful weapon of war.[43]

Paul Nitze recalled in his memoirs that he believed in July 1945 that Japan would surrender "even without the atomic bomb."[44] While in Japan, Nitze and his Survey analysts conducted hundreds of interrogations of Japanese military and civilian officials, which made up the preponderance of evidence for the early-surrender counterfactual. However, the bulk of those interrogations provided only very tenuous support to the counterfactual conclusion that Japan "certainly" would have surrendered before 31 December 1945, "and in all probability prior to 1 November 1945," without the atomic bombs or Russian war declaration. It was natural for Nitze to begin his analysis with a hypothesis concerning the effects of the atomic bombs on ending the war with Japan.[45] Yet Nitze remained committed to that notion even when the evidence—the interrogations of Japanese officials—did not reasonably support his conclusions. And Nitze's bold statement that his conclusions on why Japan surrendered were based on "all the facts," after a mere three months of evidence gathering, stretches the limits of believability.[46]

It is important to remember that Nitze and his fellow Survey analysts were part of a much larger American occupation of the Japanese home islands that began immediately after the Japanese surrender on 3 September 1945. The Americans who made up that occupation force brought with them certain cultural and racial attitudes—powerfully shaped by the long, brutal Pacific war—toward the Japanese. Such attitudes undoubtedly affected the way Nitze, D'Olier, Galbraith (until the end of October), and the rest thought about the Japanese wartime leaders whom they relied upon, through interrogations, for most of their evidence.[47]

Juxtapose the formal, authoritative atmosphere of the interrogations of Japanese officials with the collegiate-like atmosphere (even if sometimes strained) during the interrogation of Albert Speer in Germany four months earlier. George Ball remembered Speer to be "like us."[48] Speer himself felt toward Galbraith, Nitze, and Ball "a great sense of affinity."[49] However, there did not seem to be any sense of "affinity" between USSBS analysts and defeated Japanese wartime leaders in late October 1945, only a desire to draw out "all the facts" from the erstwhile hated enemy.

Consider for example the Survey's interrogation of Prince Fumimaro Konoye, former Japanese premier and influential advisor to the emperor and to other key leaders, on 9 November 1945. The principal interrogators were Nitze, D'Olier, Galbraith, and Paul Baran. When questioned by Nitze[50] about how much longer the war would have continued if the atom bomb had not been dropped, Konoye responded: "Probably it [the war] would have lasted all this year." Nitze then became more specific and asked if the war would have been terminated prior to 1 November; Konoye's response was "Probably would have lasted beyond that."[51]

Franklin D'Olier followed Nitze in the interrogation of Konoye and parroted Nitze's counterfactual line of questioning. D'Olier asked the former premier whether the Japanese leadership would "have been forced to surrender even if Russia had not come in or even though we had not dropped the atomic bomb?" Konoye replied that the "Army had dug themselves caves in the mountains and their idea of fighting on was fighting from every little hole or rock in the mountains." D'Olier then asked if the emperor would have allowed the army to do that. Konoye replied that the emperor "would not have let them go that far. He would have done something to stop them."[52] Although Konoye's testimony to Nitze and D'Olier provided some support for the early-surrender counterfactual, his testimony leaned heavily toward a more prolonged war, one that could have continued beyond 1 November, and perhaps even after 31 December 1945, without the atom bomb and Soviet declaration of war. But testimony by key Japanese leaders like Konoye that challenged the Survey's conclusions never made it into the pages of the published final reports.

It was noteworthy that during the Konoye interrogation only Nitze and D'Olier pursued the counterfactual questioning about ending the war with Japan. Galbraith confined his questions of Konoye to Japan's decisions in 1941 to go to war against the United

States. Paul Baran, who had become a senior member of the Pacific Survey's Economic Division, was concerned with Japan's wartime economy, and the "greater Asia co-prosperity sphere." Captain T. J. Hedding, a member of Ofstie's Naval Analysis Division, asked Konoye questions about the military's role in Japan's political and economic structure during the war.[53]

Nitze's 12 March "Very Preliminary Draft" of the *Summary Report* contained the early-surrender counterfactual as it would appear (except for some slight grammatical modifications) in the 1 July published report. The only important change was the location of the counterfactual within the overall report. The March drafts of the *Summary Report* placed the early-surrender counterfactual at the end of the report in the concluding remarks. But in April, a subsequent draft placed it at the end of a short narrative on "Japan's Struggle to End the War," which preceded the report's conclusions and recommendations.[54] Nitze most likely moved the counterfactual because it fit better with the narrative on Japan's attempts to end the war than with the report's future-looking conclusions and recommendations.[55]

Nitze's use of the counterfactual in the *Summary Report* drew no criticism from other Survey analysts. The Survey's chronicler, Major James Beveridge, noted that there was "serious controversy" among Survey analysts over some of the Survey's conclusions. But these bitter disagreements were caused by the "Military Analysis and Naval Analysis Divisions . . . over the respective contributions of the Navy and the Air Forces to the ending of the war against Japan," and not the early-surrender counterfactual. Beveridge went on to note that the Survey's recommendations concerning the postwar defense establishment brought about the fiercest debates among Survey analysts.[56]

In fact, Survey members seemed to have formed a consensus around Nitze's early-surrender counterfactual. As early as October 1945, when Survey members were still collecting evidence (but before Nitze had drafted his counterfactual), a special envoy to President Truman, Edwin Locke, noted that some Americans in Japan had already decided the atomic bombs "speeded surrender by only a few days."[57] Americans like Admiral Ofstie could accept the early-surrender counterfactual because it allowed them to claim that the decisive factor in producing victory in the Pacific was the navy's blockade around the Japanese home islands. The AAF, conversely, by citing the counterfactual, could claim that LeMay's firebombing of Japanese cities ultimately brought about unconditional surrender, not the atomic bombing of Hiroshima and Nagasaki, or the Russian declaration of war. For the hundreds of other Survey analysts, both civilian and military, Nitze's counterfactual fit neatly into their conceptual understanding of strategic bombing. They believed that the purpose of strategic bombing was to destroy the enemy's war-making capacity.[58] Since their analysis of the Pacific war showed them that the conventional bombing of the Japanese home islands coupled with the naval blockade had decisively damaged Japan's war-making capacity, the atomic bomb, for them, played only a minor role in ending the war.

But a June 1946 analysis produced under the direction of General Leslie Groves, military commander of the Manhattan Engineer District which built the bomb, disagreed. General Groves's report, "The Atomic Bombings of Hiroshima and Nagasaki," argued that "the atomic bomb did not alone win the war against Japan, but it most certainly ended it, saving the thousands of Allied lives that would have been lost in any combat invasion of Japan."[59] The Survey's secretariat, Walter Wilds, told presidential assistant Edwin Locke (who had recently arrived back from Japan as a special envoy to the president) that the Survey believed the Groves report "should not be made public at this time." Wilds informed Locke of attempts on the Survey's part to "reduce conflicts" between the two reports by providing General Groves with Survey "data." Wilds believed that the simultaneous release of the Survey's *Summary Report* and the Groves report would "promote public confusion."[60] The potential "public confusion" that concerned Wilds was most likely tied to the contradiction between the two reports over the role of the atomic bomb in "ending" the war against Japan.

Assistant Secretary of State Dean Acheson, who was heading the

American negotiations with the Soviet Union in Paris, raised a question about the *Summary Report*'s early-surrender counterfactual. In a letter to Locke, Wilds reminded him that Acheson had read the Survey's analysis on Japan's surrender decision and held "certain reservations with respect to making public at this time the sections dealing with Russia's role in the Pacific war."[61] Acheson was probably worried about the Soviet response to the counterfactual conclusion that Japan would have surrendered "even if Russia had not entered the war."

Locke himself was concerned about the Survey's early-surrender counterfactual. Wilds noted that Locke had discussed with him "certain points," "especially the language in the surrender report which describes the role of the atom bombs in terminating the war."[62] On several drafts of the *Summary Report* in Locke's "Strategic Bombing Survey" folder there are handwritten question marks in the margins next to the early-surrender counterfactual.[63] It is unclear who placed those question marks on the drafts. Probably it was Locke himself and not the president. Locke told the president that he had been following the Survey reports closely and had gone over "the preliminary drafts" and had advised the president "to the best of [his] ability."[64]

President Truman met with D'Olier and Nitze on 29 March 1946 to discuss their conclusions.[65] No transcript exists for this meeting. It is possible, though, that they talked about the necessity of using the atomic bombs to force Japan to surrender. In a May letter to the president, D'Olier asked him to recall from their recent 29 March meeting that "one of the Survey's important studies reconstruct[ed] the discussions and negotiations in Japan which led to its unconditional surrender. . . ." D'Olier then requested that the president grant him permission to have access to "ultra information" (the secret Japanese diplomatic messages that American intelligence had intercepted during the war) so that the Survey could "establish more factually and clearly the factors affecting" the Japanese decision to surrender, "especially the period from April through August 1945. . . ."[66] It is possible that President Truman questioned the early-surrender counterfactual in the late-March meeting with Nitze and D'Olier, which may have pushed them into asking for "ultra information" to provide implicit support for the *Summary Report*'s claim that Japan would have surrendered even if the United States had not dropped the atomic bomb. A few days later the president granted D'Olier permission to use Ultra intelligence "to complete the Survey's important study of the factors surrounding the unconditional surrender decision of the Japanese."[67] But in the 1 July published version of the *Summary Report,* the early-surrender counterfactual, stating the atomic bomb was unnecessary in forcing Japan to surrender, remained unchanged.

IV

There is no question that Japan was a defeated nation by very early August 1945. But would Japan have surrendered "certainly prior to 31 December 1945, and in all probability prior to 1 November 1945," without the atomic bomb or Soviet war declaration, as the *Summary Report* argued? President Truman told the American people shortly after the atomic bombing of Hiroshima, "We have used [the bomb] . . . in order to shorten the agony of war, in order to save the lives of thousands and thousands of young Americans." The *Summary Report*'s conclusion challenged President Truman's remarks that Japan would not have surrendered soon if the United States had not used the bomb.[68]

Not only did the *Summary Report*'s early-surrender counterfactual contradict official explanations of the use of the atomic bomb, it implicitly contradicted some of the other conclusions brought out in the *Summary Report* itself and other published reports from the Pacific Survey.

The *Summary Report*, though acknowledging that the war against Japanese shipping was an important factor in destroying Japan's war economy, argued that the decisive factor in persuading the Japanese leaders to surrender was the conventional strategic bombing of the home islands.[69] But two reports—the Economic Division's *The Effects of Strategic Bombing on Japan's War Economy* and the Transportation Division's *The War against Japanese Transportation*—subtly differed from the *Summary Report*'s argument. In the view of these two division studies, the antishipping campaign had virtually destroyed Japan's economy prior to the main weight of the AAF's bombing campaign, and therefore these two publications, unlike the *Summary Report*, stress the decisive role of antishipping in Japan's ultimate defeat.[70]

The fact that Japan's economy was for the most part destroyed prior to the AAF's heavy bombing attacks led the authors of these two reports to conclusions that were different in degree from those of the *Summary Report*. The differences concern the relative importance of conventional bombing of the Japanese home islands and the antishipping campaign in Japan's decision to surrender. These two applications of military power were equally important in the Economic Division's judgment: "While the outcome of the war was decided in the waters of the Pacific . . . well in advance of the strategic bomber offensive against Japan's home islands, the air offensive against Japan proper was the major factor determining the timing of Japan's surrender."[71] In this conclusion, the naval war against Japanese merchant shipping and the resulting loss of raw material were not merely one of the cumulative causes that defeated Japan but actually "decided" the outcome of the war in the Pacific.

The Pacific Survey's analysis of urban area attacks had to wrestle with the fact that in the Pacific, unlike the European theater, area attacks constituted 70 percent of the AAF's campaign. *The Effects of Air Attack on Japanese Urban Economy* credited the AAF's area attacks for causing great damage to the urban workforce and social structure. According to the report, absenteeism of workers, directly caused by air raids, turned an already critical situation into one of complete desperation. The air raids also caused widespread destruction and deprivation not only in the cities but throughout the Japanese homeland.[72] But when it came to assessing the effectiveness of the area attacks on Japanese war production, this report became less favorable to area bombing. Indeed, the report's recurring theme was that the Japanese economy was already defeated before the AAF began its air campaign: "As in Germany, the air attacks against Japanese cities were not the cause of the enemy's defeat. The defeat of Japan was assured before the urban attacks were launched. . . . The insufficiency of Japan's war economy was the underlying cause of her defeat."[73] This conclusion, which downplayed the effectiveness of urban area attacks on Japan's war production, was often followed, strangely, by statements giving much weight to the importance of area attacks in lowering Japan's morale and will to resist: "The raids brought home to the people the realization that there was no defense against the Allied aircraft; that nothing could prevent the wholesale destruction of every inhabited area in Japan and that further resistance was futile."[74] The implicit argument here was that urban area attacks had a more decisive impact on morale than on Japan's war economy.

But the Pacific Survey report *The Effects of Strategic Bombing on Japanese Morale* argued that lowered morale, resulting from conventional strategic bombing, was not the decisive factor that forced the political leadership to accept surrender. According to the report, low morale and apathy on the part of the civilian population toward continuing the war were not the decisive factors that defeated Japan: "Throughout the small nation the effects of Allied bombings were general more than specific and were not confined to the target areas. The drop in morale which took place throughout the country was not the factor that defeated Japan." The report acknowledged that regardless of the low level of morale, the Japanese people would still have continued fighting and working to support the war effort had the emperor so desired.[75]

The Survey's morale report did acknowledge that the morale of the Japanese people influenced, to varying degrees, the political leadership in its decision over whether to continue fighting or terminate the war. Members of the ruling elite, usually the militarists, might have had some concern about public morale, but they also believed that the Japanese people, regardless of their demoralized state, would have complied with the decisions made by the political and military leadership. The report concluded that morale (either political or public) was not decisive; rather, it was only "one important factor among several" in the defeat of Japan.[76]

Three conflicting conclusions emerge from the pages of various reports of the Pacific Survey: (1) approximately 70 percent of AAF attacks against the Japanese home islands were against urban areas; (2) area attacks against Japan's morale and urban economy were not decisive factors in Japan's decision to surrender; and (3) conventional strategic bombing was the decisive factor in forcing the Japanese to surrender "unconditionally." The Survey's first two findings, taken together, suggest that a major portion of the AAF's air campaign against the Japanese home islands was not decisive, and was perhaps unnecessary. The third finding—the *Summary Report*'s conclusion—therefore, requires an explanation of how the remaining 30 percent of the AAF's campaign, which consisted of precision attacks against specific military and economic targets, defeated Japan and forced a surrender. Granted the *Summary Report* argued that the main weight of the AAF's campaign against Japanese cities lowered the morale and will to resist of the Japanese leadership, thereby forcing them to accept surrender, but the Pacific Survey report on morale suggested that both factors were not critical for Japan's capitulation.

This is the dilemma that emerges from the pages of the Pacific Survey reports: How to claim the decisiveness of conventional air power when there was evidence pointing to the conclusion that a large part of the AAF's campaign, while important, was not the crucial factor in Japan's defeat? The devastating effects of the antishipping campaign and of conventional strategic bombing certainly forced the Japanese leadership to realize that defeat was inevitable. But there is a difference between the realization of defeat and the political acceptance of surrender. Here is where the atom bomb enters into the equation. If read as a collective whole, the Pacific Survey reports implicitly suggest that the atom bomb was the sufficient cause that transformed the realization of defeat into surrender, thus contradicting the early-surrender counterfactual.

Tucked away in an often-ignored appendix of *The Effects of Air Attack on Japanese Urban Economy* is a postwar analysis of strategic bombing, produced by scholars from Japan's Imperial University. Their analysis agreed with most of the Survey's main themes, except for this striking remark about the conventional air attack, the atom bomb, and the end of the war: "Though there were many different views [over whether to continue the war], the majority of leaders entirely lost heart to continue hostilities. Particularly, the debut of the atomic bombs in the Pacific war theater was *decisive*."[77] It is unclear how this statement made its way into the final report. Paul Nitze himself was one of four Survey directors whose personal approval was necessary before any reports could be released for publication.[78] Somehow those responsible for revising or rewriting "contradictory" material overlooked the Japanese scholars' findings as well as other evidence challenging the Survey's interpretation of Japan's decision to surrender.

V

Not tucked away in the midst of published Survey reports was the July 1947 study produced by Orvil Anderson's Military Analysis Division, *Air Campaigns of the Pacific War*. Making the same points that he made in his July 1946 memorandum to the secretary of war on the *Summary Report*, Anderson's *Air Campaigns* sought to bludgeon the "American Public" into accepting the idea that the national defense establishment had to be "oriented toward airpower" and that the future of air power must "not be restricted, as in pre–World War II years, by the inertia of established organizations or personalities." Anderson's report argued that the experience of World War II proved that:

> Airpower dominated its own element.
> Airpower dominated naval warfare.
> Airpower dominated ground warfare.
> Airpower was capable of forcing the capitulation of an enemy nation without surface invasion.[79]

Anderson's pamphletlike report, with its blatant air force parochialism, was certainly different in style and reasonableness of tone from the other Pacific Survey published reports. Yet it nevertheless reflected accurately the overall partiality of the Strategic Bombing Survey toward air power and an independent air force.

In stark contrast to Anderson's report was Ofstie's Naval Analysis Division's published study, *Campaigns of the Pacific War*. The navy's report was a calm, methodical narrative of the major naval battles of the Pacific war. There were no grandiose claims about the decisiveness of the navy's antishipping campaign or of its carrier-based aircraft. The most sweeping conclusion, if one can call it that, was the following:

> By January 1945, Japan was in fact a defeated nation. . . . All hope of future resistance had depended upon oil and now the tankers were sunk and the oil cut off. . . . At home the bad news began to be known and mutterings of negotiated conditional peace arose even in the armed forces. Japan was defeated: it remained only necessary to persuade her of the fact.[80]

This statement does not differ from observations found in other Pacific Survey reports: Japan's economy had been broken before the main AAF attacks; the antishipping campaign had been decisive in Japan's defeat; conventional strategic bombing had persuaded the political leadership to realize defeat and accept unconditional surrender.

The process of getting Anderson's *Air Campaigns of the Pacific War* and Ofstie's *Campaigns of the Pacific War* to the Government Printing Office for publication in late 1946 and 1947 demonstrates the powerful postwar interests of both the Army Air Forces and the navy that operated within the Pacific Survey. The process also shows that the services' representatives on the Survey, General Anderson and Admiral Ofstie, were not "evenly matched."[81] Instead, the AAF clearly had the upper hand because of the conceptual approach of directors like Nitze and, more important, the partiality of Franklin D'Olier.

Historian David MacIsaac, in his 1976 book on the Survey, *Strategic Bombing in World War Two: The Story of the United States Strategic Bombing Survey*, called the bitter disagreement between Ofstie and Anderson "The Great Anderson Navy War." MacIsaac's mistake was to portray the Survey, and especially Franklin D'Olier, as the impartial mediator between Ofstie and Anderson. D'Olier, according to MacIsaac, did his best to be "fair."[82] But the record strongly suggests that D'Olier deliberately sided with Anderson and allowed *Air Campaigns* to be published in the face of objections by Ofstie and Paul Nitze.

In early 1946, Ofstie's division wrote a report, "The Air Effort against Japan" (a different study from *Campaigns of the Pacific War* discussed above), that described and evaluated the part played by air power in the Pacific war. Yet when Ofstie submitted the galleys of this report for review, Nitze considered it not to be "an impartial or accurate account of the air effort against Japan." The Survey, said Nitze, "would not approve of its publication in its present form which incorrectly associates the Survey with it."[83] Ofstie's report argued that U.S. naval action in World War II in the Pacific "played the principal as well as the deciding part." The report concluded that "too much has been said of late of the peculiar and distinctive nature of airpower, and too little of its necessary interrelation with land and sea forces *for whose benefit it exists*."[84] Major General Lauris Norstad, who had probably been briefed about the Naval Analysis Division's report by Anderson, was worried that the report claimed to be an analysis of the overall air effort against Japan, but was really a highly biased description of the navy's carrier-based air effort.[85] As a result of these expressed concerns, and Nitze's desire to maintain "impartiality," the Survey did not publish the report.

But Ofstie did get legitimate approval from the Survey to publish *Campaigns of the Pacific War*. Ofstie remembered that "in line with the procedure for approval," his division's report was sent to the chairman's office and to Anderson's Military Analysis Division for review.[86] The report was subsequently "approved by the Survey for publication."[87] More important, a representative from Anderson's division met with Ofstie and Survey Secretariat Wilds in late summer 1946 and "agreed to the final changes" of *Campaigns of the Pacific War*.[88]

Anderson's Military Analysis Division had prepared several supporting reports on different AAF units that had fought in the Pacific, e.g., *The Fifth Air Force in the War against Japan* and *The Air Transport Command in the War against Japan*. Anderson's division, however, had not prepared a division overall report by the time the Survey had completed its work with the publication of the chairman's reports in July 1946. Ofstie remembered asking Anderson on numerous occasions if his division would have a general summary of Army Air Forces activities in the Pacific. According to Ofstie, Anderson often replied that he would have such a report to Ofstie "at the next meeting," or "in a few weeks."[89]

It was not until late 1946 (about four months after the Survey had officially finished its work, but when it still maintained a small staff under Lieutenant Colonel G. L. McMurrin to oversee remaining administrative matters) that Orvil Anderson submitted a report, "Over-All Air Effort in the War against Japan," to Nitze, who had recently taken a position in the State Department.[90] On Christmas Eve Nitze fired off a brisk reply to McMurrin telling him not to publish Anderson's report. The Survey, according to Nitze, had promised the Naval Analysis Division that it would not publish the Military Analysis Division's overall report because it had denied the navy's request to publish their overall report.[91] D'Olier, who had recently returned to the position of president of Prudential Life Insurance, agreed "100%" with Nitze's decision.[92]

Anderson's eagerness for the Survey to publish a report that would laud the accomplishments of the AAF in the Pacific war and state explicitly air power's role in the postwar defense establishment produced another report, *The Air Campaigns of the Pacific War,* in early 1947. Once Ofstie read Anderson's draft of *Air Campaigns,* he immediately told Nitze that the report was anything but "an objective study of the war." Ofstie found *Air Campaigns* "to be in major part a vicious and deliberate attempt to discredit the entire naval service." Ofstie forcefully reminded Nitze that Anderson's proposed report had not been approved by the key Survey directors as was his own *Campaigns of the Pacific War.* He considered the potential publication of *Air Campaigns* "to be directly contrary to the principles under which the Survey operated and decidedly inimical to the best interests of the armed services and the government. . . ."[93]

Nitze suggested to Ofstie that he meet with Anderson's staff "to see if an understanding could be reached on material objected to in the manuscript." But Nitze reassured Ofstie that if an agreement between the "Army and Navy representatives" could not be reached over *Air Campaigns*, "the U.S. Strategic Bombing Survey would not publish this document. . . ." Ofstie met with two of Anderson's assistants on 14 March at the Burlington Hotel in Washington, D.C., to discuss *Air Campaigns.* After that meeting Ofstie informed Secretary of the Navy James Forrestal, Nitze, and D'Olier by memorandum that no agreement had been reached. Ofstie "assumed that publication of subject manuscript" was a "closed issue" as far as the Survey was concerned.[94]

Ofstie was wrong. In July 1947, the Government Printing Office published under the auspices of the Strategic Bombing Survey, *Air Campaigns of the Pacific War.* Naval officers were furious. After reading *Air Campaigns of the Pacific War*, Ofstie's assistant, Captain G. W. Anderson, roared that the report would be better titled "Everyone's Out of Step but Orville [*sic*]." Captain Anderson then recommended to Ofstie, because the report was of the most "pernicious" nature, that it be "withdrawn from circulation and disciplinary action taken. . . ."[95]

Secretary of the Navy Forrestal was equally upset. In early September 1947, he sent a letter (prepared for him by Ofstie) to

D'Olier with copies furnished to Secretary of War Kenneth Royall and Paul Nitze. Forrestal stressed to D'Olier the crucial objection to the publication of *Air Campaigns*: it was "published by the Government Printing Office without prior reference to any representative of the Navy Department," thus violating the Survey's established procedures for approving reports for publication. Forrestal believed the report to be "highly objectionable" and "replete with malicious implication and biased opinion." He found it "decidedly derogatory to the wartime leadership of the Naval high command." He closed the letter with a strong request that D'Olier take immediate action not only "to suppress the publication but to disavow it due to errors of fact, interpretation, and conclusion."[96]

Paul Nitze soon learned how *Air Campaigns* came to be published as an official Survey report. Nitze told the deputy chief of naval operations, Admiral Forrest Sherman, that he had had no idea that *Air Campaigns* was being published under the auspices of the Survey until it had been released by the Government Printing Office and subsequently brought to his attention. Nitze, at that point, telephoned D'Olier for an explanation. D'Olier informed Nitze that he himself had reversed Nitze's decision in the spring not to publish *Air Campaigns*. D'Olier said he had informed Nitze of his decision to allow the publication of *Air Campaigns,* because of D'Olier's "desire to save [Nitze] embarrassment."[97]

VI

Franklin D'Olier was an advocate for building the postwar defense establishment around air power and an independent air force. As a former national commander of the American Legion, D'Olier sent copies of the European and Pacific *Summary Reports* to all of the forty-eight state commanders of the Legion. He agreed with Harvard law professor and erstwhile COA member W. Barton Leach that the Survey was the most "persuasive" argument made yet "of the national requirement for air power" and that it should be given the widest distribution possible.[98] He also understood the influence the Survey was having, and would continue to have, on the reorganization of the defense establishment. In late July 1947, as the Government Printing Office was releasing copies of *Air Campaigns*, D'Olier boasted to Nitze how Secretary of War Robert Patterson had told him of the important role the Survey reports had played in the unification of the armed services. "He [Patterson] said that repeatedly after many hearings our Report had been mentioned, with particular reference to our insistence upon unification."[99]

The Survey's call for unification of the armed services included a call for a separate "third establishment" that became, as a result of the National Security Act of 1947, the United States Air Force. The airmen's dreams had been fulfilled.

CHAPTER 6

A-Bombs, Budgets, and the Dilemma of Defense

Symington—

Do you realize that in accepting our new jobs and in the event of war with Russia, we will be hanged as war criminals if we lose?

There had better be some real honest to God thinking about what we need to avoid being on the losing side.

The U.S. has already set the pace for the atomic bomb, strategic bombing, and hanging war criminals.

This is no time to temporize very long with old established prerogatives of the Services, nor to tolerate inter-Service rivalry, friction, jealousy. Whoever does not cooperate should be obliterated.

GENERAL CARL SPAATZ, 1947

Anticipating his "new job" as chief of staff of the United States Air Force, General Carl A. Spaatz forcefully emphasized to the about-to-be-named secretary of the air force, W. Stuart Symington, that they must "obliterate" any opposition to the air force's plans for the postwar defense establishment.[1] The opposition that Spaatz was referring to was neither the Soviet Union nor any other external enemy to the United States. Instead, it was the United States Navy in its resistance to the unification of the armed services (that would allow for an independent air force) and its challenge to the air force's approach to strategic bombing. Retired Army General Hugh Drum summed up the problem best when he told Ferdinand Eberstadt, who was heading a navy commission to study the unification of the armed services, that the "crux of the whole controversy" was the "Air."[2]

The published reports produced by the United States Strategic Bombing Survey helped the air force and the navy explain their conception of the "air" for the national defense establishment. Both services used the Survey during the armed services unification hearings, held at various times in 1946 and 1947, to argue either for or against an independent air force. In 1948, President Truman reduced the defense budget (for fiscal year 1950) to $13.7 billion, resulting in the cancellation of production of the navy's cherished supercarrier, the USS *United States.* A series of congressional hearings followed in 1949 that probed deeply into the navy and air force's visions for the postwar defense establishment. During these hearings, the air force and the navy again relied on the Strategic Bombing Survey to support their position on controversial issues such as the air force's procurement of the B-36 strategic bomber, the roles and missions of both services, methods of strategic bombing, and the atomic bomb.

I

The first postwar congressional hearings on unification of the armed services began on 17 October 1945 when the Senate Military Affairs Committee began to explore two bills that committee members had introduced. Key issues that emerged from these early hearings were the push for a single defense department and the independent status of the air force. Since the days of Billy Mitchell, the air force had desired coequal status with the army and navy: unification was a means to achieve that end. The navy, on the other hand, opposed unification because an independent air force disrupted the traditional balance between the Navy and War Departments over budgets. An independent air force would mean that three services would be competing for funds instead of just two.[3] Lurking underneath this concern over budgets was also the emerging fear among naval officers that many Americans believed strategic air power, delivered by the air force, to be the decisive factor in future warfare.[4] Naval leaders saw in this belief the potential demise of carrier aviation and a decline in the status of their service.

During the October 1945 congressional hearings many top civilian and military leaders appeared before the committee to explain their positions on unification. Even though the Pacific portion of the Strategic Bombing Survey was still ongoing, some of its draft reports had made their way back to Washington along with the many completed reports from the European Survey. When arguing either in favor of or against unification, military leaders would often use reports from the Survey as proof of their services' accomplishments during the war. Proving which service played the decisive role in victory was closely linked to arguments over the future structure of the defense establishment. Vice-Admiral Dewitt C. Ramsey, deputy commander in chief for the Pacific fleet, told the Senate Military Affairs Committee that he vehemently disagreed with the AAF claim that carrier-based aviation had become obsolete by the closing months of the war owing to the ability of the AAF to bomb the Japanese home islands. According to Admiral Ramsey, carrier aviation played a critical role in forcing Japan to surrender unconditionally, and if a land invasion of Kyushu had been necessary, carrier aviation would have played a decisive role in that operation as well.[5] He used evidence from the Strategic Bombing Survey to support his description of the war and the navy's role in winning it. The Survey, argued Admiral Ramsey, would "set forth in the record . . . that the Navy has measured up to the confidence reposed in it by the American people in spelling doom for the Japanese dreams of conquest long before the first atomic bomb descended on Hiroshima."[6]

General Spaatz also appeared before the committee to provide his opinions on unification. In his testimony he used key passages from the Survey as justification for the air force's postwar plans for air power. An often-used passage from the European Survey's *Summary Report* states that "Allied air power was decisive in the war in western Europe."[7] General Spaatz quoted this passage to committee members when explaining the crucial role the AAF played in producing victory in the war in Europe. But unlike Admiral Ramsey, who dwelled extensively on wartime accomplishments, General Spaatz quickly moved the discussion toward the future role of air power:

> The plain fact is that coasts and seas no longer have their old significance for defense. Distance has been telescoped. . . . In the air power age the Air Force is vitally concerned with the development of jet propulsion, supersonic speeds, guided missiles; not to speak of the potentials of harnessed atomic energy. The Air Force should be free from control by interests which may be influenced more by things of the past or present than by ideas for, and of, the future.[8]

General James H. Doolittle echoed these same air force sentiments when appearing before the committee. He referenced an unnamed "study" by the Survey that analyzed the effects of strategic bombing on Japanese cities (perhaps the findings from the Pacific Survey's Urban Areas Division). General Doolittle stressed the level of destruction in over forty Japanese cities wrought by B-29 attacks and the strategic bomber's decisive role in the war with Japan: "The Navy had the transport to make the invasion of Japan possible; the Ground Forces had the power to make it successful and the B-29 made it unnecessary." The essence of General Doolittle's argument was that strategic air power had changed the face of warfare by obviating the need for a ground invasion of the Japanese home islands. The past, argued General Doolittle, proved that "Air, due to the facility and speed with which we move through it and the inherent limitations of land and sea, is the medium through which the weapons of the future will travel."[9]

Throughout 1946 and into 1947, the battle lines hardened between the air force and the army on one side, and the navy on the other, over the unification of the armed services and the independent status of the air force. The festering issue of naval air power was at the center of debate between the air force and the navy.

In a November 1946 speech to the Air Force Association, General Doolittle wondered why the United States needed "two air forces any more than we need two armies or two navies." He further stated: "All land based planes must be under one command in order to achieve not only the most economical air power possible, but the most effective air power possible." That "command," noted Doolittle, would be an independent American air force.[10] General Spaatz insisted to the Joint Chiefs that the air force should subsume all naval land-based aviation.[11] The navy's budget for 1947 concerned Secretary Symington because of the navy's demand for "land based planes to protect their ships. . . ." Symington reminded President Truman that the navy's request was "millions of dollars more than the Air Force's [for] the purchase of airplanes." Land-based air, according to Symington, was the responsibility of the air force.[12] Many airmen came to believe that the navy's effort to maintain its land-based airplanes indicated a desire on the navy's part to take away the strategic bombing mission from the air force. General Ira Eaker noted to Symington in April 1946 that the navy was offering air force B-29 pilots regular commissions in the navy, proving to Eaker "the Navy's intention to build up strategic bombing."[13]

In the summer of 1946, President Truman caused great concern among navy officers by sending to the secretaries of war and navy a memorandum arguing that naval reconnaissance and antisubmarine warfare should be performed by airmen. They sensed that the president's memorandum was an indication of "just the initial step in a continuing campaign by the Army Air Force people to absorb all Naval aviation."[14] Navy officers believed that the navy had to maintain its land-based airplanes to accomplish part of their wartime mission of naval reconnaissance and antisubmarine warfare.

About a year later, in June 1947, the House Committee on Expenditures in the Executive Department heard closing arguments by service leaders on the unification of the armed services. The navy maintained its position that there should not be an independent air force, and naturally air officers argued the opposite. Echoing the same statements that Generals Spaatz and Doolittle had made at earlier hearings, Major General Lauris Norstad told the committee that owing to the decisive results produced by strategic bombing in

World War II, the Army Air Forces should be granted independent status within a unified defense establishment because it was the service best suited to carry out the revolutionary methods of strategic air warfare. To support his position, General Norstad used the concluding passage from the Pacific Survey *Summary Report* that called for, "in addition to the Army and Navy . . . an equal and coordinate position for a third establishment."[15]

Yet a naval officer who testified to the committee shortly after General Norstad raised some troubling questions about pressure put on some Survey authors to reach conclusions claiming the decisiveness of strategic bombing in World War II and the need for a postwar independent air force. The Pacific Survey's Naval Analysis Division director, Admiral Ofstie, told the committee about his frustrating experience with the writing of the Pacific Survey *Summary Report*. He provided draft versions of the Pacific Survey *Summary Report* that showed the gradual shift from concluding that an independent air force was not desirable to the published report's implicit call for a coequal air arm.[16] The draft versions disclosed by Admiral Ofstie demonstrated to the committee the partial, not impartial, nature of Survey conclusions.

Military officers were not the only ones relying on Survey reports to support their positions in the unification debates. Representative W. J. Dorn of the House Committee on Expenditures in the Executive Department obtained a number of unpublished Survey interrogations of key Japanese and German military and political leaders. The congressman provided a litany of statements made by these individuals attesting to the importance of strategic bombing in defeating Germany and Japan. The excerpts that Congressman Dorn used also expressed the notion that both Germany and Japan would have done better in the war if they had had an independent strategic air force. He included in the hearing record the conclusion from the Pacific Survey *Summary Report* about the need for a "third establishment" that would be responsible for strategic air power. The *Summary Report*'s conclusion supported Dorn's desire for an air arm of coequal status with the army and navy.[17]

Although President Truman signed the unification of the armed services into law in July 1947, there remained strong disagreements between the services over roles and missions. In the summer and fall of 1948, service leaders met with Secretary of Defense James Forrestal at Key West, Florida, and Newport, Rhode Island, to iron out some of these problems. Although the meetings did reduce tensions, important questions remained unanswered over which service would control the atomic bomb and the method for dropping it in a potential war against the Soviet Union.

II

The atomic bomb posed a dilemma for the airmen's vision for the postwar defense establishment. On the one hand, the airmen committed themselves to a strong public speaking and writing campaign, professing that the atomic bomb had revolutionized warfare and that the nation's defense should be centered on the air force's ability to deliver the bomb against the Soviet Union. But on the other, senior airmen knew that too much emphasis on the atomic bomb as the central part of the national defense establishment would raise troubling questions in Congress about their proposed seventy-group air force that was based largely on a conventional nonatomic strategic bombing mission.[18]

In the spring of 1947, Major General Frederick Anderson, the air force assistant chief of staff for personnel and public relations, and a number of senior airmen helped a journalist write an article for the popular magazine *Readers Digest*. The purpose of the article was to strike fear into the hearts of many Americans and convince them of the need for the air force to have the capability of delivering an atomic attack against the Soviet Union. The draft of the article started off by warning the American people of the great potential danger that atomic bombs posed to the United States. Although the Soviet Union did not possess the bomb, the article argued that the United States would "shortly be exposed" to a devastating atomic attack. The solution, according to the article, was for the American people to form "atomic councils" and demand that their government authorize an "immediate activation of an Air Striking Force adequate to blow out any aggressor" with atomic bombs.[19]

General Spaatz told the editors of the Washington, D.C., newspaper *Evening Star* that their ongoing writing on the importance of air power reflected "in large measure the interest of the American people in their security in this Atomic Air Age." General Spaatz noted that the effects of the atomic bomb would have "far reaching" consequences on the American defense establishment. He closed the letter by suggesting to the editors that much of the "misdirection of thought and effort [concerning defense issues] could be eliminated if the Naval Air Force became a part of the United States Air Force. . . ."[20]

Air force advisor W. Barton Leach recommended to Spaatz and Symington that they emphasize, when speaking in public, that the air force in peacetime must have a "long range striking force, capable of delivering atomic weapons." Leach pointed out that aggressors could "be deterred, not by defensive measures but by a force in being which can strike them hard and hurt them badly if they start a fight."[21] General Spaatz's successor as chief of staff of the air force, General Hoyt Vandenberg, told a "civilian seminar" in 1948 that the air force's primary wartime mission was to launch an "air counter-offensive" at the "earliest possible moment" with America's "most powerful weapons."[22]

Both generals, though, along with Secretary of the Air Force Stuart Symington, downplayed the importance of the atomic bomb in national strategy when they briefed the Congressional Air Policy Board in early 1948 on the air force's proposed seventy-group program. Since the end of World War II, the seventy-group air force had come to define what the airmen believed to be adequate air power for the national defense. The core of the seventy-group program was twenty-five very heavy bomber groups that could deliver a conventional, strategic bombing attack against the Soviet Union, and possibly an atomic attack as well.[23] General Vandenberg told the congressmen of the Air Policy Board that the seventy-group program that he was recommending dealt solely with "conventional types of bombs, and [did] not include atomic weapons, which should be regarded as a complement to conventional bombs, rather than as a basis on which an entire plan should be built." That seventy-group program, which would cost $7.5 billion, was the "minimum force" that the United States should maintain in peacetime, argued General Vandenberg.[24]

During the discussion period that followed General Vandenberg's presentation, the first remark made by Congressman John Hinshaw, the board's head, pointed out that the general's presentation "omitted any mention of the use of atomic weapons." This was perplexing to the congressman because of all the published statements he had read touting the exceptional power of atomic weapons as compared with conventional bombs. Congressman Hinshaw noted that some of the figures that he had in mind placed one atomic bomb as having "270 times the capacity of one B29" that would drop only conventional bombs. Since General Vandenberg had not mentioned the great power of atomic bombs during his briefing, Congressman Hinshaw wondered "how the use of that weapon affects the plan." General Spaatz responded by emphasizing the secrecy surrounding the bomb and the airmen's inability, due to security requirements, to discuss it with the congressmen: "When you talk about the atomic weapon, you get right into the atomic security act and the question is rather difficult to answer right off."[25]

Without getting into actual numbers and technical information relating to the bomb, Vandenberg was still able to explain to the congressmen the airmen's (nonpublic) belief that the atomic bomb should be an ancillary weapon to the seventy-group air force's mission of carrying out a conventional bombing attack against the Soviet Union. Even after five or six years of further development and production of atomic weapons, according to Vandenberg, there was "only the bare possibility of winning the war [against the Soviets] by forcing capitulation" if the United States relied heavily on atomic weapons. The airmen therefore looked at the atomic bomb "from the standpoint of an additional weapon" to support a conventional bombing campaign against the Soviet Union.[26]

Simply put, conventional strategic bombing required many, many very heavy bombers that justified the air force's seventy-group program. Heavy reliance on the atomic bomb would have logically called into question the great number of airplanes that the airmen were asking Congress to buy. General Spaatz acknowledged that "200 plane loads" of conventional bombs would "accomplish the same result" as one atomic bomb attack.[27] For the airmen and their seventy-group program, the nemesis was in the arithmetic.

A second nemesis was the conception put forward by military strategist Bernard Brodie that the atomic bomb had become the "absolute weapon." The air force's seventy-group program was based largely on the World War II experience of the Army Air Forces. Yet Brodie argued that the atomic bomb seemed to have erased the World War II pattern of strategic bombing because of the new weapon's huge destructive capacity. Brodie believed that World War II had proven the decisiveness of strategic bombing, but the atomic bomb had changed the way strategic bombing would be conducted in a future war. Probably Brodie's most challenging argument was this: "Thus far the chief purpose of our military establishment has been to win wars. From now on its chief purpose must be to avert them. It can have no other useful purpose."[28] Yet the seventy-group program that Generals Spaatz and Vandenberg presented to the Air Policy Board was not a program fundamentally based on the ability of the air force to deter a war with the Soviets. Instead, the mission of the proposed seventy-group air force would ultimately be to fight and win a war against the Soviet Union by relying heavily on conventional strategic bombing. Symington told the congressmen of the Air Policy Board: "The more air you can get us, the happier we are."[29]

III

The atomic bomb posed a different challenge to the navy and its postwar interests. If the air force had to tread cautiously in dealing with the atomic bomb, the navy struggled to demonstrate that it too could include atomic weapons in its vision for the national defense. Naval officers did this by conducting their own public relations campaign showing that the navy's carrier-based airplanes had a role to play in strategic bombing.

Navy officers did not accept the airmen's argument that strategic bombers like the B-29 and the air force's newest bomber, the B-36, had so radically altered "time and space" as to make the geographical barrier created by the Pacific and Atlantic Oceans irrelevant for the nation's defense. One navy officer argued that naval aviation was "the frontier defense of the United States." In this line of thinking, because the oceans still provided the United States with geographical protection from enemy attack, the navy and its carrier-based airplanes would be able to operate on the edge of that "frontier" and protect the United States "from surprise attack."[30] Admiral Ofstie told a 1948 Navy Day audience that he did not believe the Soviet Union could launch a long-range conventional bombing attack against the United States. The great oceans that separated Russia and the United States were still America's best lines of defense, and the navy's wartime mission was to control that defensive area.[31]

Navy officers also argued that carrier-based aviation would be more capable of carrying "the war to the enemy." Admiral Chester Nimitz noted in his 1947 valedictory address that for "several years to come," the air force's bombers would not be able to make "two way trips between the continents."[32] The navy's carrier-based aircraft would be the most logical choice, according to Nimitz, to conduct strategic bombing operations against the Soviet Union. Responding to Nimitz's remarks, General Spaatz lamented to Symington that an article in a New York newspaper covering the Nimitz valedictory highlighted the admiral's position that aircraft carriers and their planes could "deal shattering blows to an enemy's industrial potential far inland in the event of war. . . ." Spaatz was upset because in his mind the navy was going far beyond the notion that naval aviation would be used only to support "fleet operations." Spaatz interpreted the navy's public statements as an attempt to convince the public that the navy should be allowed to take part in strategic bombing operations.[33]

Spaatz's concern was justified. The navy's assistant secretary for air, John Nicholas Brown, was reported to have testified to the Eberstadt committee on defense unification: "In any future war, the Navy, through its carrier task forces, will carry the war to the enemy. . . . In the early stages of any future war, long range bombers of the U.S. Air Force will not be able to reach the industrial heart of the enemy."[34]

Carrier-based aircraft, argued navy officers, would be most effective in dropping atomic bombs on targets inside of the Soviet Union. Since the air force's long-range bombers would have to fly great distances to reach critical targets within the Soviet Union, navy officers believed that their accuracy and the probability of their delivering the bombs would be quite low. The atomic bomb, claimed Admiral Ofstie in a speech to the Aviation Writers Association in 1948, was "of no use unless it [could] be delivered to the right spot. To my mind this, the delivery of the 'A' bomb, should be and probably is a major consideration today in the war plans of the Air Force and of Naval aviation."[35]

The navy did not disagree in principle with what I have called the American conceptual approach to strategic bombing—the use of strategic air power to attack the war-making capacity of the enemy. But the navy did want to be able to participate in strategic bombing operations in a potential war with the Soviet Union. Claiming a role to play in strategic bombing operations would give the navy leverage in the interservice "war" with the air force over defense dollars.

IV

The post–World War II plans for war against the Soviet Union, produced by the Joint Chiefs of Staff, called for "a prompt strategic air offensive" that would "destroy the Soviet war-making capacity." In the war plans written between 1945 and 1950, the atomic bomb was a critical component of that air offensive because the United States held sole ownership (until the Soviets exploded their first atomic bomb in August 1949) of atomic weapons. According to the planners, that produced a "distinct advantage" over the Soviet Union.[36] War with the USSR, according to the plans, would be "total" and would involve the industrial power of both nations. In order for the United States to destroy the Soviet will to resist, it would first have to destroy the "effectiveness of her [the Soviet Union's] war-machine."[37]

The first plans written in early 1946 for a potential war against the Soviet Union—the PINCHER plans—placed a heavy reliance on attacking Soviet industrial systems such as transportation, petroleum production, tank factories, ball-bearing plants, and other war industry. The PINCHER plans noted that most of these Soviet industries were located in major urban areas, therefore requiring a strategic bombing campaign that would attack Soviet cities. Urban areas, according to PINCHER, "would remain highly important for very long range air operations. The industrial structure . . . together with the known industrial dispositions abatable to the Soviets in western Europe, constitutes a sound premise on which to select [targets] for strategic air operations."[38]

The PINCHER plans and supporting intelligence estimates assumed that the Soviet Union did not pose an immediate military threat to Western Europe. According to these early postwar studies, the Soviet Union had a considerable conventional advantage over American, British, and French forces in Europe. But the studies also contended that the Soviets, for several years, would try to avoid a major conflict with the United States. Only a "miscalculation" of "the risks involved" on the part of the Soviets would lead to a "war between the USSR on one side and the United States and the British Empire on the other." The plans and intelligence estimates posited that once war began it would be "total" and fought to the fullest ability of America's industrial might.[39]

In November 1947 the Joint Chiefs approved war plan BROILER. In certain ways BROILER was similar to PINCHER. Both plans relied heavily on an early strategic air campaign against the Soviet Union employing atomic bombs. Both saw the need for advanced bases to launch this air offensive. But whereas the PINCHER series assumed that the massive American force requirements to carry out the plan would be met, BROILER was premised on the current American forces available for war in 1948.[40]

BROILER did acknowledge that atomic attacks directed at Soviet industry located in major urban areas would at the same time kill large numbers of civilians and destroy political control centers. Target areas, as the plan pointed out, "should be selected so that the maximum effect, both of physical destruction of war-making potential and destruction of the will to continue to resist, is attained."[41] Yet the actual target lists for BROILER still emphasized a strategic air campaign using atomic bombs to attack industrial systems like transportation, petroleum, and armament and munitions factories. Although the Soviet population in these proposed attacks would suffer greatly, this was seen as a bonus effect, the primary mission still being the destruction of the Soviet war-making capacity.[42]

As war planning evolved during the first five years following the end of World War II, a number of factors helped to shape the plans' overall approach to fighting a war with the Soviet Union. There was a political need to maintain unity among friendly European nations against perceived Soviet aggression. War planners, therefore, moved away from the earlier concept in the PINCHER series of withdrawing completely from Europe and adopted a new approach by 1948, one that saw American and British forces conducting a fighting retreat in Europe that would hold the Soviets at the Rhine River. The massive American ground invasion of the Soviet Union envisioned in the PINCHER series became an unrealistic concept based on the force structure of the American army in the late 1940s. Finally, the Soviet explosion of its first atomic device in 1949 had an impact on war planning. In their plans, the Joint Chiefs became increasingly concerned with "retarding" and "blunting" Russia's ability to occupy Western Europe and attack the United States with atomic weapons.[43]

Yet the core concept in almost every war plan and study during these years was a quick and devastating strategic air attack, relying heavily on atomic bombs, to destroy the industrial structure of the Soviet Union. No external threat, international event, domestic issue, or interservice wrangling over budgets would change this conceptual approach to fighting modern wars.

Consider the May 1948 war plan CRANKSHAFT that followed BROILER. Although in CRANKSHAFT the Chiefs made some important modifications from earlier plans concerning America's desire to defend Western Europe, the war-fighting approach in CRANKSHAFT showed remarkable continuity with that of both the BROILER and PINCHER series. CRANKSHAFT's mission statement read: "To impose the National War Objectives of the United States on the USSR."[44] In order to force the Soviet Union to accept American objectives, CRANKSHAFT called for creating "conditions within the USSR which will insure the abandonment of Soviet political and military aggression." The way to do this, as CRANKSHAFT pointed out, was to "initiate an air-offensive against vital strategic elements of the Soviet war-making capacity."[45]

The targeting approach in CRANKSHAFT focused on using strategic bombers to attack eight critical war-making elements of the Soviet Union: key government and control facilities; urban industrial areas; the petroleum industry; submarine bases; construction and repair facilities; transportation systems; the aircraft industry; the coke, iron, and steel industry; and the electric power system.[46] CRANKSHAFT recognized that most of the above war-making elements were located in large Soviet urban areas. Thus the preponderance of American attacks would be directed against Soviet cities. Like war plan BROILER, CRANKSHAFT considered the possibility of directly attacking morale by killing people in Soviet urban areas. Interestingly, at one point, CRANKSHAFT acknowledged that "it may become advisable to abandon the concept of destruction of the enemy's physical means to wage war in favor of a concept involving destruction of his will through [a] massive attack [against the Soviet] people." But the planners withdrew from this divergent concept by stating that a more thorough understanding was needed of the link between directly attacking the Soviet people and the possible breakdown of Soviet will to resist.[47]

The planners realized that strategic bombing against Soviet cities would kill millions of Soviet noncombatants. Their conception of modern warfare, tied to a deep-rooted understanding of a modern industrialized society, however, caused them to view the application of strategic air power in a war with the Soviets as a method of destroying the Soviet Union's war-making capacity. The planners themselves summed this concept up best in CRANKSHAFT when explaining the probable effects of strategic air attacks against Soviet industrial areas: CRANKSHAFT pointed out that such attacks would critically impair the Soviet ability to make war by decimating "the major portion of the skilled labor, technicians, and scientific workers available to the Soviets, the loss of which would reduce their industrial capabilities greatly."[48]

There was a marked similarity between CRANKSHAFT's treatment of killing "skilled labor" and the Strategic Bombing Survey's European and Pacific reports on the effects of strategic bombing on the morale of the industrial labor force. The CRANKSHAFT planners and the Survey analysts who wrote the reports on morale shared the same conception of strategic bombing: to view the killing and injuring of civilians by strategic bombing in terms primarily of war production, not morale. An industrial labor force that was killed or maimed by strategic bombers could not go to the factories and produce industrial goods that fueled the enemy's "war machine."

In May 1949, the Joint Chiefs released the Harmon Report, which analyzed the probable effects of a strategic air campaign that used atomic bombs against seventy Soviet cities. The report was named after its head, Lieutenant General Hubert Harmon, and was staffed by a number of army, navy, and air force officers. The report concluded that the United States could launch a successful strategic air offensive against Soviet cities (General Harmon's committee assumed that all the planes would get through to their targets). But the report also pointed out that while it would destroy 30 to 40 percent of Soviet industrial capacity, the air offensive would not affect appreciably the Soviet people's will to resist. In fact the Harmon Report argued that the atomic offensive, for the majority of Soviet citizens, "would validate Soviet propaganda against the United States, unify these people and increase their will to fight." The report concluded that the most effective and tangible results of the atomic offensive would be to quickly attack the Soviet Union and "[inflict] shock and serious damage to vital elements of the Soviet war-making capacity."[49]

In many ways the Harmon Report read like so many of the Strategic Bombing Survey's European and Pacific analyses. There were points where the enemy's will was considered a possible target for strategic air power. But the postwar plans for a war against the Soviet Union, the Harmon Report, and the Strategic Bombing Survey reports shared a common conception of using strategic air power to attack the enemy's war-making capacity. In the American conception, therefore, the enemy's will to resist would be a target that was too ambiguous to plan for and evaluate.

V

The Joint Chiefs of Staff seemed to have formed a consensus over the approach to war fighting that was manifested in the series of war plans produced between 1945 and 1950. With regard to air power, the Chiefs considered the concept of strategic bombing brought out in the plans to be correct. General Omar Bradley, the army chief of staff, and Admiral Louis Denfield, the chief of naval operations, for example, told Representative Carl Vinson, the chairman of the House Armed Services Committee that was preparing to investigate allegations surrounding the air force's B-36 bomber, that the Chiefs' concept of strategic bombing was a "fundamental part of our concept of war, and that its presently planned extent is considered the best for our nation. . . ."[50]

The disagreement between especially the navy and the air force was not over the American conceptual approach to strategic bombing, which both considered "sound," but over the methods the military would use to carry out strategic bombing operations in case of war with the Soviet Union. The navy, for example, placed much importance on the need to acquire advanced overseas bases for the air force to launch its bombing operations against the Soviets. In order to acquire and support those bases, especially in the Mediterranean, the navy would have to command the sea lines of communications. The navy also believed that its carrier-based aircraft could successfully launch strategic bombing operations against Russia's "military machine."[51] The air force, conversely, argued that the B-36 strategic bomber, based in the United States, was the most effective weapon system for carrying out a strategic bombing campaign against the "industrial heart" of the Soviet Union. Control over sea lanes, which was so important for the navy, became less important for the air force.[52]

Two critical events crystallized the debate between the navy and the air force that resulted in the B-36 investigation by Representative Carl Vinson's House Armed Services Committee. In March 1949, the newly appointed secretary of defense, Louis Johnson, canceled production of the navy's cherished supercarrier, the USS *United States*. The navy responded with a deliberate attack on the strategic vision and performance capability of the air force's newest bomber, the B-36. In the midst of this service battle over future weapon systems, President Truman announced in August 1949 the reduction of the 1951 fiscal year defense budget to $13 billion, about $2 billion less than the services had originally planned.[53]

With Carl Vinson as chairman, the House Armed Services Committee opened the B-36 hearings in August 1949. The air officers who testified naturally wished to disprove the charges that the B-36 was not the most economical bomber for the defense dollar and further to establish the efficacy of their method of strategic bombing in the postwar world. The atomic bomb and the air force's ability to deliver it were an important part of the air force's case to Congress. General Curtis LeMay, who at the time of the hearings was commanding the Strategic Air Command (SAC), provided expert testimony and convinced most committee members that the B-36 was a sound bomber capable of delivering the atomic bomb with decisive results. Ruminating over the proper course for the defense establishment to take, committee member Dewey Short wondered why "this government . . . should be spending billions of dollars in arming the countries of western Europe? Should we not, perhaps, put more emphasis on building and improving the B-36s here, because we can get them out and get them back without relying on anyone else?"[54] General LeMay's response to the congressman was shrewd and bureaucratically astute. By agreeing with Short, General LeMay would have confirmed the allegations of many naval officers that the air force was relying too heavily on atomic weapons for the nation's defense. Instead, General LeMay argued that the bombers would get through, but would not necessarily "win the war." For that would require, according to the general, a balanced mix of forces. Yet LeMay's testimony, coupled with that of other air force officers, confirmed in the minds of many congressman, and many Americans, that the atomic bomb, delivered by air force bombers, was the decisive weapon in modern combat.[55]

Curiously, the reports of the Strategic Bombing Survey provided little help to air force officers during the B-36 hearings. The most significant use of Survey reports was in a negative way by Air Force Chief of Staff General Hoyt S. Vandenberg. He told committee members that there "had been many attempts to discredit the value of strategic bombing by quoting [out of context] excerpts from the Strategic Bombing Survey." [56] This type of critique would become quite common with air force proponents when attacking the credibility of Survey "abusers." According to air proponents, the "consensus" conclusions of the Survey were to be found in the chairman's *Summary Reports*, not in the many other division studies. Indeed, when air force officers referred to the Survey during unification hearings, it was usually to either the Pacific or the European *Summary Report* proclaiming the decisiveness of air power in World War II. When detractors of air power deviated from those reports into the murkiness of the other supporting studies, air proponents would often claim Survey "abuse."[57]

There were extreme cases, however, when detractors of the air force's method of strategic bombing clearly made outlandish arguments based on Survey reports. The B-36 hearings ended in late August 1949, but Committee Chairman Carl Vinson, responding to complaints from naval officers that they did not get a chance to present their side of the story, reopened the hearings on 5 October to hear navy testimony on strategic air power and naval aviation.[58] One of the more junior naval officers to testify was Commander Eugene Tatom, head of the navy's aviation ordnance branch. On 10 October, Commander Tatom made an unbelievable assertion about the destructive qualities of the atom bomb. Tatom told the committee that an individual "could stand in the open at one end of the north-south runway at the Washington National Airport, with no more protection than the clothes you now have on, and have an atom bomb explode at the other end of the runway without serious injury to you."[59] Committee Chairman Vinson pressed Tatom for substantiation of this remarkable assertion. Tatom then read excerpts from the Pacific Survey report, *The Effects of Atomic Bombs on Health and Medical Services in Hiroshima and Nagasaki.* He pointed to data collected by the Survey showing how the effects of radiation and flash burns greatly diminished beyond 6,500 feet from ground zero.[60] But quoting this statistic from the above report downplays the destructive power of the atomic bombs that another report from the Pacific Survey, *Effects of the Atomic Bombs on Hiroshima and Nagasaki,* makes abundantly clear.[61]

Appearing shortly after Commander Tatom, Stuart Symington echoed General Vandenberg's earlier concern that certain individuals were using excerpts from the Survey to discredit strategic bombing. Symington criticized an "anonymous" article, "The Strategic Bombing Myth," that was appearing in various forms in many newspapers across the country and that had made it into the hands of key congressmen of the House Armed Services Committee. The document was written to thoroughly discredit the capabilities of the B-36 bomber and the air force's method of strategic bombing.[62]

The anonymous author of "The Strategic Bombing Myth" used

selected passages from Survey reports to show how the AAF's methods of strategic bombing in World War II had been a "total failure." According to "The Strategic Bombing Myth," the AAF's reliance on area bombing in World War II was immoral because it killed innocent civilians and ineffective because it did not destroy the war-making capacity of either Germany or Japan. But the article concluded that certain methods of bombing during World War II were quite effective. Bombing German transportation during World War II, according to "The Strategic Bombing Myth," proved to be a "decisive factor in the collapse of the Germany Army."[63]

Symington correctly pointed out in his testimony to the congressmen that "The Strategic Bombing Myth" rested in large part on highly selected portions of the Strategic Bombing Survey. He presented to the committee a letter written by former Survey chairman Franklin D'Olier that argued that "The Strategic Bombing Myth" grossly misstated the major conclusions of the Survey.[64] Explicitly, the secretary sought to attack the credibility of the article, but he had ulterior motives as well. The naval officers who appeared prior to Secretary Symington had relied largely on the Survey to attack air force methods of strategic air warfare. By attacking the use of the Survey in extreme form ("The Strategic Bombing Myth" and the Tatom testimony), Secretary Symington hoped to place doubt in the minds of committee members about the navy's use of the Survey in preceding and subsequent testimony.

But navy officers, during the hearings, were able to make shrewd use of the Survey to discredit what they saw as the air force's flawed method of strategic bombing. Admiral Arthur W. Radford, Commander in Chief, Pacific Fleet, was called back to Washington by Admiral Denfield to organize and present the navy's case to the congressional committee.[65] He testified that the B-36 was not a precision bomber and the atomic bomb was not a precision weapon. The air force, according to Admiral Radford, would therefore have to use the B-36 to conduct mass area bombings of Soviet cities using atomic bombs. Based on his reading of the Strategic Bombing Survey, area bombings of cities had not worked in World War II, nor would this type of strategic bombing prove decisive in a potential war with the Soviet Union. The admiral was in favor of strategic bombing and using the atom bomb, but only on military targets, not "the indiscriminate bombing of cities."[66]

The heart of the navy's critique was that the air force's method of strategic warfare was based on a flawed understanding of the past. In Admiral Radford's mind, the popular belief that strategic bombing had revolutionized warfare by making armies and navies less important was wrong; in future wars sea lanes would still have to be secured and the navy would still play an integral role in the nation's defense. Other naval officers who appeared after Admiral Radford argued this same point. When proclaiming the relevance of tactical aviation in a potential war with the Soviet Union, Brigadier General Vernon E. Megee, a Marine Corps aviator, based his argument on Survey findings on the role that tactical aviation played in destroying transportation networks in Germany and Japan during World War II.[67] Admiral W. H. P. Blandy, commander in chief of the Atlantic Fleet, embellished a point that Admiral Radford had made a few days earlier that an all-out atomic attack on Soviet cities would not break the Soviet people's will to resist. Admiral Blandy's reading of the Survey showed that strategic bombing "in the latter part of the war, had a very great effect on Germany's oil and steel industries and her transportation, plus a marked effect upon her general economy, and the morale of her people." But Blandy added that strategic bombing operations in World War II that killed large numbers of civilians did not lead to "an actual breakdown of the will of the people to resist." The lessons from the past that should be applied to present and future defense strategy was that there was no such thing as an "atomic Blitz." Instead, wars would continue to be fought with the army and navy destroying the enemy's capacity to resist, stated Blandy.[68]

Erstwhile USSBS director Admiral Ralph A. Ofstie, appearing again before the committee, pointed out what naval officers saw as the air force's misconception of the past and its flawed vision for future defense strategy. He began his testimony, like other naval and marine officers before him, by citing Survey findings that demonstrated the impact strategic bombing had had on German and Japanese "military targets," such as oil and transportation. With this historical foundation laid, Admiral Ofstie then explained the navy's method for using strategic bombing in a potential war with the Soviets. Since, as Ofstie believed, atomic attacks on Soviet cities would be ineffective based on World War II experience, the first Soviet targets that should be hit in the initial stages of a war were the ones that had proved most decisive in World War II, oil and transportation. The navy, according to Admiral Ofstie, because of its unique ability to control sea lanes and project air power, would have the primary role "in such offensive actions." For Ofstie, lessons from the past only proved the incorrectness of the air force's methods and the correctness of the navy's. He asked:

> Must the Italian Douhet continue as our prophet because certain zealots grasped the false doctrines many years ago and refuse to relinquish this discredited theory in the face of vast costly experience? Must we translate the historical mistake of World War II into a permanent concept merely to avoid clouding the prestige of those who led us down the wrong road in the past? . . . [We must] build the armed forces of this country on the basis of experience rather than hope, hard fact rather than wishful prophecy, balanced power rather than the single-shot philosophy.[69]

Note the resemblance in this passage to Orvil Anderson's Survey report, *Air Campaigns of the Pacific War*. In that report, it was the "established organizations" (like the navy) who were preventing the air force from realizing its future vision for the security of the United States. Admiral Ofstie, however, turned this argument on its head and labeled air proponents "zealots" for pulling the nation's defense into the future with a flawed understanding of the past.

But attacking the air force's method of strategic bombing on the grounds of military ineffectiveness was only part of the navy's overall critique. Building on their argument (based on Survey reports) that strategic bombing in World War II was deeply flawed for military reasons, naval officers argued that it was also immoral. Admiral Ofstie told committee members that the United States was morally wrong for bombing civilians during World War II and Americans would be equally immoral if they had to kill civilians in a war with the Soviet Union. According to the admiral, the American people were in "strong opposition to military methods [area bombings of cities] so contrary to our fundamental ideals."[70]

What was striking about the moral tack of the navy's critique was that the majority of senior naval officers followed it. Admiral Radford "condemned" the potential area bombing of Soviet cities and did not "believe in [the] mass killing of noncombatants" based on what he had learned since the war. Admiral Thomas Kinkaid referred to the strategic bombing of Germany and Japan as "terrorizing bombardments" that violated established laws of war. When discussing with committee members the appropriate targets if the United States had to fight the Soviet Union, Admiral Blandy stated that "no sane man would derive any satisfaction from killing women and children" because it constituted the "slaughter of innocent people."[71]

Yet some troubling contradictions emerge out of these 1949 hearings that are worth considering. If the issue of morality was so important to naval officers, why did it not emerge before the 1949 supercarrier cancellation and defense budget reductions? By the late 1950s, the navy was developing a strategic nuclear-tipped missile launched from submarines that would be predominantly used as an area weapon against enemy cities. What happened to the morality issue? Taking the longer view strongly suggests that the navy's 1949 moral critique of the air force was only a tactic in the navy's interservice "war" to claim a larger share of the defense budget.[72]

VI

Admiral Ofstie, for example, about a year prior to the 1949 hearings, had no problem with "knock[ing] hell out of Moscow with atomic bombs." The United States should also use atomic bombs, according to the admiral, on the other "major urban and industrial areas" in the Soviet Union. In a classified memorandum to the navy's General Board (a group of high-ranking naval officers who advised the secretary of the navy), Ofstie noted that the United States would "hesitate to use bacteriological warfare involving the mass destruction of persons until after the enemy had shown good evidence they had intended to use it." But Ofstie did believe the United States should attack Soviet "grain crops" as soon as "we had the advantage and knew that the Soviets could not retaliate effectively against us. This would then be merely a quicker way of bringing the enemy to submission." Ofstie also hinted at a willingness to launch a surprise bacteriological attack against the Soviets providing there was "evidence" that the Soviets were intending to attack the United States with biological weapons. Killing civilians, therefore, with weapons of mass destruction did not pose a moral dilemma for Ofstie in 1948.[73]

In this same classified memorandum, Ofstie strongly advocated a heavily nuclear preventive war against the Soviets. According to Ofstie's "personal view," the United States

> should go to war at that time when Russia is approaching industrial self sufficiency in that part of Europe which is outside Russia. . . . The obvious advantage would be that this would make it possible for us to win the war. The alternative would be a stalemate and subsequent decreased relative potential between the U.S. and the Soviet. Such a course of action (preventive war) would be possible in this country if the public were educated up to fully understanding the true position. . . . It would be very difficult to make full preparations for a "planned war" without publicly revealing that intent. However, the ace up our sleeve here would be our ability to prepare fully for atomic warfare since the weapons themselves are already in existence and the aircraft (land and carrier based) are needed in only small numbers of inauspicious types, and necessary installations afloat and ashore can be prepared without any particular show. . . . It would appear to me that the selection of 'D' Day would, in some measure at

> least, be guided by casting a balance between our atomic readiness (stockpile of bombs, planes able to penetrate, and bases within range) and the growing war capability of the USSR.[74]

This passage demonstrates Ofstie's belief in the soundness of a strategic bombing campaign against the Soviets, as long as the methods used in that strategic bombing campaign involved the navy's carrier-based aircraft. It also shows that a senior, influential military officer like Ofstie was willing to call for, in a classified memorandum, a surprise atomic attack against the Soviet Union in order to prevent the Soviets from attacking the United States first. And Ofstie's memorandum referred to "educating the public" to accept the "true position," which meant America needed to have the political will to launch a "preventive war" against the Soviet Union.

Ofstie made the same argument to the Joint Chiefs of Staff when he served as a board member for the evaluation of the July 1946 Bikini Island atomic tests. The "Operation Crossroads" evaluation team was headed by Massachusetts Institute of Technology President Karl T. Compton and also included General J. W. Stilwell, General Albert Wedemeyer, and Admiral D. S. Parsons as special advisors.[75] The evaluation team that Ofstie served on released its final report to the Joint Chiefs on 29 December 1947. The report concluded that atomic bombs, used in conjunction with other weapons of mass destruction such as biological and chemical weapons, would "depopulate vast areas of the earth's surface, leaving only vestigial remnants of man's material works." Since an enemy nation in the possession of such weapons could launch a surprise attack on the United States, the report stated that America needed to revise its

> traditional attitudes toward what constitutes acts of aggression so that our armed forces may plan and operate in accordance with the realities of atomic warfare. Our attitude of national defense must provide for the employment of every practical means to prevent surprise attack. Offensive measures will be the only generally effective means of defense, and the United States must be prepared to employ them before a potential enemy can inflict significant damage upon us.[76]

When reviewing the report's findings, the respective members of the Joint Chiefs of Staff disagreed over a number of its conclusions.[77] The issue of which service would have primary control over atomic weapon development brought about sharp debate. But there was no disagreement among the service chiefs over the recommendation that the president should consider reorienting national military policy to allow for an offensive strike against the Soviet Union.

Indeed, when the Chiefs forwarded the Crossroads report to the White House they bracketed the paragraphs concerning preventive war so that President Truman could carefully consider this proposed crucial shift in policy. The Chiefs acknowledged in a cover memorandum to the president that a substantial shift in policy toward preventive war was a political decision that the commander in chief would have to make.[78] Secretary of Defense Forrestal attached a cover letter to the Chiefs' memorandum pointing out to the president that the bracketed portions related to "the enactment of legislation which would establish new definitions of acts of aggression and incipient attack. Such legislation would make it the duty of the President of the United States, as Commander in Chief of its Armed Forces, and after consultation with the Cabinet, to order atomic bomb retaliation when such retaliation was necessary to prevent or frustrate an atomic energy attack upon us."[79] By using the term "retaliation" the secretary hedged on fully advocating to the president a shift in policy toward preventive war. Yet Forrestal's implicit suggestion was that America was already at war with the Soviets, albeit a cold one, and in this context retaliation became synonymous with prevention, or launching a surprise attack on the Soviets to "frustrate an atomic energy attack" on the United States.

Not hedging whatsoever in advocating preventive war with a potential "enemy" was Orvil Anderson's Strategic Bombing Survey Report, *Air Campaigns of the Pacific War*. Anderson's report stated that the American public must be kept "informed with respect to the dangers of accepting the first blow in a future war." *Air Campaigns* argued further that the American people "must recognize that an overt act of war has been committed by an enemy when that enemy builds a military force intended for our eventual destruction, and that destruction of that force before it can be launched or employed is defensive action and not aggression."[80] Interestingly, when Admiral Ofstie read the published version of *Air Campaigns* he made lacerating marginal comments at many points in the report, but he made no comments on the margins where Anderson advocated preventive war.[81]

The notion of preventive war was not a new concept for Orvil Anderson. As early as 1943 he told an interviewer that if America wanted to "prevent getting hit" by a potential aggressor, it should "hit" first. On 6 August 1945, the same day the United States dropped an atomic bomb on Hiroshima, Anderson told another interviewer that America had to "accept a national policy of prevention. If necessary we have to shoot to do it, but we will shoot quick. Nip it in the bud; don't let him become a big bear or he will roll all over you; take him while he is a cub or before he is a cub." Anderson added that if the United States saw an enemy nation starting to develop a weapon "such as the bursting of the atom," it should "just say no" to that enemy nation. But if the enemy refused to listen to the United States, argued the general, then "we will hit them."[82]

In 1947, as commandant of the Air War College, Anderson perceptively understood the dilemma that strategic air power posed for the concepts of defense and offense. Anderson argued in a lecture to students that an enemy's strategic bombing attack against the United States would mostly "get through to their targets." Even though the United States would try to defend against such an attack by trying to shoot down the enemy's aircraft, "a well planned mass attack, well might be decisive" against the United States. Anderson then posited that the only way to "defend" successfully against such an attack would be to take the "offensive" by destroying the enemy's war-making capacity that produced its strategic air power.[83] Thus, in Anderson's conception, what appeared to be an offensive attack against an enemy nation was in fact defensive because it prevented that enemy from attacking the United States first.

This line of thinking allowed Anderson in September 1950 to

recommend publicly a preventive war against the Soviets. Anderson stated in an interview to an Alabama newspaper reporter:

> Give me the order to do it, and I can break up Russia's five A-bomb nests in a week! And when I went to Christ, I think I could explain to Him why I wanted to do it now before it's too late. I think I could explain to Him that I had saved civilization. . . . This doctrine of waiting until you're hit first—even when you know the first blow will kill you, is queer. . . . Right now, today, this nation is committing the greatest sin in history—the sin of not providing for the assurance and security of our own posterity. Damn it! We are obligated to them. . . . There's no realism here! . . . We're at war, damn it! We want to call it a police action [the Korean War], but American lives and dollars and time are being lost in that action. It has all the features of war except the definition! . . . With it [the A-bomb], used in time, we can immobilize a foe, reduce his crime before it has happened. . . . If you take the heart out of the enemy's body, you don't have to cut his fingers off. . . . Realism, oh, for a little realism in America before it is too late![84]

Anderson's frightening remarks anticipated the deranged movie character of "General Jack D. Ripper," who on his own volition initiates a preventive war against the Soviet Union, in Stanley Kubrick's 1964 satire of American nuclear strategy, *Dr. Strangelove*.[85]

The Anderson interview was in fact a very accurate representation of the general's view of air power strategy and his deeply felt belief that the United States should launch a surprise attack on the Soviet Union to prevent it from attacking the United States first. But for stating those beliefs on strategy and preventive war in a public forum, Air Force Chief of Staff General Hoyt Vandenberg relieved Orvil Arson Anderson of his post as commandant of the Air War College. Even though a good number of other military officers would have agreed with Anderson in private, stating those thoughts in a public forum challenged the official policy of containing (not rolling back) the Soviet Union and terrified the majority of the American people.[86] Simply put, Anderson crossed the line by stating in public what he and many others believed about strategic air power and the Soviet Union.

VII

Anderson's Survey report, *Air Campaigns*, and his outspoken rhetoric on preventive war contradicted Paul Nitze's conclusions concerning air power and national security in the Pacific Survey *Summary Report*. Nitze admitted in the *Summary Report* that it would be impossible to completely protect the United States from an enemy's strategic bombers and guided missiles. It therefore behooved the United States, according to Nitze, "to accept the possibility that at least a small number of enemy planes or guided missiles may be able to evade all our defenses and to attack any objective within range." The defense of the United States would come from "the threat of immediate retaliation with a striking force of our own," which "should deter any aggressor from attacking."[87] For Nitze, America's defense should come from the threat of immediate retaliation. For Orvil Anderson, America's defense should come from offensive action that would destroy the enemy's war-making capability before it could be brought to bear against the United States.

The contradiction between the Survey reports of Anderson and Nitze over retaliation versus preventive war manifested the dilemma that strategic air power posed for the military's defense of the United States. In the logic of air power theory, if the enemy's forces could be destroyed in a first strike, the surest way to defend the United States was through offensive, not defensive, action. In a very troubling but truthful way, Orvil Anderson was one of the few military officers who understood the dilemma, explained it publicly, and advocated a strident solution. The contradiction also demonstrates how the Survey, by its published reports and the ideas of its analysts, reflected the American conceptual approach to strategic bombing and the dilemma that conception posed for American security in the postwar world.

Strategist Bernard Brodie wrote a personal note to Orvil Anderson shortly after the general's relief from his post as commandant of the Air War College. Brodie told Anderson that the relief had presented the general's view on preventive war to the nation "in a much more forceful and commanding way . . . than would otherwise have been possible."[88] When Brodie wrote this letter to Anderson, the strategist was preparing to leave Yale University to become a special advisor to the chief of staff of the air force, General Hoyt Vandenberg, on air power doctrine and military strategy.[89] General Anderson maintained a file containing the correspondence he received after his relief from the Air War College, and the only letter there from an influential military establishment member, either civilian or military, was from Bernard Brodie.

Perhaps Brodie understood better than anyone else the dilemma that atomic weapons posed for American security and the logic of General Anderson's public statements on preventive war. In a lecture to the Air War College two years after Anderson's relief, Brodie referred to "preventive war" as an "alternative strategy to be considered," and he blamed his "social science colleagues for the fact that they have turned their faces away from any consideration of this problem."[90]

VIII

Bernard Brodie and other postwar analysts used the reports of the USSBS to help them think through the problems that nuclear weapons and air power posed for American national security. In his 1946 book *The Absolute Weapon*, Brodie argued that atomic bombs had revolutionized warfare. Brodie contended that any future war with the Soviets would not be similar to the great land battles of World War II. Instead, Brodie saw the next major war being fought primarily, and decisively, with atomic bombs.[91] Partly because Brodie believed that atomic weapons had changed the way wars in the future would be fought, he was judicious and cautious in using the Survey to support his theories. For Brodie, if there was any meaningful continuity between strategic bombing in World War II and future atomic war, it had to be analyzed rigorously for the development of atomic strategy.

The Survey's numerous reports on the successes and failures of bombing various targets in World War II did, however, emphasize to Brodie the crucial importance of choosing the right targets before an atomic war began with the Soviet Union.[92] The main lesson Brodie drew from strategic bombing in World War II was that proper target selection depended on an analysis of the enemy nation's political economy and social structure. Brodie stressed that planning for a potential nuclear war had to be based on a thorough, contemporary analysis of all relevant factors for a particular enemy. In 1952, while serving as a special air force advisor, Brodie criticized the Air Targets Division for basing postwar target selection in the Soviet Union on a USSBS conclusion that German electrical power facilities were vulnerable to bombing and that if they had been attacked, it would have had a crippling effect on the economy.[93] While electrical facilities might have been the right targets in the war against Germany, he questioned whether they were necessarily the correct targets for a nuclear war with the Soviets.[94]

Perhaps the antithesis of Brodie when it came to defining and applying the lessons of World War II was P. M. S. Blackett, a Nobel Prize-winning physicist, a creator of operations research, and a member of Britain's Advisory Committee on Atomic Energy. Blackett's 1948 book *Military and Political Consequences of Atomic Energy Weapons* critiqued postwar American perceptions about the absolute nature of atomic weapons. According to Blackett, the American people had concluded, incorrectly, that the atomic bombings of Hiroshima and Nagasaki had militarily defeated Japan. This led them to the erroneous belief that a future war with the Soviet Union could be decided quickly and decisively with atomic weapons.[95] To deny the absolute nature of atomic weapons, to demystify them, and to assign them a proper military role, Blackett analyzed strategic bombing in World War II to establish his theories on military strategy.

In arguing for the indecisiveness of atomic weapons and strategic air power, Blackett relied heavily on many of the Survey's conclusions, including especially the European Economic Division's report, *The Effects of Strategic Bombing on the German War Economy.* It argued that most German war production increased up to mid-1944 in the face of Allied bombing attacks. After the June 1944 Normandy invasion, according to the Survey, strategic bombing did cause considerable damage to German industry, but it was the cumulative effect of the ground offensive that moved rapidly into the heart of Germany as well as strategic bombing that produced Germany's collapse.[96] In light of this Survey conclusion, Blackett argued that even after acknowledging "the great developments of air power, it is clear that Germany's defeat in the second world war, as in the first, was brought about primarily by her huge loss in man-power and material incurred in the land battles. . . . Air power played, of course, a decisively important role in all the great land battles."[97] In Blackett's judgment, strategic bombing had produced decisive results only in conjunction with the "great land battles" of World War II, and military strategy based solely on the purported decisiveness of atomic weapons did not take into account this "lesson" of history.

Blackett also argued that atomic bombs, because of their widely destructive capabilities, could be used only against large cities. According to Blackett, the relative inaccuracy of contemporary delivery systems and the bomb's overwhelming destructive power made atomic weapons inappropriate for destroying smaller "precision" targets such as industrial factories or transportation centers. He therefore concluded that the most efficient use of atomic weapons would be against large, highly populated cities. The United States, consequently, would have to target large urban areas in a major war with the Soviet Union. Using the Survey's conclusion that urban area attacks did not substantially reduce Germany's war production in World War II, Blackett contended that nuclear attacks on large Soviet urban areas would have the same negative result.[98]

The *New York Times* military correspondent, Hanson Baldwin, an Annapolis graduate, relied on the Pacific Survey *Summary Report* to support his argument that the combat use of the bomb was unnecessary. In his 1949 book *The Great Mistakes of the War,*

Baldwin used the often-cited conclusion from the *Summary Report* that, owing primarily to conventional strategic bombing, Japan would have surrendered very probably by 1 November and certainly by 31 December 1945 even if the United States had not dropped the atomic bomb. He cited this conclusion together with another from a Pacific Survey report, *The Effects of Strategic Bombing on Japan's War Economy*, to demonstrate that the antishipping campaign had effectively undermined the Japanese war economy before the atomic bombings of 6 and 9 August 1945.[99]

Among the first to use the Survey's findings to defend Truman's decision to drop the bomb was former secretary of war Henry L. Stimson. In a widely read 1947 article in *Harper's Magazine* (actually authored by his young aide, McGeorge Bundy, whose role was not revealed at the time), Stimson cited the Survey report *Japan's Struggle to End the War* and concluded: "All the *evidence* I have seen indicates that the controlling factor in the final Japanese decision to accept our terms of surrender was the atomic bomb."[100]

Stimson's statement is an early example of how conclusions drawn from the narrative portion of *Japan's Struggle to End the War* could be much different from the ending portion of the report, which stated verbatim (from the *Summary Report*) Nitze's early-surrender counterfactual. But for Stimson, the narrative in *Japan's Struggle to End the War,* by itself, indicated that the Japanese cabinet was deadlocked over whether to accept the Potsdam terms or continue the war in August 1945, and thus the atom bomb made the decisive difference. Unlike the Survey, Stimson concluded from the narrative that the United States had to drop the bomb to end the war quickly and save American lives.

Stimson, though, did not explicitly seek to rebut the Survey's "official" explanation for Japan's surrender (even though Stimson's explanation contradicted Nitze's counterfactual conclusion). He sought to avoid controversy and formal argumentation in an intentional rhetorical strategy urged by close advisors.[101] Stimson's implicit critique, though, was still potent because it suggested that Nitze had incorrectly interpreted his evidence.

Franklin D'Olier knew that Nitze's Pacific Survey's counterfactual conclusion raised troubling questions about the end of World War II in the Pacific. Shortly after *Harper's Magazine* published Henry Stimson's article on President Truman's decision to use the bomb, University of Chicago theologian Fred Eastman told D'Olier that he was "struck by the difference between "the two explanations for Japan's surrender." Eastman wondered if Stimson had read the Pacific Survey report (that argued the bomb was unnecessary) "before [Stimson] wrote his article." D'Olier informed Eastman that he had never read Stimson's article.[102] D'Olier chose not to confront the two contradictory statements concerning Japan's surrender and the necessity of the atomic bomb. Instead, he simply provided Eastman with a restatement of the presidential directives that established the Survey. It is unclear why D'Olier did not try to resolve the apparent contradiction between Stimson's and the Survey's explanation for Japan's surrender.

Back in December 1944 Franklin D'Olier gave a welcome speech to many of the Survey's newly arrived analysts. He used a metaphor to explain to them his concept of strategic bombing. According to D'Olier, tactical bombing took off the arms and legs of the "cow," but strategic bombing destroyed the whole "cow," arms and legs and all.[103] D'Olier's Bombing Survey did its part to demonstrate that American strategic air power had slain the "cow" of German and Japanese war-making capacity during World War II. But in the Pacific, the United States did it, according to the Survey, without the atomic bomb. In 1946–47, that conclusion did not seem threatening to air power, to the sense of U.S. history, or to the military services.

The Strategic Bombing Survey would continue to influence thinking about strategic bombing and military strategy beyond the immediate post–World War II years. For example, Gar Alperovitz, in his 1964 book *Atomic Diplomacy*, challenged Stimson's official explanation of the A-bomb. Using Paul Nitze's Pacific Survey counterfactual as evidence, Alperovitz argued that President Truman used the bomb not to end the war, because he knew that Japan would soon surrender, but to intimidate the Soviet Union.[104] In the early 1970s, journalists like David Halberstam and I. F. Stone used selected portions of the Survey to support their criticisms of President Richard Nixon's bombing campaign against North Vietnam.[105] More recently, the Survey has been used by analysts writing on the use of air power in Kosovo and Yugoslavia. In an April 1999 editorial that heavily criticized NATO's air campaign in the Balkans, the *Nation*, citing USSBS conclusions as proof, argued that the use of air strikes would not break Serbia's will.[106]

The conclusions contained in the published reports of the United States Strategic Bombing Survey have tended to be perceived as facts, rather than interpretations, of strategic bombing in World War II. The Survey's published reports, unfortunately, have taken on the mystique of "biblical" truth. Trying to tell the truth about air power in the Persian Gulf War almost a half century after the USSBS completed its work, the analysts of the Gulf War Air Power Survey (GWAPS) understood that their conclusions were interpretations, based on facts, about air power in Southwest Asia.

CHAPTER 7

A Comparison of the United States Strategic Bombing Survey with the Gulf War Air Power Survey

[According to Pentagon gossip] it appears we are in the grip of historians.
ELIOT COHEN, 1992

After World War II, Bernard Brodie and other defense analysts read, and often used, many of the United States Strategic Bombing Survey (USSBS) conclusions in their postwar writings on military strategy and defense policy and organization. The Survey's published studies provided postwar analysts with a wealth of evidence to support their wide-ranging arguments. The reports of the USSBS also helped the air force in its postwar fight for independence, and provided support to both the air force and the navy in the fierce interservice battles over defense funding in 1949.

The "internal war" between the military services over defense dollars and organization turned to actual war in late June 1950 when North Korea attacked South Korea across the 38th parallel. The Korean War was indeed a very different type of war to the American military, especially the United States Air Force.[1] If the political objectives of World War II that airmen helped to achieve were the unconditional surrenders of Germany and Japan, the political objectives of the Truman Administration in Korea were much more limited. Instead of attacking what most airmen believed to be the root cause of the war in Korea—the Soviet Union and later China—President Truman restricted the use of American air power to the

Korean Peninsula.[2] The airmen were thus limited to bombing a small number of strategic targets in North Korea and to supporting the ground operations of the army.[3]

When it came to evaluating the effects of air power in the Korean War, members of the Air Staff thought that another study like the World War II USSBS was unnecessary since the preponderance of air power used in Korea was "tactical interdiction."[4] The Korean War did not fit airmen's conceptual understanding of the primary use of strategic air power and therefore did not warrant a civilian-led evaluation on the scale of the USSBS. Neither would the next limited war fought by the United States after Korea.

In 1965, as the United States was beginning its large-scale military involvement in the Vietnam War, erstwhile air force chief of staff General Curtis E. LeMay boasted that in order for the United States to win in South East Asia it should use strategic air power to bomb North Vietnam "back into the Stone Age."[5] LeMay ignored the relative fact that, compared with the industrial might of the United States, North Vietnam was already in the "Stone Age."

The World War II USSBS informed the airmen that the way to use strategic air power in Vietnam was to bomb the enemy's war-making capacity. The American air chiefs believed that the air force's approach to fighting a strategic air war—shaped by the World War II experience much more than by Korea—was adaptable to any type of conflict, including a limited war in Vietnam.[6]

As the war progressed, however, airmen were unhappy with the gradual, limited approach to bombing North Vietnam forced upon them by their civilian masters. Rolling Thunder, the air campaign from 1965 to 1968 designed to apply incremental pressure on the North Vietnamese leadership, seemed wrong to air officers because it placed what they saw as artificial limits and restrictions on the use of air power. According to airmen, Rolling Thunder did not allow the air force to apply overwhelming air power on a strategic level quickly and decisively against North Vietnam.[7]

In 1972 American airmen began to use strategic air power the way they believed it should be used. The Linebacker I air campaign

(May–October 1972) halted North Vietnamese conventional attacks into South Vietnam by air interdiction and close air support. In December 1972 (the so-called Christmas Bombings), President Nixon ordered the air force to conduct Linebacker II: a large-scale air power attack against strategic targets centered in Hanoi and Haiphong to compel the North Vietnamese leadership to accept a cease-fire and thus allow American forces to withdraw from South Vietnam. Since the North Vietnamese government accepted cease-fire terms shortly after Linebacker II, many airmen believed that it was American strategic air power that finally got the United States out of the Vietnam War. Former president Richard Nixon commented on the television show *Meet the Press* sixteen years later that had the United States bombed North Vietnam in 1969 as it did during the Linebacker campaigns, "we would have ended the war in 1969 rather than in 1973."[8]

Within the air force since the end of the Vietnam War, an "unhealthy" myth has emerged that posits that the Linebacker campaigns "won" the war for the United States.[9] While the Linebacker I and II campaigns stopped the North Vietnamese conventional attack and brought them back to the diplomatic bargaining table, it is wrong to suggest that a similar approach would have ended the war in 1969 or even in 1965, as some airmen have suggested. The Linebacker campaigns were relatively successful because they attacked certain North Vietnamese capabilities in 1972 that were vulnerable to air power. During the years of Rolling Thunder, conversely, since the communist forces in the South did not rely substantially on the war-making capability of the North, air power's effectiveness was limited.[10] However, these realities often went unnoticed by airmen in the years following Vietnam. Thus with the myth of the Linebacker campaigns firmly placed in their minds, the airmen moved on to prepare again to fight the Soviet Union in a nuclear air war, just as they did after Korea. And as with Korea, since their experience in Vietnam was inconclusive and not adaptable to textbook explanations,[11] an extensive civilian-led evaluation of air power after the Vietnam War was not conducted.

I

Uncertainties about the use of American air power in the Korean and Vietnam Wars changed to certainty within the Air Force about the effectiveness of air power in the Persian Gulf War. Indeed, in early January 1991, shortly before the United States initiated its aerial assault on Iraq and Kuwait, Colonel John A. Warden III, air force deputy director for war-fighting concepts in the Pentagon, believed that another World War II-type survey was needed if the United States carried out its planned air campaign. Colonel Warden subsequently sent a memorandum to the air force vice-chief of staff, General John M. Loh, pointing out that a "bombing survey would be extremely valuable" and should be performed by an "independent commission." Colonel Warden later pursued the idea of what became known as the Gulf War Air Power Survey (GWAPS) with former USSBS director Paul Nitze. In fact Colonel Warden prepared a special briefing for Nitze and made a strong "pitch for an independent bombing survey."[12] Undoubtedly, Colonel Warden and other airmen saw great success in their efforts against Iraq; an "independent study" would assuredly confirm the decisiveness of American air power in the Gulf War just as airmen intended the USSBS to do after World War II.

In a certain way, however, the GWAPS was unlike the USSBS. American airmen played a strong role in establishing the USSBS's organizational structure and in shaping the questions that it answered, and airmen influenced the conclusions reached by the USSBS about strategic bombing in World War II. The USSBS thus fit neatly within the AAF's conceptual approach to air power, and served its postwar interests in establishing an independent air arm. The GWAPS was different. Powerful air force interests did try to influence the conclusions reached by the GWAPS. However, those interests did not substantially affect the GWAPS ability to conduct an independent study of the use of air power in the Gulf War.

Analyzing this shift from the USSBS to the GWAPS is important because it sheds light on the subtle interplay of advocacy and assessment between the air force and its civilian-led studies of major bombing operations. Exploring the shift also illuminates the culture of military institutions and how they arrive at "lessons learned" from military operations and apply them to future defense policy, organization, and operations.

II

Iraq's invasion of Kuwait on 1 August 1990 surprised many Americans. Once President George Bush authorized an American military deployment to the Gulf to help defend Saudi Arabia against a possible Iraqi attack, F-15s and other aircraft assigned to the command of Lieutenant General Charles Horner, commander of Central Air Force (CENTAF), arrived in Saudi Arabia on 9 August 1990. The arrival of General Horner's aircraft and airmen was the start of a large buildup of American military forces that eventually reached over five hundred thousand personnel. Desert Shield, as the buildup became known, changed to Desert Storm on 16 January when the United States and other coalition forces launched an air campaign against a wide array of Iraqi targets in Iraq and Kuwait. Many airmen, including Colonel Warden (the conceptual "founding father" of the air campaign against Iraq called Instant Thunder),[13] hoped that air power alone could eject Iraqi forces from Kuwait, a key political goal for the United States.[14] Yet on 24 February, after more than a month of continuous bombing, the United States and coalition forces launched a ground campaign to achieve the goals that air power may or may not have been able to accomplish if left on its own.[15] Relying heavily on the conditions created by the air campaign, the ground offensive took a mere four days to defeat the Iraqi forces in Kuwait and compelled the Iraqi leadership to accept a cease-fire on coalition terms.

Like the airmen at the end of World War II, air officers after the Gulf War perceived great success in their application of air power to achieve American objectives.[16] And there was a similar desire among at least a few airmen to prove success through a civilian-led, independent survey of air power's effectiveness in the Gulf War.

On 25 July 1991, Secretary of the Air Force Donald B. Rice made a phone call to Eliot A. Cohen, a professor of strategic studies at the Paul H. Nitze School of Advanced International Studies at Johns Hopkins University, inviting him to serve as the editor-in-chief (or director) of what became known as the Gulf War Air Power Survey. Secretary Rice, in a follow-up memorandum, pointed out to Cohen that the GWAPS would "form conclusions on the implications for future Air Force organization, training and force structure." However, for the GWAPS to be accepted as a credible source of analysis on air power in the Gulf, it needed to "conduct its study according to the highest standards of professional and intellectual integrity and objectivity." Cohen accepted the secretary's invitation to head the GWAPS, agreeing wholeheartedly that the air force should "establish the most accurate possible record of DESERT SHIELD and STORM and learn from it."[17] Cohen also apparently received a promise from Rice that the GWAPS reports would not be "staffed," or reviewed, by air force agencies.[18]

Secretary Rice's memorandum to Eliot Cohen established the GWAPS by providing it with "terms of reference" for the conduct of its study.[19] The GWAPS mandate was "to review all aspects of air warfare in the Persian Gulf," but focusing its analysis on the operational aspects of the American air campaign against Iraq.[20] The GWAPS was civilian-led and included more than one hundred civilian and military analysts. It also included a review committee of prominent American statesmen, retired military officers, and scholars to provide advice and criticism on the GWAPS analytical approach and published studies. The review committee's chairman was Paul Nitze.

From August 1991 to January 1993 (and slightly beyond), GWAPS members conducted extensive research and wrote a five-volume study (to include an executive *Summary Report*) on air power in the Gulf War. The GWAPS was organized into "task forces," all but one being civilian-led. Each task force focused its analysis on thematic aspects of the Gulf War such as operations and effects, logistics, and command and control, to name a few.[21] The GWAPS conducted most of its work out of Crystal City in the Washington, D.C., area.

Arguably, the GWAPS is comparable in stature and magnitude to the World War II USSBS. The fact that the USSBS had over one thousand civilian and military analysts, while the GWAPS had just slightly over one hundred, suggests that the former conducted a much greater amount of research and analysis simply in terms of raw numbers of personnel. It is important to note, though, that the GWAPS did not have to man numerous field teams to collect evidence inside Iraq, simply because Iraq, unlike Germany and Japan, was not occupied by American forces after the war. Moreover, regarding the collection of evidence, modern technologies and information systems provided the GWAPS access to large amounts of data, thereby reducing the need for substantial numbers of analysts to conduct research. One could also point out that the USSBS produced over three hundred reports and studies, while the GWAPS wrote "only" five volumes. Such a comparison can be misleading because many of the USSBS's published studies were supporting documents (field team reports on specific bombed targets) for each of its divisions' overall reports. Writing to the director of the joint staff in January 1992, Colonel L. E. Trapp, Jr., military assistant to the secretary of the air force, anticipated the importance of the GWAPS by noting that it would be "equivalent in depth and impact to the landmark Strategic Bombing Survey of World War II."[22]

III

The intellectual beginnings of the USSBS and the GWAPS came not from outside the air force but from the airmen themselves. After the negative experience General Arnold had with the report produced by the Committee of Historians in early 1944, he determined that another civilian-led evaluation of air power's effects against Germany would be necessary, although not manned by historians. Likewise, even before the United States started bombing Iraq in January 1991, air officers like Colonel John Warden began exploring the idea of a civilian-run evaluation of air power in the Gulf War.

Yet while there was general consensus among airmen to conduct a civilian-led evaluation after World War II, after the Gulf War many senior airmen sought to keep air force-sponsored evaluations under their own institutional control. From January to July 1991, the recommended approach by senior airmen would be to have three different types of evaluations, or "lessons learned," managed by the vice-chief of staff of the air force. The Office of Air Force History, according to this line of thinking, would document "objectively the results of all deployment and combat operations much like the historical analyses performed following WWII, Korea, and Vietnam."[23] Another study would be contracted out to various "think tanks" such as RAND. Tactical Air Command (TAC) would write the third evaluation providing a "combat Lessons Learned" analysis from an "operational perspective."[24]

Major General Robert M. Alexander, air force director of plans, presented the air force's approach to Secretary Rice in a briefing on 24 July 1991. It appeared, however, that the air force's "ownership" of the evaluations being written on air power in the Gulf worried Secretary Rice because of the potential for bias. The secretary commented during the briefing about the possibility of getting "pabulum," thus creating a negative view from the "outside" about the "product and process" of the proposed evaluation. Secretary Rice noted that "if there [was] even a hint that we cooked the books, the value of the product will be destroyed."[25] Historian Wayne Thompson (who later became the historical advisor to the GWAPS) sensed after speaking to Rice that the secretary "was not satisfied" with the proposed "approach to studying the war." Echoing Secretary Rice's concerns, Colonel David A. Tretler, the acting air force historian, cautioned that "no one should exercise coordination, management, or approval authority over the historical studies" written by his agency. Colonel Tretler pointed out that even back in World War II General Hap Arnold understood the need for an "objective" record of the air force's wartime accomplishments.[26]

"Objectivity" was the sine qua non of the USSBS and the GWAPS. Indeed, when one reviews the many memorandums, letters, and directives that surrounded the beginnings of both surveys, the purported desire to produce "objective" and "truthful" evaluations of air power permeates the dialogue. In early 1944, when they were forming the USSBS, Generals Arnold and Spaatz recognized that the USSBS must produce reports that would be perceived as "unbiased and completely impartial" if they were to be received favorably. General Arnold himself understood how a report written by civilian experts could provide the "objective" historical record needed by the airmen in their future fight for independence.[27] Although by 1991 the independence of the American air force was no longer in doubt as it was for General Arnold in 1944, the "future" was still dependent on an "objective" and "truthful" rendering of the air force's performance in the Gulf War. Secretary Rice evidently understood this imperative and thus formed the civilian-led Gulf War Air Power Survey.

When the GWAPS began its work in August 1991, director Eliot Cohen provided his team of analysts with a set of "guiding concepts" for their studies. The approach outlined by Cohen was "at all costs" to maintain a strong sense of "objectivity, honesty, [and] integrity." Cohen drew on the "lineage" of the USSBS by emphasizing what he saw as its "integrity" and presentation of work in "clear English." Early on Cohen recognized the "symbolic ties" of the USSBS to the GWAPS.[28]

Making the rhetorical connection from the GWAPS to the USSBS was much more than just symbolism. Throughout the early days of the GWAPS, and up through the writing of its final reports, references were often made to the need to be like the USSBS, especially in terms of "objectivity." In April 1992, as the task forces were heavily engaged with the writing of their final reports, Eliot Cohen told Secretary Rice that he was using the USSBS as a model "in terms of precision, pungency, and clarity."[29] In the foreword of each published GWAPS volume and in the *Summary Report* is an introductory comment stating that "in the spirit of impartiality and scholarly rigor . . . [GWAPS] members had as their standard the observation of Mr. Franklin D'Olier, chairman of the United States Strategic Bombing Survey . . . [which was to] 'burn into everybody's souls the fact that the survey's responsibility was to ascertain facts and to seek truth, eliminating completely any preconceived theories or dogmas.'"[30]

As Survey director, however, there were few similarities between Franklin D'Olier and Eliot Cohen. D'Olier was a corporate manager and Cohen a scholar. Aside from his limited military experience as a staff officer in World War I, D'Olier had little understanding of the strategic and operational levels of war. Cohen, conversely, after graduating from Harvard with a Ph.D. in political science, spent four years at the Naval War College teaching strategy and also served on the Policy Planning Staff for the secretary of defense.[31] While D'Olier was "the amiable figurehead"[32] of the USSBS and made no intellectual contributions to the Survey's work, Cohen was closely involved with the daily running of the GWAPS, and, more important, was the intellectual leader during the research and writing of GWAPS volumes. Like D'Olier, who relied on Henry Alexander for managerial and intellectual leadership, Cohen came to rely greatly on historian Thomas Keaney, especially for the writing of the important GWAPS *Summary Report*.[33] Barry Watts noted that Keaney's role in crafting the *Summary Report* made him "the single most important participant after Cohen."[34]

Probably the most important difference between Cohen and D'Olier was in the degree of impartiality. Although D'Olier often proclaimed the need to get at the facts, to tell the truth, and to eliminate any predetermined "dogmas," his actions proved otherwise. Actually, D'Olier was quite dogmatic in his desire to help the airmen gain independence from the army.

True, there was strong bias among certain members of the GWAPS toward shaping GWAPS conclusions that would look favorably on air force parochial interests. But Eliot Cohen and other senior leaders of the GWAPS took strong steps to avoid an air force-centered, doctrinaire approach to the GWAPS's evaluation of air power in the Gulf War.

In the spring of 1992, as GWAPS analysts were writing early drafts of their findings and critiquing each other's work, Cohen rejected a rather hyperbolic phrase concerning the final events in the ground war to drive the Iraqi army from Kuwait. The phrase boasted that for the retreating Iraqis, "the incredible destruction on the misnamed Highway of Death, [was] where at least some of these poltroons received their just desserts at the hand of coalition air forces." Cohen responded that this type of "overblown rhetoric" was "unacceptable for the Survey," and was not in line with what he considered to be the GWAPS "analytical and level-headed" approach.[35]

A few months later at another review session one of the serving military officers on the GWAPS argued that the American air force's focus on strategic attacks during the Gulf War was reminiscent of Douhet's idea of using air power to "obviate the use of ground forces." According to this officer Desert Storm was a "return to decisive battle," but unlike past wars it was the "air rather than ground" that produced victory for the coalition. Cohen and Barry Watts seemed concerned with the parochial nature of the officer's comments. Watts pointed out that it was important for the GWAPS not to fixate on American air operations in the Gulf but rather to consider the other American services and the Allied contributions as well. Eliot Cohen got more to the point of the problem when he told the group that he sensed in the officer's response the "smell" of doctrine.[36]

By late 1992 the GWAPS task forces were completing the final drafts of their volumes. Cohen wanted to ensure that their work not be made public—to the press or to interested airmen and civilian analysts outside of the GWAPS—until all the revisions had been made and the volumes reviewed by the review committee and Secretary Rice. He noted to GWAPS members that they owed it to Secretary Rice to share their "conclusions with him first." Cohen forcefully told

GWAPS analysts that "no one, but no one, gets access to all or part" of the draft reports. There were GWAPS members who disregarded his directive and leaked draft reports to interested airmen and civilian analysts, who later sought to suppress the publication of GWAPS volumes.[37] Generally speaking, however, most GWAPS analysts understood the need for impartiality, intellectual honesty, and independence from air force interests during the conduct of their study.

IV

It is useful to compare the professional backgrounds of the USSBS analysts with those of the GWAPS. Paul Nitze perceptively pointed out to GWAPS leaders at a review board meeting that the USSBS, "in its attempt to be independent, selected people who had no expertise in the areas they were to study."[38] Nitze may have been getting at the lack of professional military experience of most of the USSBS personnel, including himself.

Of course one must acknowledge the historical context in which the USSBS conducted its evaluation. The reason why the USSBS had virtually no analysts with professional military backgrounds (save for the professional military officers like Orvil Anderson and Ralph Ofstie) was that a defense establishment simply did not exist during the years leading up to World War II. Very few Americans served in the armed services during the 1930s, so very few USSBS members would have had professional military service in their records. More important, the link between the military and academic institutions for research and development was only in its infancy during World War II.

When the GWAPS conducted its study in the early 1990s, a close institutional relationship between the military and civilian experts had developed within the American defense establishment. As a result, most of the GWAPS analysts were drawn from the defense establishment and had been involved in defense issues (and actions).

For example, Alexander S. Cochran, chief of the Strategy and

Plans Task Force, had been a combat infantryman in Vietnam and later served as a branch chief at the army's Center for Military History. The chief of the Operations and Effects Task Force, Barry Watts, was a former career air force officer. During his service with the air force, Watts flew 158 combat missions in Southeast Asia in F-4s, of which 100 were over Vietnam. He had also taught philosophy at the Air Force Academy. Like other senior GWAPS members, Watts had written numerous published works on military history and defense issues. In addition to Watts, John F. Guilmartin, chief of the Weapons, Tactics, and Training Task Force, was a former career military officer. He too had flown combat missions in Vietnam. Guilmartin took a leave of absence from his position as an associate professor of history at Ohio State University to serve on the GWAPS. Although Thomas C. Hone, head of the Task Force on Command, Control, and Organization, did not have professional military experience like Watts and Guilmartin, he did teach strategy at the Naval War College and served as a contract historian for the Office of Air Force History. The executive director of the GWAPS, Colonel Emery M. Kiraly, was a serving air force officer and had been Colonel John Warden's deputy during the development of the Instant Thunder air campaign plan against Iraq. Thomas A. Keaney, chief of the *Summary Report*, a retired air force officer and a B-52 pilot, had flown combat missions over Vietnam. Keaney, like Watts, had taught at the Air Force Academy, and had taught at the National War College before coming to the GWAPS.[39]

The professional experiences of GWAPS and USSBS personnel shaped the analytical framework that they brought to their evaluation of air power in the Gulf War and World War II, respectively. USSBS members were for the most part industrialists, financiers, economists, and engineers, with a small number of lawyers and behavioral scientists. Their professional experience fit comfortably with the American conceptual approach toward strategic bombing of attacking "national economic structures." Moreover, the strident effort on the part of the airmen to shape the organizational structure of the USSBS and the questions that it would answer caused

USSBS analysts to accept the American conceptual approach to strategic bombing as their framework for analysis. Certainly, GWAPS analysts shared a common framework for analysis, but it was very different from that of the USSBS.

In the late 1970s and early 1980s, after the American military's traumatic experience in Vietnam, there was a renewed interest among defense intellectuals (both military and civilian) in the operational level of war, the level between strategy and tactics. Harry G. Summers in his well-known book *On Strategy: A Critical Analysis of the Vietnam War* created a kind of populist movement within the American military that partly blamed America's loss in Vietnam on a lack of operational vision.[40] A more deep-rooted and sophisticated understanding of the operational level of war—informed by the Prussian military theorist Carl von Clausewitz—began to take hold in the defense establishment. Many civilian and military defense intellectuals especially embraced the notion of operational art—the creative part of war that links political objectives to the tactical application of military force—as a way of rejuvenating an intellectual approach to warfare in American defense circles. This way of thinking about warfare manifested itself in the late 1980s with the army's Airland Battle doctrine and Colonel John Warden's book *The Air Campaign*; both were profoundly shaped by the concept of operational art.[41] Even in the late 1990s Clausewitz still shaped the thinking of many defense analysts. A professor of strategic studies at the Marine War College noted that "the Clausewitzian theory of war remains huge within the American DOD/National Security community—among academics and practitioners alike."[42]

At least some of the primary contributors to the GWAPS volumes, including the task force chiefs, were influenced by Clausewitzian theory. For example, Mark Clodfelter, a contributing author to the GWAPS *Planning* volume, wrote an important book in 1989, *The Limits of Air Power: The American Bombing of North Vietnam*. In the book, Clodfelter argued that Clausewitz's famous dictum that war was "a continuation of political activity by other means" was the only "true measure for evaluating air power's effectiveness" against North

Vietnam. Barry Watts authored a short study that analyzed futu using the Clausewitzian construct of "friction."[43] Moreover, the foreword of each GWAPS volume pointed out that its analysis concentrated on the "operational level of war in the belief that this level of warfare is at once one of the most difficult to characterize and one of the most important to understand."[44]

It would be wrong, however, to think that being connected to the defense establishment and focusing their analysis of air power in the Gulf War at the operational level forced GWAPS members into a doctrinaire approach to their work. Political scientist John Mersheimer has argued that the best tool available for lessening the possibility that flawed ideas will affect defense policy and strategy is "intellectual pluralism. A healthy national policy depends on independent-minded defense intellectuals challenging the government and one another."[45] Comparing the intellectual environment of the USSBS with that of the GWAPS can bring Mersheimer's point out more clearly.

David MacIsaac lamented in his 1976 book *Strategic Bombing in World War Two* that the USSBS needed historians to provide a balanced interpretation of evidence. MacIsaac acknowledged that debate over findings did occur among USSBS analysts, but the USSBS was "ruled" by "an insurance man (D'Olier) and two investment bankers (Alexander and Nitze)," who firmly held "the reins of authority."[46] The majority of GWAPS task force chiefs, including the director, had Ph.D.'s in either political science or history and had spent many collective years in academe. This is not to say that an academic background necessarily guarantees objectivity. Yet a "scholarly" approach did instill in the GWAPS greater intellectual rigor and independence. Cohen noted that the GWAPS, "unlike many studies, [was] leaving an audit trail, in the form of footnotes, bibliographic essays, and open statements of where large uncertainties remain."[47] The USSBS members certainly challenged each other over evidence and conclusions. They were probably less effective, though, than the GWAPS in establishing an intellectual climate that would lead to a more independent and impartial study.

This is the most balanced chapter of the book. Fewer attempts are made to malign the USAF + air power in general. Fairly presented using primary source data and actual correspondence from the participants of GWAPS

V

One thing that the GWAPS had to help it ensure impartiality and independence that the USSBS did not was the GWAPS review committee.[48] The purpose of the review committee was to bring together a group of distinguished scholars, statesmen, and senior military leaders to act as a corporate body to review the GWAPS work, providing it with the "credibility and prestige necessary to support the final product." The review committee was not, however, intended "to serve as ornaments" for GWAPS credibility. Instead the committee played a "key role in both the study process and the final" GWAPS volumes by recommending analytical methods and by "identifying gaps in the overall project."[49]

The committee met formally in March 1992 and in January 1993 to review the work of the GWAPS. Bernard Lewis, a professor of political science at Princeton University, cautioned Eliot Cohen and his task force leaders to maintain balance in their analysis by keeping "in mind that losers tend to study what went wrong while winners study what went right." Another one of the review committee's civilian scholars, Richard Kohn of the University of North Carolina at Chapel Hill, advised the group that they needed to be very careful in the use of counterfactual speculation. Aware of the controversy over the USSBS's counterfactual about Japan's surrender at the end of World War II, Kohn noted that it would be very difficult for the GWAPS "to answer what if questions." He doubted they could assess events that did not happen.[50]

There were retired senior military officers on the GWAPS review committee like General Michael J. Dugan of the air force, Admiral Huntington Hardisty of the navy, and General Maxwell Thurman of the army. These retired officers certainly had strong vested interests in their respective services. One might have expected interservice wrangling over GWAPS conclusions similar to the fierce parochial debates between Admiral Ralph Ofstie and General Orvil Anderson of the Pacific USSBS. Yet in comparison to the USSBS, the GWAPS review committee seems remarkable in its desire to avoid service parochialism and bias. Instead, their overall goal was to advise the GWAPS analysts on the best ways to produce a balanced assessment of air power in the Gulf War. Secretary of the Air Force Donald Rice and Cohen agreed that there were "ferocious battles during the writing of the USSBS" over service interests. Both men also acknowledged that even though there would be "creative tension" within the GWAPS and the review committee over "differences of opinion," it would be nothing along the lines of the USSBS.[51]

Paul Nitze (who of course was caught in the middle of the battle between Ofstie and Anderson over certain USSBS conclusions) told the review committee that he believed the job GWAPS analysts had done on their respective volumes to be "superb." Yet in an informal discussion with Eliot Cohen, Nitze thought that the most critical issue for the GWAPS to address was the effectiveness of "the strategic air campaign against Iraq."[52] Nitze may have sensed an underlying problem with evidence that Cohen and other GWAPS analysts were confronting as they conducted their research and analysis.

VI

If the USSBS's focus was on the effects of strategic bombing on Germany's and Japan's war-making capacity, the GWAPS directed most of its analysis toward the operational aspects of American air power in the Persian Gulf War. The GWAPS did produce a volume on the effects of the air campaign against Iraq; however, unlike the World War II USSBS, which had access to evidence in Germany and Japan, the GWAPS could not enter Iraq once the war ended. Access to Germany and Japan was important for the USSBS because its analysts could collect evidence on the effects of strategic bombing and interview key enemy wartime leaders.

Air power was used in the Persian Gulf War not as an end in itself but to bring about specific effects upon the enemy. Arguably, then, the GWAPS volume, *Effects and Effectiveness,* was crucial because it would explore the raison d'être for the air campaign against Iraq: to produce effects on the enemy in support of American and coalition objectives. Cohen and other GWAPS analysts were aware of their problems with evidence, especially regarding the effects of the bombing. Cohen did not want the GWAPS to come to definitive conclusions if it did not have the requisite evidence. And he knew well of the problems that the USSBS had had with the interpretation of evidence. At a meeting in late August 1991 with the faculty of the Air University at Maxwell Air Force Base, Cohen discussed with Mark Clodfelter the issue of evidence. Clodfelter told him that the biggest issue for the GWAPS was the lack of "access to Iraq." Cohen agreed and noted that the GWAPS needed "to be more forthright than [the] USSBS on holes in our data."[53]

The primary authors of the GWAPS volume *Effects and Effectiveness*, Thomas Keaney and Barry Watts, argued that their own study, "because of its focus on operational-strategic effectiveness, ended up being closer in content and intent to USSBS volumes . . . than any other GWAPS reports." Watts and Keaney also admitted that there were some important differences "between the two, particularly regarding data and sources." They pointed out that the most critical "hole" in evidence was the fact that without access to Iraqi leaders and prewar plans, their volume was limited in its ability to discern Iraqi "intentions, before and during the Gulf War." However, the *Effects* volume argued that since the aim of the air campaign was not to overwhelmingly attack the Iraqi economic infrastructure, extensive evidence of the Iraqi war effort was not necessary. Moreover, modern technologies such as satellite imagery of bomb damage used during the Gulf War provided GWAPS analysts with a good deal of evidence on effects.[54] Too, reports from inside Iraq after the war by groups like United Nations inspections teams investigating Iraqi nuclear, biological, and chemical weapons production facilities provided *Effects* volume analysts with helpful information. Still, the authors of the volume understood the problem they had with evidence. As a result, they used the USSBS as a "baseline" to "mitigate" the problem.

In a June 1992 GWAPS review session on the *Effects and Effectiveness* volume, Alexander S. Cochran (task force leader for Strategy and Plans) recommended that since the air force rejected the lessons they should have learned from Vietnam and Korea, the *Effects* volume should "refer back to World War II." Colonel Emery M. Kiraly followed Cochran by suggesting that in order to "validate" the "findings" of the volume, the authors should make a comparison of the GWAPS and the USSBS. Making such a comparison would, according to Thomas Keaney, provide a "baseline" for the GWAPS. Establishing a "baseline" was critical for the authors of the *Effects and Effectiveness* study because of their inability to gain access to Iraq to collect evidence.[55]

The "baseline" discerned from the USSBS allowed the volume's authors to deemphasize the problems that they had with access to Iraq by showing how their volume would go beyond the more narrow approach taken by John Kenneth Galbraith's USSBS Economic Division report. The *Effects* volume noted that if one used only physical damage as a measure of strategic bombing's effectiveness, then bombing attacks on a given target could be considered successful simply if they did physical damage to the target. However, physical destruction of structures did not always produce the effects desired on an enemy political, economic, or military system. According to the authors of the *Effects* volume, Galbraith's report, *The Effects of Strategic Bombing on the German War Economy*, was unable to make nuanced distinctions between effects and effectiveness. In light of the "neglect of such effects in parts of the World War II survey," the authors believed that they should try to move beyond these shortcomings in their evaluation of the effects of the air campaign against Iraq.[56]

Thus the GWAPS *Effects* volume drew attention away from its existing problem of lack of evidence by creating a pejorative distinction between itself and Galbraith's USSBS report. But in so doing the GWAPS volume overly emphasized Galbraith's reliance on statistics and "indices" and downplayed the economists' sophisticated understanding of the German war economy as a "system" and the effects of strategic bombing thereon. Watts and Keaney also tended to conflate some of Galbraith's post-USSBS writings on air power—which were decidedly hypercritical of air power and American military policy in general—with the economist's USSBS report.

The GWAPS *Effects* volume argued that Galbraith's USSBS report, *The Effects of Strategic Bombing on the German War Economy,* narrowly focused its analysis on economic statistics rather than trying to determine the second- and third-order effects—or effectiveness—of strategic bombing on the German war economy.[57] This was a narrow rendering of Galbraith's USSBS argument. In fact a close reading of Galbraith's USSBS report shows that it did acknowledge the decisive effects of strategic bombing on the German war economy precisely because of its appreciation for the second- and third-order effects of bombing on enemy economic "systems."[58] The discussions between Galbraith and his Economic Effects Division further demonstrated that they were not solely fixated on economic statistics and "indices" in their evaluation of the overall effectiveness of strategic bombing.[59]

To be fair to Watts and Keaney, they both believed that Galbraith focused his USSBS analysis exclusively on the effects of strategic bombing on the German war economy to the detriment of "the actual goals of the air commanders at specific points in time."[60] Understanding operational objectives of air leaders was understandably important to Watts and Keaney because that was going to be a crucial factor in their study of air power in the Gulf War. But to be equally fair to Galbraith, the USSBS intentionally focused its analysis on the effects of strategic bombing on the German and Japanese war economies and not on the tactical and operational problems of the AAF.

Watts and Keaney also rolled together some of Galbraith's very critical post-USSBS writings on air power with his USSBS report. [61] Galbraith claimed in his memoirs that the data he and other Survey members had collected proved the "disastrous failures" of strategic bombing in World War II.[62] Neither his report nor any of the other published USSBS studies ever used such language or made such bombastic generalizations.[63] Still, many analysts who have read the economists' post-Survey writings have tended to allow them to negatively color Galbraith's USSBS report.[64] It should be remembered, however, that in 1945, when Galbraith was a USSBS director, he was highly respected for his judgment, balanced approach, and analytical acumen. Air power champion and USSBS director General Orvil Anderson thought Galbraith to be "one of the most valuable men on the Survey, if not the most valuable."[65]

Yet in comparison with what Paul Nitze did when he drew conclusions about why Japan had surrendered at the end of World War II, the use of Galbraith's economic report by the GWAPS *Effects* volume was only a minor foible. Indeed, for the analysts of the Pacific portion of the USSBS there was clearly competing evidence (based largely on interviews with Japanese leaders) as to why the war ended. Yet Nitze seems to have been less concerned with acknowledging contradictions than with proving his argument about the decisiveness of conventional strategic air power and the indecisiveness of the Soviet war declaration and atomic bomb. The result was the well-known counterfactual stating that Japan would have surrendered "certainly prior to 31 December 1945, and in all probability prior to 1 November 1945 . . . even if the atomic bombs had not been dropped, even if Russia had not entered the war, and even if no invasion had been planned or contemplated." Prudence called for such a bold statement to be followed with a discussion on evidence, but none was forthcoming. GWAPS analysts writing on air power's effects almost forty years later would be more forthright than the USSBS about problems with evidence.

Understanding the limits of evidence kept GWAPS authors from taking the same step toward bold counterfactual speculation that Nitze had taken many years earlier. The *Effects* volume argued that even after accepting the fact that the air campaign had destroyed "large amounts of Iraqi equipment . . . whether or for how long the Iraqi troops could have held on even without a ground attack can be no more than matters of speculation."[66] One can clearly see the authors' desire to avoid a counterfactual statement arguing that

Iraq would have surrendered soon owing to crippling air attacks even if coalition forces had never conducted a ground invasion.

The *Effects* volume, therefore, did not make exorbitant claims about the effectiveness of air power against Iraq. In fact the principal authors, Watts and Keaney, concluded the volume by cautioning against the view held by many airmen that the application of American air power in the Gulf War indicated a revolutionary change in the nature of war, especially regarding the use of radar-evading stealth bombers and precision guided bombs. The two authors argued that instead of demonstrating inconsistency with past wars, the Gulf War demonstrated the "limits to strategic air attack encountered at least as far back as World War II."[67]

There are, however, still those willing to go the distance and champion the cause of air power in future debates over defense policy and organization. The United States Air Force historian, Richard P. Hallion, argued in his 1992 book *Storm over Iraq: Air Power in the Gulf War* that the ground war against Iraq "could not be decisive in the way that earlier ground wars had been." Hallion then professed that the Gulf War had proven that "Air power can hold territory by denying an enemy the ability to seize it, and by denying an enemy the use of his forces. And it [air power] can seize territory by controlling access to that territory and movement across it."[68]

Hallion wrote *Storm over Iraq* around the same time that GWAPS analysts were reaching their conclusions about air power in the Gulf War. Hallion was not at all happy with the GWAPS reports because he believed they would produce a negative reaction among the public toward the American air force's performance against Iraq.[69]

Like Hallion, the air force was very uncomfortable with the GWAPS conclusions, which did not provide the expected glowing endorsement for the dominance of air power in the Gulf War. Some members of the GWAPS felt they were pressured to mute their criticism, and Hallion warned the administrative assistant to the secretary of the air force that there should be a forceful reconsideration of "the implications of releasing" the GWAPS reports. Hallion went on to caution that whatever "positive statements" the GWAPS volumes made would "be gradually lost in much the same way that those of the USSBS" were lost after World War II.[70]

It is interesting to note that like the USSBS European and Pacific *Summary Reports*, but unlike any of the GWAPS volumes, Hallion's book finished with a section titled "Toward the Future." Like the two USSBS reports, Hallion called for a future defense policy to be based on air power. Using a favorite word of General Orvil Arson Anderson, Hallion boasted that "today, air power is the *dominant* form of military power."[71]

Ironically it was an air force historian who tried to suppress the GWAPS reports, reduce the number of GWAPS published copies, and ultimately champion the air force cause in a book about air power in the Gulf. When we remember the "headache" that the Committee of Historians gave Edward Mead Earle and General Arnold over their report in 1943 and the intentional exclusion of historians from the USSBS, historian Richard Hallion's pitched battle against the GWAPS is indeed ironic. Furthermore, about a year before the release of the GWAPS volumes, Eliot Cohen had been told that "gossip" from the Pentagon had it that they were in the "grip of historians."[72] The implication of this statement was that since many historians made up the ranks of the GWAPS, their conclusions about air power against Iraq would not be favorable to the air force's performance. Yet it was a historian who would try to mend the perceived damage to the future interests of the air force from the release of the GWAPS reports.

The GWAPS was simply not willing to make defense policy recommendations, as did the two USSBS *Summary Reports* and Hallion's book, *Storm over Iraq*. Eliot Cohen noted in a letter to the review committee in August 1992 that the GWAPS volumes were written "with an awareness of the policy issues" that the Gulf War raised. The volumes were not, however, crafted to "make specific recommendations for future policy."[73]

The GWAPS volumes certainly acknowledged the achievements of air power in the war against Iraq, but they also pointed out the shortcomings. The *Command and Control* volume, for example, concluded that the American air force "did win an overwhelming victory" in Desert Storm. But the primary authors of the volume (Thomas C. Hone, Mark D. Mandeles, and Lieutenant Colonel Sanford S. Terry) cautioned that the advanced technology used in the Gulf War by the air force to "solve old command and control problems" had in fact "created new problems" in managing air power assets in combat.[74] Williamson Murray, the principal author for the *Operations* volume, agreed that the air campaign was decisive and "destroyed whatever willingness" the Iraqis might have had to fight a ground war against the American-led coalition. But like the authors of the other GWAPS volumes, Murray warned against claiming too much for the air campaign: "In the end, the campaign was relatively successful, but only because the time and air assets that were available to attack those enemy forces were almost limitless. . . ."[75] The GWAPS volumes thus brought out both the good and the bad of the American-led air campaign against Iraq.[76]

So too did the USSBS's evaluation of strategic bombing in World War II. Yet the conclusions drawn by the USSBS were shaped and influenced by the powerful postwar interests of the AAF. For the GWAPS in the early 1990s there were clearly similar air force interests at work trying to affect the outcome of the GWAPS reports. The GWAPS, however, based on the available documentary evidence, was able to keep those interests at bay, allowing for an independent study of air power in the Gulf War.

AFTERWORD

Six years after the GWAPS completed its study of air power in the Gulf War, the United States led a North Atlantic Treaty Organization (NATO) air campaign in the Balkans against Yugoslavia. The apparent aim of the campaign was to force the Yugoslavian president, Slobodan Milosevic, to stop the ethnic cleansing of Albanians in Kosovo and to pull his military forces out of Kosovo. Air power was expected to help achieve those objectives.

The American-dominated NATO air campaign over Yugoslavia demonstrates that problems still exist with the use of strategic bombing in war and conflict. First, the type of targets bombed in Yugoslavia and the attitudes of certain senior airmen toward the air campaign show that the traditional American concept of strategic bombing continues to shape Air Force thinking. Second, as in previous conflicts involving the application of air power—World War II, Korea, Vietnam, and the Gulf War—efforts to prove the effectiveness of strategic bombing remain clouded with ambiguity. Third, because it is difficult to assess the effectiveness of strategic bombing, a need remains for experts—civilian experts—to conduct evaluations along the lines of the USSBS and GWAPS. Finally, appreciating the importance of such studies, advocates of air power will try to shape conclusions about the effectiveness of air power; depending on the independence of the evaluation, objectivity may be the victim.

Consider the continuity between the concept of strategic bombing developed by Haywood Hansell and his fellow ACTS theorists in the late 1930s and the conceptual underpinnings to the Yugoslavia air campaign. In World War II, American airmen sought to destroy the war-making capacity of Germany and Japan by bombing critical economic systems such as transportation and electrical power. By the closing days of air operations over Yugoslavia and Kosovo, American airmen were bombing electrical power and transportation facilities with the intent of destroying, or at least reducing, Serbian capacity to conduct military operations.[1] And like American airmen in World War II who believed that strategic air power should not be used against military forces in the field, airmen in 1999 wanted to concentrate on strategic targets in Serbia rather than "plinking" tactical targets like tanks and artillery pieces in Kosovo.

Also, airmen during the Yugoslavia air campaign firmly believed that if the United States used air power correctly—with overwhelming force and applied quickly throughout the depth of the enemy homeland—it would force a decision and end the war sooner on NATO's terms. Too, airmen at the start of World War II believed that if left unrestricted and unfettered by other requirements, strategic bombing might very well end the war without the use of ground forces. Following World War II and into the cold war, the lament of many airmen looking back on Korea and Vietnam was that air power never got its proper chance to "win" both wars. Testifying to Congress in October 1999, just four months after the end of the Yugoslavia air campaign, Lieutenant General Michael C. Short, commander of NATO air forces flying in the campaign, argued that if it had been left up to him he would have severed "the head of the snake on the first night" by bombing strategic targets in Belgrade. Such an approach, according to General Short, would have stopped Serbian ethnic cleansing in Kosovo by putting "a dagger in the heart" of the Serbian leadership.[2]

However, General Short and other contemporary airmen have the same problem that General H. H. Arnold had in World War II and even Colonel John A. Warden had in the Gulf War: the problem of proving strategic bombing's effectiveness. One can make bombastic, metaphor-laden claims that inflate the expectations of what air power could have accomplished. But the fundamental problem of determining the effects of strategic bombing has not gone away. Indeed, the Yugoslavia air campaign shows that when an enemy leader remains in power and is unlikely to tell the world what made him act, the effectiveness of strategic bombing is even more difficult to know.

There are some questions to think of regarding the American-led air campaign in the Balkans: Was it the impact of air power on Serbian infrastructure that caused Milosevic to withdraw his forces from Kosovo? Or did the bombing of targets in Serbian cities like Belgrade create hardships and terror among the civilian population that in turn somehow influenced Milosevic's actions? Did the threat of a ground invasion by NATO armies ultimately persuade the Serbian leader that he had to accept NATO and U.N. demands? Finally, what effect did Russia's removal of support for Serbia have on Milosevic's decision? If modifications are made to the language and context of these questions, they appear strikingly similar to the questions that Paul Nitze and his fellow USSBS analysts asked about the role of strategic bombing in the unconditional surrender of Japan in 1945.

Back in the fall of 1945, General Orvil Arson Anderson stridently believed that he knew the answer to why Japan surrendered unconditionally: American strategic bombing. He subsequently applied a heavy parochial hand to the writing of Pacific Survey reports to shape conclusions that were favorable to the interests of the airmen and their institution. The civilian analysts of the USSBS accepted the American conceptual approach to strategic bombing of General Anderson and other airmen, made it the analytical framework for their evaluation, and wrote conclusions about air power in World War II that vindicated that conception.

Shortly after the Yugoslavia air campaign ended in 1999, American airmen proclaimed in a manner similar to that of General Anderson in 1945 that air power "prevailed."[3] Yet understanding whether or not, or to what degree, air power "prevailed" along with other factors in Kosovo will require an independent evaluation by analysts who strive for objectivity. Since proving the effectiveness of a critical component of air power—strategic bombing—brings out such strong feelings in proponents, opponents, and even zealots, a thoughtful and independent study is essential. Once analysts produce evaluations of American air power like the USSBS and the GWAPS, the challenge is then to use them wisely, not slavishly, in order to help understand a crucial part of the past and to recognize how a partial view of that past may have shaped later policies, perceptions, and polemics.

Talk about calling the kettle black! If this guy isn't biased and parochial about the so-called ineffectiveness of strat bombing as an army officer, I don't know who is!

NOTES

Notes to the Introduction

1. With apologies to "Major King Kong," played by actor Slim Pickens in the 1964 movie *Dr. Strangelove; Or, How I Learned to Stop Worrying and Love the Bomb.*

2. Gar Alperovitz, *Atomic Diplomacy: Hiroshima and Potsdam* (1965; New York: Penguin Books, 1985), 286–87.

3. United States Strategic Bombing Survey (USSBS), Chairman's Office, *Summary Report (Pacific War)* (Washington, D.C.: USGPO, 1946), 26.

4. Barton J. Bernstein, "Roosevelt, Truman, and the Atomic Bomb, 1941–1945: A Reinterpretation," *Political Science Quarterly* 90 (spring 1975): 24.

5. Haywood S. Hansell to David MacIsaac, 27 July 1970, box 3, folder 5, Haywood S. Hansell Papers, U.S. Air Force Academy Library.

6. On the issue of "truth" in historical writing, see Eric Hobsbawm, *On History* (New York: New Press, 1997), viii; also see Chris Lorenz, "Can Histories Be True? Narrativism, Positivism, and the 'Metaphorical Turn,'" and Thomas Haskell, "Farewell to Fallibilism," in *History and Theory* 37 (1998): 309–29, 347–69.

7. David MacIsaac, *Strategic Bombing in World War Two: The Story of the United States Strategic Bombing Survey* (New York: Garland Publishing, 1976); also see MacIsaac, "What the Bombing Survey Really Says," *Air Force Magazine* 56 (June 1973): 60–63; and MacIsaac, "A New Look at Old Lessons," *Air Force Magazine* (September 1970): 121–27. The first critical analyses of the Survey's findings on Japan and the combat use of the A-bomb did not appear until 1995; see Barton J. Bernstein, "Compelling Japan's Surrender without the A-bomb, Soviet Entry, or Invasion: Reconsidering the US Bombing Survey's Early-Surrender Counterfactual," *Journal of Strategic Studies* 18 (June 1995): 101–48; Robert P. Newman, "Ending the War with Japan: Paul Nitze's Early-Surrender Counterfactual," *Pacific Historical Review* 64 (May 1995): 167–194; and Gian P.

Gentile, "Advocacy or Assessment? The United States Strategic Bombing Survey of Germany and Japan," *Pacific Historical Review* 66 (February 1997): 53–79.

8. For another account of the Survey, see Frank C. Watson, "United States Strategic Bombing Survey: A Look to the Future" (research report submitted to the Air War College Faculty, Air University, February 1983). Watson notes at the beginning of the paper that the AAF realized early on the value the Survey would have in shaping future defense policy, but he never considers the implications of the airmen's parochial interests in shaping Survey conclusions.

Notes to Chapter 1

1. Guilio Douhet, *The Command of the Air*, trans. Dino Ferrari, new imprint by the Office of Air Force History (1942; Washington, D.C.: USGPO, 1983), 57–59, 71–106. For analyses of Douhet, see David MacIsaac, "Voices from the Central Blue: The Air Power Theorists," in *Makers of Modern Strategy*, ed. Peter Paret (Princeton: Princeton University Press, 1986), 624–47; and Philip S. Meilinger, "Guilio Douhet and the Origins of Airpower Theory," in *The Paths of Heaven: The Evolution of Airpower Theory*, ed. Philip S. Meilinger (Maxwell Air Force Base, Ala.: Air University Press, 1997), 1–40.

2. Douhet, *Command of the Air*, 60.

3. Meilinger, "Guilio Douhet and the Origins of Airpower Theory," 28.

4. Douhet, *Command of the Air*, 35.

5. Ibid., 57–58.

6. Conrad C. Crane, *Bombs, Cities and Civilians: American Airpower Strategy in World War II* (Lawrence: University Press of Kansas, 1993), 17–18; Ronald Schaffer, *Wings of Judgment: American Bombing in World War II* (New York: Oxford University Press, 1985), 24; Michael S. Sherry, *The Rise of American Air Power: The Creation of Armageddon* (New Haven: Yale University Press, 1987), 52; Meilinger, "Guilio Douhet and the Origins of Airpower Theory," 33.

7. Crane, for example, in *Bombs, Cities and Civilians*, argues that by the mid-1930s Douhet's writings did influence the development of American air power strategy but only insofar as Douhet advocated an independent air arm and the decisiveness of strategic bombing (17–18). Shaffer, in

Wings of Judgment, tends to place more emphasis on Douhet's influence on Americans, especially the bombing of civilians (24). Sherry, in *The Rise of American Air Power*, sees the influence of Douhet on American airmen as a part of a greater mix of social, political, economic, and especially technological factors (52–76). An extreme case of a refusal to acknowledge Douhet's influence on American airmen is Robert T. Finney, *History of the Air Corps Tactical School, 1920–1940* (Washington, D.C.: USGPO, 1955). In an older but still useful work, Thomas H. Greer, *The Development of Air Doctrine in the Army Air Arm, 1917–1941* (Maxwell Air Force Base, Ala.: Air University Press, 1955), argues that the influence of Douhet on American thought was "indirectly and directly substantial" (49). Robert Futrell in *Ideas, Concepts, Doctrine: Basic Thinking in the United States Air Force 1907–1960* (Maxwell Air Force Base, Ala.: Air University Press, 1971), points out that many airmen in the 1930s were aware of Douhet's theory of air warfare but were unwilling to acknowledge the Italian's influence because of the fear of political repercussions over an independent air arm and public reaction to Douhet's advocacy of the direct bombing of civilians (39). The most recent analysis of Douhet by historian Philip Meilinger, "Guilio Douhet and the Origins of Airpower Theory," acknowledges Douhet's influence on American air power theory and cites the air force's experience in the Gulf War as a vindication of Douhet's general theory of air power in achieving command of the air (31).

8. Lee Kennett, *A History of Strategic Bombing* (New York: Charles Scribner's Sons, 1982), 57; Richard H. Kohn and Joseph P. Harahan, introduction to Douhet, *Command of the Air*, viii.

9. Finney, *History of the Air Corps Tactical School*; Haywood Hansell, *The Strategic Air War against Germany and Japan: A Memoir* (Washington, D.C.: USGPO, 1986), 13.

10. According to Douhet's theory and the American conceptual approach to bombing, strategic bombers might have to attack the enemy air force either on the ground, in the air, or in production factories. But this was only the first step in achieving command of the air that would allow the bombers to attack targets in enemy territory.

11. On William Mitchell and the development of American air power, see Mark L. Clodfelter, "Molding Airpower Convictions: Development and Legacy of William Mitchell's Strategic Thought," in Meilinger, *Paths of Heaven*, 79–114; Alfred F. Hurley, *Billy Mitchell: Crusader for Airpower*

(Bloomington: Indiana University Press, 1964); and Crane, *Bombs, Cities, and Civilians*, 15–22.

12. William Mitchell, *Winged Defense: The Development and Possibilities of Modern Air Power—Economic and Military* (1921; rpt. New York: Kennikat Press, 1971), 215; Hurley, *Billy Mitchell*, 103.

13. Quoted in Crane, *Bombs, Cities and Civilians*, 16. For the Mitchell court-martial, see Clodfelter, "Molding Airpower Convictions," 101–5.

14. Futrell, *Ideas, Concepts, Doctrine*, 44–53.

15. Mitchell, *Winged Defense*, 16–17; Douhet, "The Probable Aspects of the War of the Future," in *Command of the Air*, 187–90, 194; Clodfelter, "Molding Airpower Convictions," 99.

16. Tami Davis Biddle, "British and American Approaches to Strategic Bombing: Their Origins and Implementation in the World War II Combined Bomber Offensive," *Journal of Strategic Studies* 18 (March 1995): 110–13; Greer, *Development of Air Doctrine,* 89–93; Robert Divine, *The Reluctant Belligerent: American Entry into World War II* (Austin: University of Texas Press, 1965), 8–11.

17. Memo, Major General Frank M. Andrews to Army Adjutant General, "Organization for Air Defense," 26 April 1937, box 10, record group 340, Office of the Secretary of the Air Force (RG 340), National Archives (NA), College Park, Md.

18. The Air Corps Tactical Schools, by the late 1930s, had become the "incubator" of American strategic bombing doctrine. Partly owing to the geographic detachment of Maxwell from Washington, D.C., partly because it was the only service school that was producing a coherent doctrine for strategic bombardment, and because the smartest air corps officers either were instructors or had been students at the school (e.g., Hap Arnold, Carl Spaatz, Muir Fairchild, Laurence Kuter, Orvil Anderson, Frederick Anderson, Ira Eaker, Hoyt Vandenberg, and Haywood Hansell), the school became the seedbed for developing concepts of air power within the AAF. See Peter R. Faber, "Interwar US Army Aviation and the Air Corps Tactical School: Incubators of American Airpower," in Meilinger, *Paths of Heaven*, 211–12; Crane, *Bombs, Cities and Civilians*, 22.

19. Haywood Hansell, *The Air Plan That Defeated Hitler*, (Atlanta: Higgins-MacArthur, 1974), 37; Faber, "Interwar US Army Aviation," 200.

20. Memo, Andrews to Army Adjutant General, "Organization for Air Defense," 26 April 1937, box 10, RG 340, NA.

21. Futrell, *Ideas, Concepts, Doctrine*, 92–96.

22. Memo by Lieutenant Colonel Donald Wilson, "Long Range Airplane Development," November 1938, file 168.7012-20, Air Force Historical Research Agency, Maxwell Air Force Base, Ala. (AFHRA); unnamed author, "The Unwaged War," file 168.7012-18, ibid. Greer, *Development of Air Doctrine,* 109.

23. Quoted in Hansell, *Air Plan That Defeated Hitler,* 45.

24. Air Corps Tactical School, Course: Air Force "National Economic Structure" (instructor, Muir Fairchild), pp. 1–3, 1939–1940, file 168.7001-31, AFHRA. Historian Ronald Schaffer in his important 1985 book *Wings of Judgment* implies that the emphasis of Fairchild's thirty-nine-page lecture was on attacking civilian morale for psychological effects (30–33). But Fairchild acknowledged at the beginning of the lecture that this was not the recommended method of the school. Schaffer, therefore, quotes Fairchild out of context in order to provide support for his argument that both morale and physical capacity were equally important targets for air officers as they refined their theory of air power in the late 1930s. Air officers at the Tactical School, however, did not treat both as equally important. Fairchild's lecture, at least, demonstrates that in 1939 the primary objective for strategic bombers was the enemy's war-making capacity.

25. Fairchild, "National Economic Structure," 6.

26. Clodfelter, "Molding Airpower Convictions," 96.

27. Hansell, *Strategic Air War against Germany and Japan*, 12–13; Fairchild, "National Economic Structure," 29–30.

28. Hansell, *Strategic Air War against Germany and Japan*, 12, 19; Fairchild, "National Economic Structure," 31.

29. Fairchild, "National Economic Structure," 6–7.

30. Proposed memo, General Henry H. Arnold to President, "Committee to Survey Results of Combined Bomber Offensive," April 1944, box 41, record group 243, United States Strategic Bombing Survey (RG243), NA; H. H. Arnold, *Global Mission* (New York: Harper and Brothers, 1949), 490–91; Futrell, *Ideas, Concepts, Doctrine*, 144; Thomas M. Coffey, *Hap: The Story of the U.S. Air Force and the Man Who Built It* (New York: Viking Press, 1982), 277–78.

31. Hansell, *Strategic Air War against Germany and Japan*, 21–24; Hansell, *Air Plan That Defeated Hitler*, 49–52; memo, Air Intelligence

Section to Chief of Staff, "Air Intelligence Project No. 1," 1 March 1940, box 8, Carl A. Spaatz Papers (Spaatz Papers), Manuscript Division, Library of Congress (LC); Guido R. Perera, *Leaves from My Book of Life: Washington War Years* (Boston: privately printed, 1975), 85.

32. Roosevelt to Henry Stimson, 9 July 1941, file 145.82-1, AFHRA; Futrell, *Ideas, Concepts, Doctrine*, 108–9; Arnold, *Global Mission*, 245.

33. On the writing of AWPD/1, see James C. Gaston, *Planning the American Air War: Four Men and Nine Days in 1941—An Inside Narrative* (Washington D.C.: National Defense University Press, 1982).

34. "AWPD/1, Munitions Requirements of the Army Air Forces," (AWPD/1), August 1941, pp. 1–2, file 145.82-1, AFHRA.

35. AWPD/1, p. 2; Hansell, *Air Plan That Defeated Hitler*, 80. Hansell's two books on air war planning against Germany are the best memoir accounts available. But Hansell's treatment of morale is inconsistent with the way AWPD/1 treated it in 1941. In AWPD/1, morale is fourth on the list of primary objectives to attack. The plan accepts morale attacks as a possibility. If, as the plan states, German morale under precision attacks begins "to crack, area bombing of civil concentrations may be effective." Although the entire plan, after the initial discussion of attacking morale, pays very little attention to it, morale is still listed as a primary objective on page 2 of the plan. But Hansell in both of his memoir accounts of war planning—*The Air Plan That Defeated Hitler* (1972) and *The Strategic Air War against Germany and Japan* (1986)—when recounting AWPD/1, does not include morale in the list of primary objectives. *The Air Plan That Defeated Hitler* mentions obliquely (two pages after the first three objectives are listed) that morale was considered as an objective for bombing.

36. Memo for the Chief of Staff, "Munitions Requirements of the Army Air Forces for the Defeat of Our Potential Enemies," August 1941, file 145.82-1, AFHRA.

37. Hansell, *Air Plan That Defeated Hitler*, 86.

38. AWPD/42, "Requirements for Air Ascendancy," 9 September 1942, tab b-1, box 206, Map Room Files, Franklin Delano Roosevelt Library, Hyde Park, New York (FDR Library); Hansell, *Strategic Air War against Germany and Japan*, 58; Futrell, *Ideas, Concepts, Doctrine*, 131.

39. Wesley Frank Craven and James Lea Cate, *The Army Air Forces in World War II* (Chicago: University of Chicago Press, 1948), 2: 224–27.

40. Ibid., 1:352–53.

41. Arnold, *Global Mission*, 333–34; Craven and Cate, *Army Air Forces in World War II*, 1:353.

42. Craven and Cate, *Army Air Forces in World War II*, 1:353–54; James McGregor Burns, *Roosevelt: The Soldier of Freedom* (New York: Harcourt Brace Jovanovich, 1970), 345.

43. Arnold to Assistant Chief of Air Staff, Management Control, "Research and Analysis to Fix Earliest Practicable Date for Invasion of Western Europe," 9 December 1942, History of the COA, file 118.01, AFHRA.

44. "Western Axis Oil Industry as Bombardment Target," undated, History of the COA, file 118.01, AFHRA.

45. Committee of Operations Analysts report, "Vulnerability of Japanese Economic Objectives to Strategic Air Bombardment," 6 February 1944, box 167, Map Room Files; Perera, *Leaves from My Book of Life*, 110, 114. The term urban area attacks has often been employed to describe the use of strategic bombers in World War II to attack German and Japanese cities with the intention of striking civilians targets, thereby directly attacking their morale. Urban area attacks, in this conception, become synonymous with the direct attack on morale as an *objective*. But for American airmen and civilian analysts during World War II, urban area attacks, like the precise bombing of specific industrial targets (precision bombing), was a *method* (albeit a very destructive one) of strategic bombing with the *objective* usually being the German and Japanese war-making capacity. An urban area attack, as a *method*, could have had morale as an *objective*, but the two were logically distinct, and not automatically synonymous.

46. Edward Mead Earle to Winfield Riefler, 23 December 1942, History of the COA, file 118.01, AFHRA.

47. Biddle, "British and American Approaches to Strategic Bombing," 118–20; Schaffer, *Wings of Judgment*, 36–38; Charles Webster and Noble Frankland, *The Strategic Air Offensive against Germany, 1939–1945*, vol. 2: *Endeavor* (London: Her Majesty's Stationary Office, 1961), 12.

48. Memo, Committee of Operations Analysts to Arnold, "Report of Committee of Operations Analysts with Respect to Economic Targets within the Western Axis," 8 March 1943, reproduced in James Beveridge, "History of the United States Strategic Bombing Survey," four-volume typescript, microfilm copy from AFHRA, roll no. 1123 or 1154 (Beveridge, Europe or Pacific), frames 1339–40.

49. Ibid., frame 1339.

50. Other agencies that took part in target selection and evaluation were the Economic Warfare Division of the American Embassy in England (of which the Economic Objectives Unit was a part), the Army Air Forces' Air Board, and the Joint Target Group (JTG), which later replaced the COA to select and evaluate strategic targets in Japan; see Craven and Cate, *Army Air Forces in World War II,* vol. 2, 363–65; Futrell, *Ideas, Concepts, Doctrine,* 142–44, 162–63.

51. R&A Branch, OSS London, "War Diary," [Rostow Report], 13 September 1942–April 1945, file 520.056-167, AFHRA; Leslie H. Arps, "Report, Operational Analysis Section, Eighth Air Force," October 1942–June 1945, file 520.303-3, AFHRA; Craven and Cate, *Army Air Forces in World War II,* vol. 3: 72–79.

52. "War Diary," [Rostow Report]; also see Charles W. McArthur, *Operations Analysis in the U.S. Army Eighth Air Force in World War II* (Providence: American Mathematical Society, 1990).

53. Memo, Arnold to President, 27 January 1944; Committee of Historians, "Germany's War Potential: An Appraisal," December 1943, revised 18 January 1944, p. 41, box 164, Map Room Files, FDR Library; Barney M. Giles to Assistant Chief of Air Staff, Intelligence, "Committee of Historians to Analyze and Appraise Current Conditions and Prospective Developments in Germany," 29 September 1943, box 20, Edward Mead Earle Papers (Earle Papers), Seely G. Mudd Library, Princeton University (Princeton); Earle to Theodore Sorensen, 21 October 1943, ibid.

54. Frank Monaghan to Edward Mead Earle, 15 October 1943, box 20, Earle Papers. The names Carl Becker, Henry Commager, and Edward Mead Earle are generally familiar to contemporary historians. But a cursory check of the other members of the group shows that they too were historians of the first rank. Bernadotte Schmitt, for example, won the Pulitzer Prize for history in 1931 for his book *The Coming of War: 1914* and served as editor of the *Journal of Modern History* from 1929 to 1946. Louis Gottschalk, scholar of French history at the University of Chicago, wrote biographies on Marat and Lafayette and became a leading scholar in comparative studies of revolution. See Lucian Boia, ed., *Great Historians of the Modern Age: An International Dictionary* (New York: Greenwood Press, 1991), and S. William Halperin, *Some 20th Century Historians: Essays on Eminent Europeans* (Chicago: University of Chicago Press, 1961), xii–xvii.

55. Memo, Giles to Assistant Chief of Air Staff, Intelligence, "Committee of Historians to Analyze and Appraise Current Conditions and Prospective Developments in Germany," 29 September 1943, file 142.16-12C, v. 7, AFHRA.

56. Note of transmittal to "Germany's War Potential," p. 2 (italics mine).

57. For a still useful evaluation of facts and history, see E. H. Carr, *What Is History?* (New York: Vintage Books, 1961), 3–29; MacIsaac, *Strategic Bombing in World War Two,* 22.

58. AAF Committee of Historians, "Meeting of 30 October 1943," file 142.16-12, v. 2, AFHRA.

59. Memo, Giles to Assistant Chief of Air Staff, Intelligence, 29 September 1943.

60. Memo, Monaghan to Committee of Historians, "Memorandum No. 2," 11 November 1943, file 142.16-12C, v. 12, AFHRA.

61. Perera, *Leaves from My Book of Life*, 78.

62. Committee of Historians, "Germany's War Potential," 19–20. The USSBS's Economic Division report later disproved the historians' conclusion that Germany's war economy was "totally mobilized."

63. Committee of Historians, "Germany's War Potential," pp. 24–25 (emphasis in original).

64. Ibid., 32–33.

65. "Memo for the Commanding General, Army Air Forces," 29 December 1943, file 142.16-12C, v. 10, AFHRA.

66. Committee of Historians, "Germany's War Potential," pp. 41–42.

67. Earle to Sorensen, 29 November 1943, 3 January 1944, box 20, Earle Papers.

68. Sherry, *Rise of American Air Power*, 259–60; Crane, *Bombs, Cities and Civilians*, 93, 98.

69. In the report's cover memorandum to the president of 27 January 1944, Arnold mentions that exploring the analogy was a stated purpose for the committee. Arnold probably had discussed the analogy to 1918 Germany with the president during November 1943 on the their way to the Cairo conference on board the battleship *Iowa.* Arnold did meet privately with the president and the other Chiefs on the trip across the Atlantic; see *Foreign Relations of the United States* (FRUS), "The Conferences at Cairo and Tehran, 1943" (Washington, D.C.: USGPO, 1961), 273–90; Arnold, *Global Mission*, 453–56, 490.

70. Committee of Historians, "Germany's War Potential," appendix 1: "Is There a Valid Analogy between 1918 and 1944?" p. 53.

71. Memo, Arnold to President, 27 January 1944 (italics mine).

72. General Arnold was not averse to writing cover memorandums that stated his disagreements with, or modifications to, conclusions brought out in other evaluations; see, for example, foreword by Commanding General, Army Air Forces, to "Evaluation of Results of Strategic Bombardment against the Western Axis," 27 January 1944, file 118.01, History of the COA, AFHRA.

73. MacIsaac, *Strategic Bombing in World War Two*, 161.

74. Ibid., 160. Peter Novick, in *That Noble Dream: The "Objectivity Question" and the American Historical Profession* (Cambridge: Cambridge University Press, 1988), obliquely mentions a recommendation made by Becker to the Pentagon cautioning "against accepting grandiose Air Corps claims that their bombing would break German morale," but does not explicitly mention the report or the committee (303).

75. Dr. Bruce Hopper, interview with Major General Orvil Anderson, 6 August 1945, p. 1, file 168.7006-2, AFHRA; memo, Marshall to Commanding General, Mediterranean Theater of Operations, 3 November 1944, box 14, RG 243, NA. Strobe Talbott uses the term "calipers" when describing Paul Nitze's analytical approach to evaluating strategic bombing; see Talbott, *The Master of the Game: Paul Nitze and the Nuclear Peace* (New York: Alfred A. Knopf, 1988), 32.

Notes to Chapter 2

1. Stimson to Franklin D'Olier, 3 November 1944, box 14, RG 243, NA. The "United States Strategic Bombing Survey" was officially named as such by memorandum no. 100, "Redesignation of US Bombing Research Mission," 29 October 1944, box 225, Spaatz Papers, LC. Prior to its name redesignation, the Survey was referred to by a number of different titles: "Strategic Bombing Effects Survey"; "Post-Armistice Damage Evaluation Committee"; "Committee to Survey Results of Combined Bomber Offensive"; "Bombing Research Unit." For simplicity and to avoid confusion, the terms Survey, Strategic Bombing Survey, and USSBS will be used to describe the evaluation that the AAF had in mind even though at a given time before 29 October 1944 it was not referred to by that title.

2. It is acknowledged that in the chairman's *Summary Report* of the European and later Pacific portions of the Survey, there were passages that addressed the relevance of air power to national military strategy and policy. But it was only in these two reports that the issue was addressed. In the conduct of their lengthy evaluation and in their numerous other published reports, Survey analysts did not question the relevance of air power: they only evaluated the degree of its effectiveness.

3. Sherry, *Rise of American Air Power*, 194.

4. Edward Mead Earle, interview with Major General General F. L. Anderson and Colonel Robert Hughes, 1 May 1944, box 24, Earle Papers.

5. Memo, Lieutenant Colonel James B. Ames to General F. L. Anderson, "Proposed Committee to Survey Results of Combined Bomber Offensive," 28 March 1944, Beveridge, Europe, frames 1360–61. Beveridge's organizational history of the Survey contains an excellent appendix with many of the letters and memorandums that established it. His history and attached documents are available in boxes 24–26, RG 243, NA, and on microfilm from the NA and the AFHRA.

6. Memo, Major Ralph A. Colbert to General Thomas D. White, "Post-Armistice Damage Evaluation Commission," 27 March 1944, Beveridge, frames 1356–57.

7. Beveridge, Europe, frame 761.

8. Futrell, *Ideas, Concepts, Doctrine*, 142–44; MacIsaac, *Strategic Bombing in World War Two*, 21–22.

9. General Carl A. Spaatz to Arnold, 5 April 1944, Beveridge, frame 1365.

10. Memo for the Joint Chiefs of Staff, "Post-Armistice Evaluation of the Strategic Bombardment of Europe," undated, Beveridge, Europe, frames 1373–74.

11. Arnold to Spaatz, 21 April 1944, box 41, RG 243, NA; Haywood S. Hansell, Jr., *Strategic Air War against Japan* (Washington, D.C.: USGPO, 1980), 30–32.

12. Memo for Brigadier General Giles from Guido R. Perera of the COA, "Progress Report," 24 September 1943, History of the COA, file 118.01, AFHRA; Hansell to F. L. Anderson, 15 April 1944, box 25, Earle Papers; Perera, *Leaves from My Book of Life*, 108, 115; Schaffer, *Wings of Judgment*, 121–22.

13. Spaatz to Arnold, 13 June 1944, box 225, Spaatz Papers; Laurence Kuter to Spaatz, June 1944, ibid.

14. F. L. Anderson to Spaatz, 3 April 1944, Beveridge, Europe, frames 1363–65; Spaatz to Arnold, 5 April 1944, ibid.; Arnold to Spaatz, 5 June 1944, box 225, Spaatz Papers.

15. Memo, Colonel John H. McCormick to Assistant Chief of Staff, Plans, "Survey of Results of Combined Bomber Offensive," 9 May 1944, box 225, Spaatz Papers.

16. "Mission to Study the Effects of the Strategic Bomber Offensive on the German War Effort," minutes of the meeting held in the Upper Room, Air Ministry, Whitehall, 17 June 1944, Beveridge, Europe, frames 1420–21; MacIsaac, *Strategic Bombing in World War Two*, 36–37.

17. AAF Evaluation Board and U.S. Strategic Bombing Survey, "Extracts from Notes on People Contacted from November 7 to December 7, 1944," box 389, Adlai Stevenson Papers (Stevenson Papers), Princeton.

18. Memo, White to Assistant Chief of Air Staff, Plans, "Survey of Results of Combined Bomber Offensive," 7 May 1944, box 225, Spaatz Papers.

19. Spaatz to Arnold, 12 May 1944, box 225, Spaatz Papers; memo, "Organization of Machinery for Cooperation with British and Soviets in Survey of Results of Bomber Offensive," 30 May 1944, Beveridge, Europe, frame 1433.

20. Crane, *Bombs, Cities and Civilians*, 10. For an alternative interpretation that argues that the AAF, by 1944, had switched from precision attacks to area attacks, with German morale as the primary objective, see Schaffer, *Wings of Judgment*, 103.

21. Memo from Air Vice Marshall, Policy, "Bombardment Policy," 29 October 1942, box 84, Spaatz Papers; Max Hastings, *Bomber Command: The Myths and Reality of the Strategic Bombing Offensive, 1939–1945* (New York: Dial Press, 1979), 136; Webster and Frankland, *Strategic Air Offensive against Germany, 1939–1945*, 1:322–23.

22. General Eaker's press conference, 6 October 1943, pp. 1–3, box 18, Ira C. Eaker Papers (Eaker Papers), LC; Ira Eaker, "The Case for Day Bombing," undated, box 21, ibid.; Crane, *Bombs, Cities and Civilians*, 42–48.

23. Conrad C. Crane, "The Cigar Who Ignited the Fire Wind: Curtis LeMay and the Incendiary Bombing of Urban Areas," unpublished, undated; personal copy provided by Crane to author. Also see Biddle, "British and American Approaches to Strategic Bombing," 91, 117.

24. Memo, F. L. Anderson to Spaatz, "Attached Study on Air Attack on German Civilian Morale," 17 August 1944, box 84, Spaatz Papers.

25. Memo, Ames to Arnold, "Post-Armistice Evaluation of the Strategic Bombardment of Europe," undated, Beveridge, Europe, frame 1358.

26. Memo, Air Chief of Staff to Deputy Air Chiefs of Staff, "Survey of Results of Combined Bomber Offensive," 28 April 1944, Beveridge, Europe, frames 1403–4.

27. Memo, Charles Kindleberger to Ames, "Post V-Day Investigation of the Effects of the Combined Bomber Offensive," 6 April 1944, box 225, Spaatz Papers. It is noteworthy that a later set of questions for the Survey posed by the EOU in August left out completely the objective of evaluating the relevance of strategic bombing; see "Outline Notes on the Strategic Bombardment Survey," 9 August 1944, Beveridge, Europe, frames 1485–95.

28. Colbert to White, "Memorandum for Brig. Gen. T. D. White," 27 March 1944, Beveridge, Europe, frame 1356.

29. Joint Target Group, "Memorandum on Assessment of Damage by Air Bombardment in the European Theater," 10 November 1944, USSBS Records, microfilm no. A1154, frames 1615–22, AFHRA; Futrell, *Ideas, Concepts, Doctrine*, 162–63; Craven and Cate, *Army Air Forces in World War II*, 5:624–25.

30. Memo, AC/AS, Plans to the Air Inspector, "Survey of Results of Combined Bomber Offensive," 10 May 1944, box 225, Spaatz Papers.

31. Memo, William Barrett to the Air Surgeon, "Recommendations for the Study of the Psychological Effects of Strategic Bombing on Germany," 1 October 1944, box 41, file 381, RG 243, NA.

32. Theodore J. Koenig, "Strategic Bombing Effects Survey: Report of Progress, 5 July 1944–1 September 1944," 5 September 1944, pp. 11–13, Beveridge, Europe, frames, 1447–65.

33. In their memoirs, both Paul Nitze and Guido Perera assume that the real planning and organizational work for the Survey did not begin until after the assignment of the chairman and civilian directors in October and November 1944. Yet it is clear from the record that the AAF had recognized the importance of the Survey and had gone to great lengths to establish the organizational framework of the Survey and the questions that it would answer. This misconception of Perera and Nitze as well as other memoirists and historians of the Survey was probably due to the notion that since the Survey was to be headed by civilians, the roots of the Survey

began in late 1944 rather than much earlier. See Paul H. Nitze, *From Hiroshima to Glasnost: At the Center of Decision* (New York: Grove Weidenfeld, 1989), 26; and Perera, *Leaves from My Book of Life,* 122.

34. Thomas D. Upton, "Scope of Strategic Bombing Effects Survey," 5 August 1944, box 41, RG 243, NA.

35. Theodore J. Koenig, "Program for the Strategic Bombing Effects Survey," 5 September 1944, Beveridge, Europe, frame 1453.

36. It is unclear whether or not this proposed memorandum ever made it to the president's desk. But considering the importance that General Arnold placed on the Survey, it is almost certain that the president was made aware of the Survey as early as March 1944, if not sooner.

37. Memo, Arnold to President, "Committee to Survey Results of Combined Bomber Offensive," undated, Beveridge, Europe, frames 1370–71.

38. George W. Ball, *The Past Has Another Pattern*: *Memoirs* (New York: W. W. Norton, 1983), 55.

39. Quoted in Talbott, *Master of the Game*, 37. Although Talbott's analysis of Nitze provides some useful insights, it is documented very poorly, making it difficult to determine exact references. This quote Talbott most likely took from a postwar interview of Nitze by the U.S. Air Force Oral History Interview, Albert F. Simpson Historical Research Center, Office of Air Force History, 1981.

40. Roosevelt to Stimson, 9 September 1944, box 14, RG 243, NA.

41. Stimson to D'Olier, 3 November 1944, box 14, RG 243, NA; Perera, *Leaves from My Book of Life*, 121; Beveridge, Europe, frames 836–41; MacIsaac, *Strategic Bombing in World War Two,* 52–53.

42. Arnold to Spaatz, 5 June 1944, box 225, Spaatz Papers; Perera, *Leaves from My Book of Life*, 121; Arnold, *Global Mission*, 490.

43. James G. Hershberg, *James B. Conant: Harvard to Hiroshima and the Making of the Nuclear Age* (New York: Alfred A. Knopf, 1993), 903–4 n. 18; MacIsaac, *Strategic Bombing in World War Two*, 44; Perera, *Leaves from My Book of Life*, 121.

44. Colbert to Upton, 16 September 1944, Beveridge, frame 1516; Spaatz to Arnold, 20 April 1944, Beveridge, frame 1369.

45. Hershberg, *James B. Conant,* 611–12.

46. MacIsaac, *Strategic Bombing in World War Two*, 189; Perera, *Leaves from My Book of Life*, 121.

47. Ball, *Past Has Another Pattern*, 44; John Kenneth Galbraith, *A Life in Our Times: Memoirs* (Boston: Houghton Mifflin, 1981), 196.

48. Focus is placed on Survey directors Nitze, Ball, Galbraith, and General Orvil Anderson (and later Admiral Ralph A. Ofstie) for two reasons. First, they were the directors who provided the Survey with its intellectual direction, and in the case of the two military officers, the intense interservice rivalry that became apparent as the Survey moved to the Pacific. Second, the three civilian directors (Ball, Nitze, and Galbraith) produced memoir accounts of their duty with the Survey, and they (plus the two military directors) have archival collections that contain in varying degrees excellent primary documents pertaining to the Survey and their work on it.

49. Memo, Major W. S. Harris, "Description of Research Personnel Required for Work of the Strategic Bombing Effects Survey," box 225, Spaatz Papers.

50. Perera, *Leaves from My Book of Life*, 120–24; MacIsaac, *Strategic Bombing in World War II*, 25.

51. Perera, *Leaves from My Book of Live*, 124; Ball, *Past Has Another Pattern*, 43–45; Futrell, *Ideas, Concepts, Doctrine*, 144–45.

52. Beveridge, Europe, frames 1281–82.

53. Ball, *Past Has Another Pattern*, 69.

54. Beveridge, Europe, frames 1293–95; Nitze, *From Hiroshima to Glasnost*, xv–xxiii, 3–7, 22–24.

55. Perera, *Leaves from My Book of Life*, 125; Nitze, *From Hiroshima to Glasnost*, 26.

56. Galbraith, *Life in Our Times*, 233; Beveridge, Europe, frames 1287–88.

57. Beveridge, Europe, frame 1280.

58. Perera, *Leaves from My Book of Life*, 130; memo, White to Assistant Chief of Air Staff, Plans, "Survey of Results of Combined Bomber Offensive," 7 May 1944, box 225, Spaatz Papers.

59. Dr. Bruce Hopper, interview with Major General Orvil Anderson, 6 August 1945, p. 1, file 168.7006-2, AFHRA.

60. Perera, *Leaves from My Book of Life*, 124–25; Beveridge, Europe, frames 1274–77.

61. Hopper, O. A. Anderson interview, 6 August 1945, p. 12.

62. Nitze, *From Hiroshima to Glasnost*, 26.

63. Memo, D'Olier and Perera to Vice Chairman, U.S. Strategic Bombing Survey, "Conference with Major Muir S. Fairchild," 28 October 1944, box 2, file 337, RG 243, NA.

64. Major Muir S. Fairchild to Henry Alexander, 30 December 1944,

box 28, file 319.4, RG 243, NA; Conference Held Widewing, 8 November 1944, members present: D'Olier, Alexander, O. A. Anderson, McDonald, Koenig, and Perera, "Purpose of Conference: To Discuss Requirements and Plans for the Survey," box 225, Spaatz Papers; Nitze, *From Hiroshima to Glasnost*, 26; Perera, *Leaves from My Book of Life*, 126–27.

65. Nitze, *From Hiroshima to Glasnost*, 29; Paul Nitze to D'Olier, "Conversation with Colonel Frederick Castle . . . November 22, 1944," box 41, file 373.11, RG 243, NA; F. W. Castle, "Air Power in This War and the Following Peace," undated, box 21, Eaker Papers.

66. Nitze to John Kenneth Galbraith, 13 October 1949, box 165, Paul H. Nitze Papers (Nitze Papers), LC.

67. Hamilton Dearborn, "Orientation—Introductory Lecture," 15 December 1944, box 40, file 353.02, RG 243, NA. Arguably, Douhet and Mitchell had established a theory of air power that underpinned the American approach to strategic bombing, which Dearborn failed to recognize in his lecture to Survey members.

68. Walter W. Rostow, "The History of Strategic Bombing," 18 December 1944, box 389, Adlai E. Stevenson Papers; Dr. Barger, "Damage Caused by Strategic Bombing," 19 December 1944.

69. Rostow, "History of Strategic Bombing"; T. Dennis, "Lecture on the Economic Effect of Air Attacks," 20 December 1944, box 389, Stevenson Papers.

70. Andrews to F. L. Anderson, 5 November 1944, box 225, Spaatz Papers.

Notes to Chapter 3

1. "Minutes of Meeting Held, 1 April 1945," recorded by Paul Nitze, box 2, file 001, RG 243, NA.

2. Ball, *Past Has Another Pattern,* 61; Galbraith, *Life in Our Times,* 225–26.

3. Lieutenant Colonel John Bereta to Harry F. Bowman, 1 May 1945, box 28, file 319.4, RG 243, NA.

4. A reference guide to Survey reports and studies is Gordon Daniels, *A Guide to the Reports of the United States Strategic Bombing Survey* (London, 1981); also see USSBS, *Index to Records of the United States Strategic Bombing Survey* (Washington, D.C.: USGPO, 1947). Many of the Euro-

pean Survey reports contain two publication dates, 1945–46 and 1947. This was due to the renumbering of all Survey published reports in 1947. The European published reports referred to hereafter were completed and published in late 1945, although some have a 1947 publication date. The contents of these reports are unchanged from the first edition. See Maria B. Guptil and Maida Loescher, "Final Reports of the United States Strategic Bombing Survey," undated; this summary was prepared for the microfilm collection of RG 243 by the National Archives.

5. USSBS, Morale Division, *The Effects of Strategic Bombing on German Morale* (Washington, D.C.: USGPO, 1947), 1:1–2; USSBS, Area Studies Division, Area Studies Division Report (Washington, D.C.: USGPO, 1945), 23–24.

6. USSBS, Chairman's Office, *Over-all Report* (European War), (Washington, D.C.: USGPO, 1945), 107.

7. Memo, Alexander to Survey Directors, "Plant Reports," 11 May 1945, box 13, file 300.6, RG 243, NA.

8. "Statement of Functions," undated, box 34, file 322, RG 243, NA.

9. Memo for Division Directors from Alexander, "Material to Be Prepared Prior to Writing of Final Report," 28 April 1945, box 13, file 300.6, RG 243, NA.

10. Perera, *Leaves from My Book of Life,* 124.

11. "Minutes of Meeting Held 1 April 1945," box 2, file 001, RG 243, NA.

12. Overall Effects Division, "Memorandum on the Investigation of the Effects of Strategic Bombing," undated, box 18, file 300.6, RG 243, NA.

13. "Standard Operating Procedures for Field Operations of Survey Teams—Area Studies Division," undated, box 16, file 300.6, RG 243, NA.

14. Office of the Chairman, "Method and Sources of Data for Overall Economic Survey," 31 January 1945, box 14, file 300.6, RG 243, NA (italics mine).

15. USSBS, *Summary Report* (Pacific War), 26.

16. The Survey had an ongoing problem with gaining access to bombed targets in the Russian occupation zones; see Outgoing Message, 3 April 1945, box 42, file 384.4, RG 243, NA.

17. D'Olier to Division Directors, "Interim Reports," 11 May 1945, box 13, file 300.6, RG 243, NA.

18. Galbraith, *Life In Our Times,* 200–201; MacIsaac, Strategic Bombing in World War II, 95–96; USSBS Berlin Field Team, "Daily Record of

USSBS Spearhead Team . . ." 16 July 1945, USSBS Records, microfilm no. A1154, frame 1644, AFHRA.

19. Ball, *Past Has Another Pattern,* 54; also see Ball to D'Olier, 16 May 1945, USSBS Records, microfilm no. A1154, frame 1698, AFHRA.

20. "Preliminary Appraisal of Achievements of Strategic Bombing of Germany," undated, box 203, Spaatz Papers. The folder that contains this report is titled "The Galbraith Report," hereafter referred to as such.

21. Nitze to his mother, 16 June 1945, box 165, folder 5, Nitze Papers. Nitze also relied heavily on the Speer interrogation when explaining to Ferdinand Eberstadt the effects of strategic bombing on Germany; see "Memorandum of Interview with Paul Nitze," 19 July 1945, box 7, Ferdinand Eberstadt Papers (Eberstadt Papers), Princeton.

22. MacIsaac, *Strategic Bombing in World War Two,* 117–18.

23. Ball's translation of the interrogation of Albert Speer, 21 May 1945, pp. 22–23, box 167, George W. Ball Papers (Ball Papers), Princeton; Albert Speer, Inside the Third Reich: Memoirs (New York: Collier Books, 1981), 284, 499; Gita Sereny, *Albert Speer: His Battle with Truth* (Alfred A. Knopf: New York, 1995), 546–50.

24. Ball, *Past Has Another Pattern,* 61.

25. Ibid. Galbraith and Nitze in their memoirs also describe their experiences with the interrogation of Speer: Galbraith, *Life in Our Times,* 207–19; Nitze, *From Hiroshima to Glasnost,* 31–34.

26. Bernard Brodie, *Strategy in the Missile Age* (Princeton: Princeton University Press, 1959), 123. Brodie based his analysis on numerous European Survey reports.

27. Notes taken at meeting held 15 January 1945, box 2, file 001, RG 243, NA; Memo, William Mitchell to D'Olier and George Ball, "Importance of Electric Power Plant Bombing in Japanese War," 29 May 1945, box 21, file 300.6, ibid.; Morale Division, "Introductory Statement," 8 June 1945, box 17, file 300.6, ibid.

28. Paul Baran to John Kenneth Galbraith, "Activities of the Berlin Teams," 19 July 1945, box 28, file 319.4, RG 243, NA.

29. Galbraith, *Life in Our Times,* 233. MacIsaac also suggests that the Survey may have wanted to disassociate itself from the fire raids against Japanese cities, see MacIsaac, *Strategic Bombing in World War Two,* 102.

30. Crane, *Bombs, Cities and Civilians,* 147.

31. Area Studies Division, "The Objective of the Area Studies Division," 12 February 1945, box 225, Spaatz Papers.

32. Minutes taken at meeting held 20 January 1945, box 2, file 001, RG 243, NA.

33. USSBS, *Effects of Strategic Bombing on German Morale,* 1: 53.

34. Ibid., 1: 2–3.

35. Morale Division, "Analysis of Captured Civilian Mail," 8 June 1945, box 17, file 300.6, RG 243, NA.

36. Albert E. Cowdrey, *Fighting for Life: American Military Medicine in World War II* (New York: Free Press, 1994), 142; Stephen Ambrose, *Citizen Soldiers* (New York: Simon and Schuster, 1997), 329–30; Medical Department, United States Army, *Neuropsychiatry in World War II* (Washington, D.C.: Office of the Surgeon General, 1966), 275, 337.

37. [Name unrecognizable] to Thompson, 15 February 1945, box 17, file 300.6, RG 243, NA; memo, J. W. Frampton to Charles Hurley, "Scientific Information for Medical Section of Morale Section," 15 February 1945, ibid.

38. USSBS Intelligence Summary, 21 June 1945, USSBS Records, microfilm no. A1154, frame 404, AFHRA; Kuter to F. L. Anderson, 15 August 1944, box 153, Spaatz Papers.

39. USSBS, *Effects of Strategic Bombing on German Morale,* 1: 1–2.

40. George B. McDonald, "Study of Results Achieved by Operation Clarion," 26 March 1945, box 170, Spaatz Papers; Crane, *Bombs, Cities and Civilians,* 111.

41. USSBS, *Effects of Strategic Bombing on German Morale,* 1: 1.

42. Ibid., 1: 53.

43. Headquarters Eighth Air Force, "Target Priorities of the Eighth Air Force: A Resume of the Bombardment Directives and Concepts Underlying Them," 15 May 1945, pp. 1–2, box 41, file 383.8, RG 243, NA.

44. C.C.S 166/1, 21 January 1943, quoted in Craven and Cate, *Army Air Forces in World War II,* vol. 2: 305 (italics mine).

45. It was not uncommon for the Survey to request information from the AAF on a wide range of issues such as targeting, strategy, doctrine, operations, etc.; see memorandum from John Glover to Secretariat, "Comparison of Target Systems in Various Plans," 2 May 1945, AFHRA, USSBS microfilm no. A1154, frame 387.

46. Schaffer, *Wings of Judgment,* 103–5 (italics mine); also see Gordon Wright, *The Ordeal of Total War, 1939–1945* (New York: Harper & Row, 1968), 182; Richard Rhodes, *The Making of the Atomic Bomb* (New York: Simon & Schuster, 1986), 650; John D. Chappell, *Before the Bomb: How*

America Approached the End of the Pacific War (Lexington: University of Kentucky Press, 1997), 106–7.

47. Crane, "Cigar Who Ignited the Fire Wind," 15–20.

48. "Outline of Final Survey Report," 26 July 1945, box 14, RG 243, NA.

49. Overall Effects Division, "Memorandum on the Investigation of the Effects of Strategic Bombing," undated, box 18, file 300.6, RG 243, NA; Area Studies Division, "Short Statement of Objectives," 25 February 1945, AFHRA, USSBS microfilm no. A1154, 2098, EO 11652, frames 820–22.

50. Area Studies Division, "Suggested Procedures for Field Operations of Survey Teams," 18 April 1945, box 16, file 300.6, RG 243, NA; Office of the Chairman to all Division Directors, "Outline of Final Industry Report," 22 May 1945, box 13, file 300.6, RG 243, NA.

51. The division did make distinctions between the men, women, and children of the civilian workforce. For example, to the Area Division (and the Morale Division), women industrial workers were more likely to be absent from work after a bombing attack because of their responsibility to take care of the home. Women, according to the Morale Division, were also more prone to be absent from work because they would often go off to visit husbands who were stationed at military posts or home on leave from military service; see USSBS, *Area Studies Division Report,* 10–11; and USSBS, *Effects of Strategic Bombing on German Morale,* 1: 64–65.

52. USSBS, Area Studies Division, *A Detailed Study of the Effects of Area Bombing on Hamburg, Germany* (Washington, D.C.: USGPO, 1946), 1.

53. Ibid., 2.

54. USSBS, *Area Studies Division Report,* 23.

55. Ibid., 8–9; Stevenson to Director, Area Studies Division, "Preliminary Report on the Effect of Area Raids, 9 June 1945, box 16, file 300.6, RG 243, NA.

56. Hansell, *Air Plan That Defeated Hitler,* 80.

57. "AWPD/1, Munitions Requirements of the Army Air Forces," August 1941, pp. 1–2, file 145.82-1, AFHRA.

58. Hansell, *Strategic Air War against Germany and Japan,* 125–30.

59. USSBS, Chairman's Office, *Summary Report (European War)* (Washington, D.C.: USGPO, 1945), 12.

60. Ibid., 14.

61. Memo, Galbraith to John Black, October 1949, box 70, John Kenneth Galbraith Papers (Galbraith Papers), John F. Kennedy Library,

Boston, Mass. (JFK Library); MacIsaac, *Strategic Bombing in World War Two,* 71–72.

62. Bereta to Bowman, 1 May 1945, box 28, file 319.4, RG 243, NA.

63. Ibid.; record of telephone conversation, D'Olier and Alexander, 27 July 1945, box 22, file 311.3, RG 243, NA; Galbraith to Nitze, 18 October 1949, box 165, Nitze Papers.

64. Nitze, *From Hiroshima to Glasnost,* 35–36; Ball, *Past Has Another Pattern,* 62; Galbraith, *Life in Our Times,* 205.

65. Nitze, *From Hiroshima to Glasnost,* 34.

66. Craven and Cate, *Army Air Forces in World War II,* 2: 362–69.

67. Memo, Mitchell to D'Olier, "Importance of Electric Power Plant Bombing in Japanese War," 27 July 1945, box 41, file 383.8, RG 243, NA.

68. USSBS, Utilities Division, *German Electric Utilities Industry Report* (Washington, D.C.: USGPO, 1945), 3.

69. Craven and Cate, *Army Air Forces in World War II,* 3: 73–78, 651–53; also see Alfred C. Mierzejewiski, *The Collapse of the German War Economy, 1944–1945: Allied Air Power and the German National Railway* (Chapel Hill: University of North Carolina Press, 1988).

70. Memo, D'Olier to Secretary of War, "Preliminary Review of Effectiveness of the Combined Bomber Offensive in the European Theater of Operations," 11 June 1945, box 41, file 383.8, RG 243, NA.

71. D'Olier to Alexander, 14 July 1945, box 41, file 383.8, RG 243, NA; Office of the Chairman, "Japanese Targets," 5 July 1945, ibid.

72. USSBS, Transportation Division, *The Effects of Strategic Bombing on German Transportation* (Washington, D.C.: USGPO, 1945), 8.

73. Beveridge, Europe, frame 1052.

74. Memo, Galbraith to Professor Black, undated [October 1949], box 70, Harvard University File, Galbraith Papers. What appears to be an early version of Cabot's draft, dated 25 July 1945, shows Galbraith's claims to be correct. In the report's section on air power in the European war, it recognized the influence of Douhet and Mitchell on American air power theory. And the report presented what it called "the accomplishments of air power . . . as an independent striking force"; see Office of the Chairman, "Draft of Final Survey Report," 25 July 1945, box 28, file 319.4, RG 243, NA.

75. Beveridge, Europe, frame 1047.

76. Galbraith, *Life in Our Times,* 225–26. There does not appear to be any contemporaneous documents showing that a controversy over Cabot's

draft report happened, but it is referred to in too many other sources to dismiss. Hershberg, in *James B. Conant* (611–12), discusses it in the context of the 1949 attempt by the Harvard Board of Overseers (of which Cabot was a member) to block Galbraith's appointment as professor. At issue, ostensibly, was Galbraith's "intellectual dishonesty" when he challenged Cabot's version of the Survey chairman's final report. Hershberg points out, however, that attempting to prevent Galbraith's appointment as Harvard professor had more to do with Galbraith's liberal politics than his work on the Survey. Nevertheless it was Galbraith's challenge to Cabot's draft report and his purported "intellectual dishonesty" that the Harvard board used in 1949 to determine whether or not he would attain professorship. The result was a number of memorandums written by Galbraith in 1949 that explained the controversy over the writing of the chairman's final report as well as a series of letters between Galbraith and other Survey directors that addressed the early September 1945 controversy. I will therefore rely on these documents heavily when discussing the controversy over the chairman's final report.

77. Untitled and undated [remarks on exhibits for the appointment of Galbraith as professor of economics at Harvard, October 1949], box 70, Harvard University File, Galbraith Papers. Galbraith's abrasive personality also seems to have contributed to the tension. He clearly did not get along with Cabot and Perera, yet his relationship with Orvil Anderson was generally positive. Galbraith recalled his "relationship with Anderson with some pleasure." Anderson was quoted as saying, "I think Galbraith was one of the most valuable men on the Survey, if not the most valuable." See memo from Galbraith, 19 October 1949, box 70, Harvard University File, Galbraith Papers; Ramsey Potts to Galbraith, 22 March 1950, ibid.

78. Overall Economic Effects Division, "Brief Notes on the Conference with Overall Economic Effects Division at Bad Nauheim," 3 July 1945, box 14, file 300.6, RG 243, NA.

79. Galbraith Report, undated, box 203, Spaatz Papers.

80. Galbraith, *Life in Our Times*, 226. For a post-Survey account by Galbraith of the German war economy, see "Germany Was Badly Run," *Fortune*, December 1945, 200.

81. USSBS, Over-all Economic Effects Division, *The Effects of Strategic Bombing on the German War Economy* (Washington, D.C.: USGPO, 1945), 13–14.

82. Ibid., 26.

83. Gentile, "Advocacy or Assessment?" 58–62.

84. Memo from Galbraith, 19 October 1949, box 70, Harvard University File, Galbraith Papers.

85. Perera, *Leaves from My Book of Life,* 188.

86. Memo, COA to General Hansell, "Plan for Completion of the Combined Bomber Offensive of 5 March 1944," 12 March 1944, History of the COA, file 118.01, AFHRA.

87. USSBS, *Effects of Strategic Bombing on the German War Economy,* 5–14; USSBS, Aircraft Division, *Aircraft Division Industry Report* (Washington, D.C.: USGPO, 1945), 5; USSBS, Equipment Division, *The German Anti-Friction Bearings Industry* (Washington, D.C.: USGPO, 1945), 1–2; USSBS, *Effects of Strategic Bombing on German Transportation,* 3–4; USSBS, *German Electric Utilities Industry Report,* 3; these survey reports are reproduced in David MacIsaac, ed., *The United States Strategic Bombing Survey,* vols. 1–6 (New York: Garland Publishers, 1976).

88. USSBS, *Effects of Strategic Bombing on the German War Economy,* 13–14.

89. Perera, *Leaves from My Book of Life,* 188.

90. Guido R. Perera, "The Selection of Strategic Air Targets or Target Appraisal for a Bomber Offensive," 22 December 1944, box 39, file 350.001, RG 243, NA.

91. Ball to Arthur M. Schlesinger, Jr., 11 October 1949, box 43, Ball Papers. Paul Baran was much less diplomatic in expressing his contempt for Cabot (and Perera). Baran declared in a letter to Galbraith that Cabot was an "imbecile," and Perera "a low-grade S.O.B." See Baran to Galbraith, 12 October 1949, box 70, Harvard University File, Galbraith Papers.

92. Ball to Galbraith, 11 October 1949, box 43, Ball Papers.

93. MacIsaac, *Strategic Bombing in World War Two,* 143; also see "final" memo from Galbraith, undated [October 1949], box 70, Harvard University File, Galbraith Papers.

94. Historical Section, USTAAF, interview with Major General Orvil Anderson, 22 August 1945, pp. 3, 16, file 168.7006-2, AFHRA. For a scholarly biography of Anderson, see John Henry Scrivner, Jr., "Pioneer into Space: A Biography of Major General Orvil Arson Anderson," Ph.D. diss., University of Oklahoma, 1971.

95. O. A. Anderson interview, 22 August 1945, 9.

96. Ibid., 10–12.

97. USSBS, *Effects of Strategic Bombing on German Transportation,* 3–4.

98. Nitze, Ball, and Likert (along with Galbraith) confirmed that Galbraith had written the major portions of the chairman's final report; see Nitze to Galbraith, 13 October 1949, box 70, Ball Papers; Ball to Galbraith, 11 October 1949, ibid.; Likert to Galbraith, 1 November 1949, box 70, Harvard University File, Galbraith Papers; Galbraith, *Life in Our Times,* 226–27.

99. D'Olier determined that the chairman's office, in addition to the *Over-all Report,* should produce a shorter version called the *Summary Report* that would be printable in newspapers and more easily read by "the man in the street." Galbraith's Economic Division report was published under the auspices of the chairman's office because of its eclectic nature in evaluating strategic bombing's effects on the German war economy. See MacIsaac, *Strategic Bombing in World War Two,* 144, and MacIsaac's "Editors Introduction to Volume I," *United States Strategic Bombing Survey,* 1: xxxiii.

100. USSBS, *Effects of Strategic Bombing on the German War Economy,* 12–14; USSBS, *Over-all Report (European War),* 61, 64,108; USSBS, *Summary Report (European War),* 12, 16.

101. USSBS, *Over-all Report (European War),* 107–9; USSBS, *Summary Report (European War),* 15–18. MacIsaac, in *Strategic Bombing in World War Two,* did try to establish the "impartiality" of the Survey by emphasizing that the concluding remarks of the European *Summary Report* and *Over-all Report* qualify the phrase "air power was decisive" by modifying it with the adjective "Allied," and not "American" (141–43). MacIsaac fails to take into account the basic facts that the RAF did take up a good part of the strategic bombing campaign against Germany and that the Survey spent a good part of its effort evaluating the results of RAF bombing. How could the two reports have used anything but the adjective "Allied" in light of the basic facts and still claimed at least a modicum of "impartiality"? And AAF leaders probably had no problems with the adjective "Allied" preceding the phrase on air power's "decisiveness." In September 1945, when the European Reports were being published, air leaders like Anderson could happily accept the European Survey's conclusions concerning "Allied" air power and look ahead to the Pacific phase of the Survey where the Survey would only be evaluating "American" air power.

102. Memo from Galbraith, 19 October 1946, box 70, Harvard University File, Galbraith Papers; Galbraith, *Life in Our Times,* 226.

103. Thomas Alexander Hughes, *Over Lord: General Pete Quesada and the Triumph of Tactical Air Power in World War II* (New York: Free Press, 1995), 310; Gian P. Gentile, "A-Bombs, Budgets, and Morality: Using the Strategic Bombing Survey," *Air Power History* 44 (spring 1997): 20–31.

104. David R. Mets, *Master of Airpower: General Carl A. Spaatz* (Novato: Presidio Press, 1988), 308–9.

Notes to Chapter 4

1. "Excerpts from U.S. Strategic Bombing Survey Conference," 24 October 1945, USSBS, file 137.5-2, AFHRA; MacIsaac, *Strategic Bombing in World War Two,* 141–42.

2. Beveridge, Europe, frames 886–90.

3. Perera, *Leaves from My Book of Life,* 114.

4. Memo, Perera to Brigadier General Byron Gates, "Progress Report," 24 September 1943, History of the COA, file 118.01, AFHRA.

5. Crane, *Bombs, Cities and Civilians,* 126–27.

6. Gates to Vannevar Bush, 11 October 1943, History of the COA, file 118.04-2, AFHRA.

7. Committee of Operations Analysts, "Economic Effects of Successful Area Attacks on Six Japanese Cities: Summary of Findings and Conclusions," 1 November 1943, file 118.04-2, AFHRA; "Japanese Small Factories in Relation to Air Bombardment," undated, file 118.04-2, AFHRA.

8. Committee of Operations Analysts, "The Economic Effect of Attacks in Force on German Urban Areas," [January 1944], file 118.04-2, AFHRA (italics mine).

9. W. W. Glass, "Comments upon 'Japan—Incendiary Attack Data,'" 20 March 1944, History of the COA, file 118.04-2; "Japanese Earthquake and Fire of September 1, 1923," undated, file 118.04-2; AFHRA.

10. Memo for [first name unknown] Lindsay, "Attacks on Japanese Strategic Targets," 8 June 1944, file 118.01, AFHRA.

11. Horatio Bond to Perera, 6 March 1944, History of the COA, file 118.04-2, AFHRA.

12. Memo, COA to Arnold, "Revised Report of the Committee of Operations Analysts on Economic Targets in the Far East," 10 October 1944,

History of the COA, file 118.01, AFHRA; "Economic Effects of Successful Area Attacks on Six Japanese Cities[:] Summary of Findings and Conclusions," [4 September 1944], History of the COA, file 118.04-2, AFHRA; memo, Kuter to Secretary of War, "Blockade of Japan by Aerial Mining," 1 November 1944, file 168.7012-24, AFHRA. Perera, *Leaves from My Book of Life,* 113–15.

13. Perera, *Leaves from My Book of Life,* 114.

14. JCS 1965, "Analysis of Strategic Air Targets in the War against Japan: Report by the Joint Staff Planners," August 1944, file 142.6601-1, AFHRA.

15. Joint Intelligence Committee 152/2, "Optimum Use, Timing, and Deployment of V.L.R. Bombers in the War against Japan," 18 January 1944, box 115, Geographic File Japan, Joint Chiefs of Staff, record group 218 (RG 218), NA; Grace Person Hayes, *The History of the Joint Chiefs of Staff in World War II: The War against Japan* (Annapolis: Naval Institute Press, 1982), 702–3; Futrell, Ideas, Concepts, Doctrine, 163.

16. John A. Samford, "JTG Estimate No. 1: Strategic Air Deployment Suitable to the Current Strategy of the Japanese War," 23 December 1944, file 142.6602-1, AFHRA; Joint Target Group, "Selected Target Clusters Suitable as Alternative Targets for Area Bombing," 30 December 1944, file 142.6602-2, AFHRA.

17. Joint Target Group, "Japanese Urban Areas: General Analysis," 26 February 1945, file 142.6606-13, AFHRA.

18. Ibid.; Joint Target Group, "Monthly Target Intelligence Review," February 1945, file 142.6603-1, AFHRA.

19. Hansell, *Strategic Air War against Japan,* 48.

20. Crane, *Bombs, Cities and Civilians,* 125, 129, 131; XXI Bomber Command, "Analysis of Incendiary Operations against Japanese Urban Areas," [March 1945], box 37, Curtis E. LeMay Papers (LeMay Papers), LC. For an interpretation different from Crane's that argues that LeMay did receive a great deal of pressure from Arnold to shift to firebombing, see Schaffer, *Wings of Judgment,* 126; Sherry, R*ise of American Air Power,* 266.

21. Joint Target Group, "Selected Urban Industrial Concentrations," 28 March 1945, file 142.66022-76, AFHRA; Joint Target Group, "General Note," 15 January 1945, file 142.6606-11, AFHRA.

22. Joint Target Group, "Target Information Sheet, Nagasaki," 5 March 1945, file 142.6606-13, AFHRA.

23. Ibid.

24. Joint Chiefs of Staff, "Program for the Aerial Bombardment of Japan," [June 1945], 142.66021-12, AFHRA; memo from Brigadier General John A. Samford to Arnold, "Productive Capacity of Japanese Home Islands and Northeast Asiatic Mainland and Ability of Latter Area to Supply Japanese Mainland Troops," 7 June 1945, box 11, record group 341, Headquarters, United States Air Force (RG 341), NA.

25. Joint Chiefs of Staff, "Presentation of a Recommended Target Program," undated, file 142.6601-12, AFHRA.

26. Phone conference between D'Olier and Alexander, 6 June 1945, box 38, file 337.1, RG 243, NA; Beveridge, Europe, frames 886–90; MacIsaac, *Strategic Bombing in World War Two,* 101.

27. "Proceedings," conference between members of the JTG and USSBS, 9 June 1945 (hereafter referred to as JTG/USSBS Conference), box 2, file 001, RG 243, NA. There is a seventy-five-page typed transcript of the conference; some of the pages are unnumbered.

28. The questions that the conference members used to spur discussion were not attached to the transcript. The questions were attached instead to a memo from the JTG to General Eaker reporting on the outcome of the meeting; see memo, JTG to General Ira C. Eaker, "Preliminary Review of Effectiveness of the CBO in ETO," undated, box 2, file 001, RG 243, NA. The list contained sixteen questions, referred to hereafter as "Conference Questions."

29. JTG/USSBS Conference.

30. JTG/USSBS Conference.

31. Conference Questions; JTG/USSBS Conference, p. 1.

32. JTG/USSBS Conference, p. 1.

33. Conference Questions; JTG/USSBS Conference.

34. JTG/USSBS Conference, pp. 19–20.

35. On the relationship between civilian experts and the military, see Solly Zuckerman, *Scientists and War: The Impact of Science on Military and Civil Affairs* (London: Scientific Book Club, 1966), 3–25.

36. JTG/USSBS Conference, pp. 5–6.

37. Ibid., p. 6.

38. Ibid., pp. 6–7.

39. Ibid., p. 7.

40. Consider, for example, MacIsaac's *Strategic Bombing in World War Two.* MacIsaac argues on page 101: "Repeatedly [Survey members]

stressed their joint conclusion that enemy civilian morale was not a productive target, that while morale can be adversely affected by air attack, there can be no predictable translation of morale effects into behavior effects." Although MacIsaac is correct in his explanations of the Survey's position on the effects of strategic bombing on morale, he is wrong to argue that the JTG, even by July 1945, emphasized the importance of using area raids to attack Japanese morale. The JTG was primarily concerned with destroying Japanese finished war material that could be used to defend against a ground invasion.

41. There were three other meetings held between the Survey and the JTG on 12, 13, and 15 June. Apparently no transcripts exist for these meetings. It is possible, therefore, for morale to have been the center of discussion at the meetings. But this is unlikely. In their memoirs, both Ball and Nitze discuss the series of June meetings and point out that there were disagreements between the Survey and the JTG over the best way to destroy Japanese war-making capacity, but they do not claim there was a discussion—or dispute—on morale. Late in the afternoon on the day of the last meeting, D'Olier, Ball, and O. A. Anderson had a phone conversation with Cabot in London. A good part of the conversation was over providing information to the directors in Washington, D.C., to assist them in their meetings. The information requested was on transportation, coke production, and electric power. If morale was the primary point of disagreement between the Survey and the JTG during the 12, 13, and 15 June meetings, one would have expected the phone conversation on 15 June to address morale, but it did not.

42. JTG/USSBS Conference, p. 25.

43. USSBS, *Summary Report (European War)*, 15–16.

44. JTG/USSBS Conference, p. 14.

45. Ibid., p. 15.

46. JTG, "Japanese Urban Areas General Analysis," [5 July 1945], file 142.66022-79, AFHRA; XXI Bomber Command, "Monthly Activity Report," 1 July 1945, box 16, Curtis E. LeMay Papers.

47. JTG, "Current Air Estimate," 1 August 1945, file 142.6603-2, AFHRA; also see memo from Major General Lauris Norstad to Eaker, with attached report by the Air Staff in response to General Arnold's request "to have a study prepared considering factors essential to intensification of the bombing effort against Japan," 29 June 1945, box 11, RG 341, NA.

48. Memo, Brigadier General A. W. Kissner to Kuter, "Comments of XXI B.C. on JTG Study ES-S12," 22 June 1945, file 142.66021-12, AFHRA.

49. Joint Chiefs of Staff, "Program for the Aerial Bombardment of Japan," undated, file 142.66021-12, AFHRA.

50. Craven and Cate, *Army Air Forces in World War II,* 4: 636.

51. Memo, D'Olier to Secretary of War, "Preliminary Review of Effectiveness of the Combined Bomber Offensive in the European Theater of Operations," 11 June 1945, box 27, file 319.1(A), RG 243, NA; "Report on USSBS and JTG Conferences," undated, box 27, file 319.1, RG 243, NA.

52. Beveridge, Europe, frame 889; MacIsaac, *Strategic Bombing in World War Two,* 99–100.

53. Diary of Henry L. Stimson, 19 June 1945, microfilm copy on file at the United States Military Academy (italics mine).

54. Stimson Diary, 1 June and 6 June 1945; Crane, *Bombs, Cities and Civilians,* 135–36; Gar Alperovitz, *The Decision to Use the Atomic Bomb and the Architecture of an American Myth* (New York: Alfred A. Knopf, 1995), 463–64.

55. Nitze, *From Hiroshima to Glasnost,* 36.

56. Galbraith, *Life in Our Times,* 233.

57. Nitze, *From Hiroshima to Glasnost,* 36–37.

58. Draft of Japanese Targets [July 1945], box 27, file 319.1, RG 243, NA; "Review of Information concerning Japanese Gasoline and Synthetic Nitrogen," 2 July 1945, box 27, file 319.1, RG 243, NA. Around the same time that Nitze was writing the Survey's alternate bombing plan, Major General Claire Chennault, commander of the Fourteenth Air Force in the Pacific, suggested to LeMay "one last scheme for giving pain to the Jap." Chennault, like Nitze, recommended that the AAF bomb Japanese "rice paddies" with some sort of herbicide; see Chennault to LeMay, 9 July 1945, box 11, LeMay Papers.

59. "Japanese Targets," 5 July 1945 (revised in London on 1 August 1945), box 41, file 383.8, RG 243, NA.

60. Ibid.; "Japanese Rail Transport as a Target for Strategic Bombing," undated, box 41, file 383.8, RG 243, NA.

61. Memo, Robert A. Lovett to Secretary of War, 31 July 1945, with attached "Report on USSBS and JTG Conferences," Aircraft File, record group 107, Office of the Secretary of War (RG 107), NA; Craven and Cate, *Army Air Forces in World War II,* 4: 4, 624–25.

62. "Report on USSBS and JTG Conferences."

63. Draft of Japanese Targets [July 1945], box 27, file 319.1, RG 243, NA; "Review of Information concerning Japanese Gasoline and Synthetic Nitrogen," 2 July 1945, box 27, file 319.1, RG 243, NA.

64. Quoted in Robert P. Newman, *Truman and the Hiroshima Cult* (East Lansing: Michigan State University Press, 1995), 37.

65. On the issue of casualties for the planned invasion of Japan, see Barton J. Bernstein, "Reconsidering Truman's Claim of 'Half a Million American Lives' Saved: The Construction and Deconstruction of a Myth," *Journal of Strategic Studies* 22 (1999): 54–95; and Newman, *Truman and the Hiroshima Cult,* 185–97.

66. MacIsaac, *Strategic Bombing in World War Two,* 101

67. Nitze to Alexander, 14 July 1945, box 41, file 383.4, RG 243, NA.

68. "Record of Telephone Conversation, 18 July 1945," box 22, file 311.3, RG 243, NA.

69. Eaker to Arnold, 18 July 1945, box 2, file 001, RG 243, NA.

70. Mets, *Master of Airpower,* 303; also see Albert Wedemeyer to George A. Lincoln, 10 July 1945, box 5, George A. Lincoln Papers (Lincoln Papers), United States Military Academy, Special Collections, West Point, N.Y. (USMA).

71. Message, Arnold to Spaatz, 4 August 1945, box 11, LeMay Papers; Sherry, *Rise of American Air Power,* 308.

72. Crane, *Bombs, Cities and Civilians,* 139; Mets, *Master of Airpower,* 302–3.

73. Minutes of meeting held at the White House, 18 June 1945, CCS 381, RG 218, NA; memo, Handy to Chief of Staff, "Amplifying Comments on Planners' Paper for Presentation to the President," 17 June 1945, box 6, Lincoln Papers; Charles F. Brower IV, "Sophisticated Strategist: General George A. Lincoln and the Defeat of Japan, 1944–1945, *Diplomatic History* 15 (summer 1991): 331–32; Barton J. Bernstein, "The Alarming Japanese Buildup on Southern Kyushu, Growing U.S. Fears, and Counterfactual Analysis: Would the Planned November 1945 Invasion of Southern Kyushu Have Occurred?" *Pacific Historical Review* (1999): 565–75. For an example of a JCS study suggesting that Japan might be defeated by air bombardment and naval blockade alone, see memo Daniel Gallery to members of Joint Logistic Committee, 30 April 1945, with attached Joint Intelligence Committee, "Defeat of Japan by Blockade and

Bombardment," 18 April 1945, box 118, CCS 381, record group 218, Joint Chiefs of Staff (RG218), NA.

74. Crane, *Bombs, Cities and Civilians,* 139.

75. Record of telephone conference, 7 August 1945, box 22, file 311.3, RG 243, NA.

76. D'Olier to Alexander, 14 July 1945, box 41, file 383.8, RG 243, NA.

77. Nitze, *From Hiroshima to Glasnost,* 37.

78. USSBS, *Summary Report* (Pacific War), 26.

Notes to Chapter 5

1. Testimony by Paul Nitze, Senate Special Committee on Atomic Energy, 15 February 1946, 79th Congress, p. 530.

2. Truman to D'Olier, 15 August 1945, box 14, file 300.6, RG 243, NA.

3. It was also possible that President Truman was anticipating interservice rivalry and wanted to head it off by allowing the navy to have a voice in the Pacific Survey's evaluation.

4. Beveridge, Pacific, frames 639–44.

5. Galbraith, *Life in Our Times,* 240–41.

6. Beveridge, Pacific, frame 820.

7. Nitze to his mother, 3 February 1946, box 165, folder 6, Nitze Papers.

8. Nitze, *From Hiroshima to Glasnost,* 40–43; MacIsaac, *Strategic Bombing in World War Two,* 118.

9. Beveridge, Pacific, frames 867–68; also see Urban Areas Division, "Program of Urban Areas Division," undated, USSBS Records, microfilm no. A1154, frames 1647–50, AFHRA.

10. Minutes of staff meeting, 29 October 1945, box 37, file 337., RG 243, NA.

11. Beveridge, Pacific, frames 648–50, 937.

12. Ibid., frame 666.

13. Minutes of staff meeting, 12 November 1945, box 37, file 337., RG 243, NA.

14. Ibid.

15. Beveridge, Pacific, 223. Beveridge confirms that Nitze was the primary author of the *Summary Report.* So too does Nitze himself in his memoirs, *From Hiroshima to Glasnost,* 44.

16. Nitze to his mother, 3 February 1946, box 165, folder 6, Nitze Papers.

17. Nitze to his mother, 28 April 1946, box 165, folder 6, Nitze Papers.

18. Futrell, *Ideas, Concepts, Doctrine,* 47.

19. John F. Shiner, *Foulois and the U.S. Army Air Corps, 1931–1935* (Washington, D.C.: USGPO, 1984), 28.

20. Handwritten notes by General O. A. Anderson, undated, file 168.7006-4, O. A. Anderson Papers, AFHRA. This folder contains about twenty-five pages of handwritten and some typed notes by the general. Some of the notes appear to be early drafts of Anderson's proposed conclusion section for the Pacific Survey *Summary Report* and possibly draft sections of his division's *Air Campaigns of the Pacific War.* The most likely dates for these notes are early 1946 to the middle of 1947.

21. R. A. Ofstie, "Memorandum for Naval and Marine Corps Personnel Associated with the Naval Analysis Division of the U.S. Strategic Bombing Survey (Japan)," 16 September 1945, USSBS Records, microfilm no. 1655, roll 1, frames 1274–77, NA.

22. James H. Doolittle, "Talk to Officers of Island Command," 20 August 1945, box 38, James H. Doolittle Papers (Doolittle Papers), LC.

23. Ibid. (italics mine).

24. For an analysis of the navy's vision of postwar defense, see David Alan Rosenberg, "American Postwar Air Doctrine and Organization: The Navy Experience," in *Air Power and Warfare: The Proceedings of the 8th Military History Symposium United States Air Force Academy, 18–20 October 1978,* ed. Alfred F. Hurley and Robert C. Ehrhart (Washington, D.C.: USGPO, 1979), 245–78; and Jeffrey Barlow, *Revolt of the Admirals: The Fight for Naval Aviation, 1945–1950* (Washington, D.C.: Naval Historical Center, 1994), 105–14.

25. MacIsaac, *Strategic Bombing in World War Two,* 120.

26. Nitze to his mother, 28 April 1946, box 165, folder 6, Nitze Papers.

27. Ralph A. Ofstie, "USSBS History," 9 September 1949, box 8, Special USSBS Folder, Ralph A. Ofstie Papers (Ofstie Papers), Naval Historical Center, Washington, D.C. (NHC).

28. "Very Preliminary Draft," 12 March 1946, USSBS Records, microfilm no. 1655, roll 1, frame 0999, NA; Admiral Arleigh Burke to Admiral Ralph A. Ofstie, 9 September 1949, "An Analysis of How the Conclusions Contained in the Summary Report of the U.S. Strategic Bombing Survey (Japan) Were Modified in Successive Drafts of the Report" (hereafter referred to as, Burke, Survey Analysis), box 8, Special USSBS Folder, Ofstie Papers.

29. [Outline to] "Very Preliminary Draft," 12 March 1946, USSBS Records, microfilm no. 1655, roll 1, frame 1131, NA; Burke, Survey Analysis.

30. USSBS, *Summary Report (Pacific War)*, 28.

31. [Summary Report Draft], [March 1946], USSBS Records, microfilm no. 1655, roll 1, frame 1527, NA; Burke, Survey Analysis. In another March draft of the *Summary Report*, Nitze appears to have bracketed this statement and replaced it with a statement calling for a "third establishment" within a "unified department of common defense." This term, "third establishment," would eventually appear in the 1 July published *Summary Report*; see "Recommendations," [undated], USSBS Records, microfilm no. 1655, roll 1, frames 1526, 1528, NA.

32. M.A.D. [Military Analysis Division], "Suggested Draft on Conclusions," [March–April 1946], USSBS Records, microfilm no. 1655, roll 1, frames 1556, 1562, 1569, NA. O. A. Anderson's name does not appear on this draft, but he almost certainly wrote it. The draft closely resembles a handwritten draft of a Survey report found in the O. A. Anderson Papers. Also, throughout his career, Anderson used recognizable terms such as "echelon" and "dominating" that appear in this Survey draft. The style and tone strongly appear to be Anderson's as well. For other examples of comments by AAF officers that were similar to Anderson's, see Cabell to Nitze, 24 June 1946, USSBS Records, microfilm no. 1655, roll 1, frames 1478–93, NA; Frank Everest to Nitze, undated, ibid.

33. Ofstie to Walter Wilds, 23 September 1949, box 8, special USSBS Folder, Ofstie Papers.

34. Ofstie, "USSBS History."

35. [Summary Report] "Conclusions," [Comments by] "RA Ofstie," [April 1946], USSBS Records, microfilm no. 1655, roll 1, frames 1459, 1462, 1465, 1468, NA (hereafter referred to as Ofstie's Comments).

36. Ofstie to Wilds, 23 September 1949.

37. Ofstie's Comments.

38. USSBS, Chairman's Office, *Summary Report (Pacific War)*, 27.

39. Ibid., 32.

40. O. A. Anderson to Secretary of War and Commanding General, Army Air Forces, "Summary Report, United States Strategic Bombing Survey," 11 July 1946, box 27, file 319.1 (A), RG 243, NA. In this memorandum Anderson was guilty of bad documentation. The Summary Report

wrote the term "air power" as two separate words. Yet Anderson's memorandum, when citing verbatim passages from the Summary Report, combined the two words into one: "Airpower." This was intentional (he used the term "Airpower" in this manner at least twelve times in the memorandum), to give weight to the notion that "airpower" was a new and forward-looking concept that embraced the centrality of an independent air force in the national defense. For a discussion of the uses of the term "air power," see MacIsaac, "Voices from the Central Blue."

41. USSBS, *Summary Report (Pacific War),* 26; and O. A. Anderson to Secretary of War and Commanding General, Army Air Forces, 11 July 1946, "Summary Report, United States Strategic Bombing Survey."

42. USSBS, *Summary Report (Pacific War),* 26, 29–32.

43. Talbott, *Master of the Game,* 37; Nitze, *From Hiroshima to Glasnost,* 42–43.

44. Nitze, *From Hiroshima to Glasnost,* 37.

45. Bernstein, "Compelling Japan's Surrender without the A-bomb, Soviet Entry, or Invasion," 104, 107; Barton J. Bernstein, "The Struggle Over History: Defining the Hiroshima Narrative," in *Judgment at the Smithsonian: The Bombing of Hiroshima and Nagasaki,* ed. Philip Nobile (New York: Marlowe and Company, 1995), 127–256; also see Newman "Ending the War with Japan," 175–78. For an analysis of the debate surrounding America's use of the atomic bombs against Japan, see Barton J. Bernstein, "The Atomic Bomb and American Foreign Policy, 1941–1945: An Historiographical Controversy," *Peace and Change* (spring 1974): 1–16; J. Samuel Walker, "The Decision to Use the Atomic Bomb: A Historiographical Update," *Diplomatic History* 14 (winter 1990): 97–114.

46. Newman, *Truman and the Hiroshima Cult,* 36.

47. The recent work by historian John W. Dower on the American occupation of Japan after World War II is by far the most authoritative account to date: John W. Dower, *Embracing Defeat: Japan in the Wake of World War II* (New York: W. W. Norton & Company, 1999), 65–84, 203–24. Dower explains that the American occupation forces (to include the USSBS) held a number of different, sometimes competing, conceptions of Japanese people and culture. Those conceptions ranged from the conservative mind-set of the "Japan School" of State Department experts who believed that a hierarchical structure of elites was needed to lead the submissive masses in a certain direction, to the more liberal-minded occupiers

who believed that the rank and file of Japan were capable of developing democratic institutions on their own (217–24). These conceptions, to varying degrees, undoubtedly shaped the attitudes of USSBS analysts as they conducted their work in Japan.

48. Ball, *Past Has Another Pattern,* 67.

49. Quoted in Sereny, *Albert Speer,* 554.

50. USSBS, Interrogation of Prince Konoye, 9 November 1945, interrogated aboard USS *Ancon* (hereafter referred to as Konoye Interrogation), box 166, Nitze Papers. The significance of this interrogation document found in the Nitze Papers is that it has the names of the individual interrogators followed by the questions that they asked of Konoye. The interrogation documents found in the USSBS records at the National Archives (and on microfilm) do not indicate who was asking the questions; see Interrogation of Prince Fumimaro Konoye, 9 November 1945, #373, USSBS Records, microfilm no. 1655, roll 1, frame 0433, NA.

51. Konoye Interrogation, 18.

52. Ibid., 20.

53. Ibid., 21–24.

54. USSBS, "Preliminary Draft of Chairman's Report," 10 April 1946, USSBS Records, microfilm no. 1655, roll 1, frame 1365, NA. It appears that it was in April, when the first narrative section on "Japan's Struggle to End the War" appeared in a *Summary Report* draft. This may have been due to a meeting between President Truman and D'Olier and Nitze on 29 March 1946. At that meeting the president could conceivably have requested the Survey to include an explanation for Japan's decision not only to attack the United States at Pearl Harbor in 1941 but also to end the war in 1945. In July 1946 the chairman's office would publish a separate report, *Japan's Struggle to End the War,* that seems to have expanded on the original section in the *Summary Report.*

55. Admiral Arleigh Burke, an assistant to Ofstie, argued in 1949 that the early-surrender counterfactual was moved within the *Summary Report* to strengthen the notion that "the atom bomb was of prime importance in concluding the Pacific war." Burke wrote this analysis of the *Summary Report* for Ofstie in 1949 during the bitter controversy between the air force and the navy over their respective services' roles and missions. A close reading of the *Summary Report* with the counterfactual placed in the two different locations does not support Burke's analysis. Burke was undoubtedly trying to

provide Ofstie with evidence to discredit the air force's reliance on the atomic bomb in 1949. See memorandum, Burke to Ofstie, "An Analysis of How the Conclusions Contained in the *Summary Report* of the U.S. Strategic Bombing Survey (Japan) Were Modified in Successive Drafts of the Report," 9 September 1949, box 8, Special USSBS Folder, Ofstie Papers.

56. Beveridge, Pacific, frames 980–82.

57. Locke's remarks are quoted in Dower, *Embracing Defeat,* 44.

58. For examples of this type of thinking among Pacific Survey analysts, see Shipping and Rail Transportation Division, "Tentative Outline of Work," 18 October 1945, USSBS Records, microfilm no. 1655, roll 1, frames 1622–24, NA; Urban Areas Division, "Statement of Plans and Policies," 20 October 1945, ibid., frames 1629–38; Manpower, Food, and Civilian Supplies [Division], "Tentative Outline of Report on Japanese Civilian Goods Industries," undated, ibid., frames 1672–75.

59. Manhattan Engineer District, "The Atomic Bombings of Hiroshima and Nagasaki," 30 June 1946, box 20, folder 2, Edwin Locke Papers (Locke Papers), Truman Presidential Library, Independence, Mo. (Truman Library). For General Groves's memoir account of the Manhattan Project, see Leslie M. Groves, *Now It Can Be Told: The Story of the Manhattan Project* (New York: Da Capo Press, 1962).

60. Wilds to Edwin Locke, 20 June 1946, box 20, folder 2, Locke Papers. Locke was the aide to the president responsible for reviewing the Survey's Pacific reports. He had recently returned from Japan as a special envoy.

61. Wilds to Locke, 10 July 1946, box 1519, file 651, Official File, Harry S. Truman Papers (Truman Papers), Truman Library.

62. Ibid.

63. See for example the copies of the *Summary Report* and *Japan's Struggle to End the War* in box 20, folder 1, Locke Papers.

64. Memo, Locke to President, 21 June 1946, box 1519, file 651, Official File, Truman Papers.

65. "The President's Appointments, Friday, March 29, 1946," box 83, President's Secretary Files, Truman Papers.

66. D'Olier to President, 10 May 1946, box 1519, file 651, Official File, Truman Papers. For an analysis of Ultra intelligence during World War II, see Edward Drea, *McArthur's Ultra: Codebreaking and the War against Japan, 1942–1945* (Lawrence: University Press of Kansas, 1992).

67. Truman to D'Olier, 15 May 1946, box 1519, file 651, Official File, Truman Papers.

68. Barton J. Bernstein, "Seizing the Contested Terrain of Early Nuclear History: Stimson, Conant, and Their Allies Explain the Decision to Use the Atomic Bomb," *Diplomatic History* 17 (winter 1993): 43, 49.

69. USSBS, Chairman's Office, *Summary Report (Pacific War)*, 26.

70. USSBS, Transportation Division, *The War against Japanese Transportation* (Washington, D.C.: USGPO, May 1947), 3; USSBS, Overall Economic Effects Division, *The Effects of Strategic Bombing on Japan's War Economy* (Washington, D.C.: USGPO, 1946), 32.

71. USSBS, Overall Economic Effects Division, *Effects of Strategic Bombing on Japan's War Economy*, 59. Galbraith, in his memoir, *Life in Our Times* (231), also gives equal importance to strategic bombing and naval blockade in critically reducing Japan's war production.

72. USSBS, Urban Areas Division, *The Effects of Air Attack on Japanese Urban Economy* (Washington, D.C.: USGPO,1947), vi, 24.

73. Ibid., v.

74. Ibid., vi.

75. USSBS, Morale Division, *The Effects of Strategic Bombing on Japanese Morale,* (Washington, D.C: USGPO, 1947), 1–2, 6, 23–25.

76. Ibid., 6; also see USSBS Naval Analysis Division, Interrogation of Admiral Kichisaburo Nomura, #429, 8 November 1945, USSBS Records, microfilm no. M1655, roll 1, NA. Interrogated by Admiral R. A. Ofstie, Paul Baran, and Lt. Cmdr. Spinks.

77. USSBS, *Effects of Strategic Bombing on Japanese Urban Economy*, 48 (italics mine). Interestingly, by 1950 and beyond, most Japanese scholars and pundits had turned the Imperial University scholars' conclusion on its head by accepting Nitze's counterfactual argument that the atomic bombs were unnecessary. This new line of thinking was, according to historian Sadao Asada in an important 1998 article, in line with the belief that the Japanese were "victims" of the atomic bombings. This thinking was supported by the British physicist P. M. S. Blackett, who argued that the atomic bombs were not used to end the war but to intimidate the Soviet Union. See Asada, "The Shock of the Atomic Bomb and Japan's Decision to Surrender—A Reconsideration," *Pacific Historical Review* 67 (November 1998): 477–512; P. M. S. Blackett, *Political and Military Consequences of Atomic Weapons* (London: Turnstile Press, 1948). Blackett's book was published in the United States in 1949 as *Fear, War, and the Bomb*.

78. Beveridge, Pacific, frame 944; Beveridge states that before a Survey report could be released for publication, it had to be approved by Nitze, O.

A. Anderson, Ofstie, and General Grandison Gardner. Beveridge refers to them as the "Big Four."

79. USSBS, Military Analysis Division, *Air Campaigns of the Pacific War* (Washington, D.C.: USGPO, 1947), 68–69.

80. USSBS, Naval Analysis Division, *Campaigns of the Pacific War* (Washington, D.C.: USGPO, 1946), 290.

81. MacIsaac, *Strategic Bombing in World War Two,* 133.

82. Ibid., 122; MacIsaac has the word "fair" set off in quotation marks so one can assume that D'Olier used the word at some point.

83. Nitze to John Sullivan, 27 June 1946, box 8, Special USSBS Folder, Ofstie Papers.

84. [Naval Analysis Division,] "The Air Effort against Japan," 7 February 1946, USSBS Records, microfilm no. 1655, roll 2, frames 68, 71, NA (emphasis in original).

85. Norstad to Nitze, 17 April 1946, box 166, Nitze Papers.

86. Ofstie, "USSBS History," 9 September 1949.

87. Ofstie to Nitze, 10 March 1947, box 44, file 461., RG 243, NA.

88. Quoted in MacIsaac, *Strategic Bombing in World War Two,* 128.

89. Ofstie, "USSBS History," 9 September 1949.

90. Ibid.

91. Nitze to Lieutenant Colonel G. L. McMurrin, 24 December 1946, box 166, Nitze Papers.

92. D'Olier to McMurrin, 3 January 1947, box 166, Nitze Papers.

93. Ofstie to Nitze, 10 March 1947.

94. Memorandum for file by Ofstie, "'Air Campaigns of the Pacific War,' Prepared by the Military Analysis Division, U.S. Strategic Bombing Survey," 17 March 1947, box 8, Special USSBS Folder, Ofstie Papers.

95. Memo, Captain G. W. Anderson to Ofstie, "Air Campaigns of the Pacific War," 4 September 1947, box 8, Special USSBS Folder, Ofstie Papers.

96. James Forrestal to D'Olier, 15 September 1947, box 8, Special USSBS Folder, Ofstie Papers; Forrestal to W. Stuart Symington, [September 1947], ibid.

97. Nitze to Admiral Forrest, Sherman, 16 September 1947, box 8, Special USSBS Folder, Ofstie Papers.

98. D'Olier to Nitze, 19 September 1946, box 165, Nitze Papers; W. Barton Leach to Nitze, 28 August 1946, ibid.

99. D'Olier to Nitze, 25 July 1947, box 165, Nitze Papers.

Notes to Chapter 6

1. Spaatz to Symington, [1947], box 4, Correspondence File, W. Stuart Symington Papers (Symington Papers), Truman Library (emphasis in original). The AAF officially gained its independence and became the United States Air Force by the National Security Act of 1947. Since this chapter addresses the years preceding and following the National Security Act, for simplicity the term "air force" will be used throughout the chapter, even if the AAF is referred to prior to the National Security Act of 1947.

2. General Hugh Drum to Ferdinand Eberstadt, 27 August 1945, box 4, Eberstadt Papers.

3. Barlow, *Revolt of the Admirals,* 30–32.

4. See, for example, memo, Ofstie to OP-05, 10 March 1949, box 8, AEC–Naval Member Military Liaison Folder, Ofstie Papers.

5. Statement by Vice Admiral Dewitt C. Ramsey, Senate Committee on Military Affairs, *Department of Armed Forces, Department of Military Security,* 79th Cong., 1st sess., 14 December 1945, p. 612.

6. Ibid., p. 613.

7. USSBS, *Summary Report (European War),* 107.

8. Statement by General Carl Spaatz, Senate Committee on Military Affairs, *Department of Armed Forces, Department of Military Security,* 15 November 1945, pp. 344–45.

9. Testimony by General James A. Doolittle, Senate Committee on Military Affairs, *Department of Armed Forces, Department of Military Security,* 9 November 1945, pp. 290, 295.

10. Remarks by General James H. Doolittle to the Air Force Association, 23 November 1946, box 38, Doolittle Papers.

11. Barlow, *Revolt of the Admirals,* 35.

12. Symington to President, box 13, Symington Papers.

13. Log entry, 30 January 1948, box 1, personal log, Papers of Arthur W. Radford (Radford Papers), NHC; memo, Eaker to Symington, "Navy Recruiting Program among B-29 Crews," 18 April 1946, box 5, Correspondence File, Symington Papers.

14. Quoted in Barlow, *Revolt of the Admirals,* 42.

15. Testimony by Major General Lauris Norstad, House Committee on Expenditures in the Executive Department, *National Security Act of 1947,*

80th Cong., 1st sess., 2 May 1947, pp. 198–99, 208; USSBS, *Summary Report (Pacific War),* 32.

16. Draft version excerpts from the Pacific Survey *Summary Report* provided by Admiral Ralph Ofstie, House Committee on Expenditures in the Executive Department, *National Security Act of 1947,* 30 June 1947, pp. 632–35.

17. Representative W. J. Dorn, House Committee on Expenditures in the Executive Department, *National Security Act of 1947,* 20 June 1947, pp. 535–42.

18. For two studies that focus on the centrality of the Strategic Air Command (SAC) in the postwar air force, see Walton S. Moody, *Building a Strategic Air Force* (Washington, D.C.: USGPO, 1995); William S. Borgiasz, *The Strategic Air Command: Evolution and Consolidation of Nuclear Forces, 1945–1955* (Westport, Conn.: Praeger, 1996).

19. Memo, F. L. Anderson to [first name unknown] Rawlings, with attached Draft Article, 20 May 1947, box 5, Frederick L. Anderson Papers (F. L. Anderson Papers), Hoover Institution Archives, Stanford, Cal.; "Meeting in Gen. Anderson [*sic*] Office," present at the meeting were Generals Partridge, Rawlings, Ritchie, Harbold, F. L. Anderson, and Colonel Harris Hull, 19 May 1947, ibid.; also see Carl Spaatz, "Strategic Airpower: Fulfillment of a Concept," *Foreign Affairs* 24 (April 1946): 385–96.

20. Spaatz to *Evening Star,* 28 January 1948, box 12, Spaatz Folder, Symington Papers.

21. "Outline of Statement to Be Made by Either Secretary of Air Force, or Chief of Staff of Air Force," undated, box 7, Leach Folder, Symington Papers.

22. Hoyt S. Vandenberg, "Remarks by General Hoyt S. Vendenberg at Civilian Seminar, PLACE: Air University," 12 May 1948, box 89, Hoyt S. Vandenberg Papers (Vandenberg Papers), LC.

23. Moody, *Building a Strategic Air Force,* 54; also see Michael Sherry, *Preparing for the Next War: American Plans for Postwar Defense, 1941–1945* (New Haven: Yale University Press, 1977).

24. Transcript of "General Vandenberg, Vice Chief of Staff, USAF, Before Congressional Air Policy Board on 21 January 1948," pp. 7, 11, box 12, Deputy Chief of Staff, Operations, record group 341, Headquarters, United States Air Force (RG341), NA. This transcript contains General Vandenberg's testimony to the board.

25. Transcript of "Discussion Following Air Force Presentation to the Combat Aviation Subcommittee, Congressional Aviation Policy Board, Room 4e-870, the Pentagon, 21 January 1948," (hereafter referred to as Air Policy Discussions), pp. 1–2, box 12, RG 341, NA.

26. Ibid., p. 1.

27. Ibid., pp. 2–3.

28. Bernard Brodie, "The Weapon," and, "Implications for Military Strategy," in *The Absolute Weapon,* ed. Brodie (New York: Harcourt, Brace and Company, 1946), 52, 70, 76; also see Bernard Brodie, "Critical Summary of War Department Paper," in *The Atomic Bomb and the Armed Services,* ed. Brodie and Eileen Galloway (Washington, D.C.: Library of Congress, 1947), 88.

29. Air Policy Discussions, p. 21.

30. Symington to Sullivan, 28 February 1949, box 9, Symington Papers.

31. Remarks of Rear Admiral Ralph A. Ofstie, "Navy Day," 1948, box 2, Speech File, Ofstie Papers.

32. Quoted in Barlow, *Revolt of the Admirals,* 54.

33. Spaatz to Symington, 7 January 1948, box 12, Symington Papers.

34. Memo for Symington, 19 October 1948, box 4, Symington Papers.

35. "Extracted from Remarks by Rear Admiral Ofstie before the Metropolitan Section of Aviation Writers Association," 30 June 1948, box 9, Symington Papers. Also see D. V. Gallery, "Don't Damn the Carriers: The U.S. Is Building a Giant, Floating Airstrip for Atom Age War," *Science Illustrated,* February 1949, 21.

36. It is interesting to note that while war planners relied so heavily on atomic bombs for a potential war with the Soviets, the total number of atomic bombs in the American arsenal by the end of 1946 was 9; in 1947, 13; in 1948, 50; and in 1949, 133. In *A Hollow Threat: Strategic Air Power and Containment before Korea* (Westport, Conn.: Greenwood Press, 1982), historian Harry Borowski points out that American military and political leaders based policy on America's "industrial potential" (5) that would produce large numbers of atomic bombs if war broke out with the Soviets. Also see David Alan Rosenberg, "The Origins of Overkill: Nuclear Weapons and American Strategy, 1945–1960," *International Security* 7 (spring 1983): 3–71.

37. Joint Staff Planners, "Concept of Operation Pincher, 2 March 1946," pp. 16, 17; Joint War Plans Committee, "Joint Basic Outline War

Plan Short Title: Pincher, 27 April 1946," pp. 6, 7; Joint Staff Planners, "Tentative Over-All Strategic Concept and Estimate of Initial Operations Short Title, Pincher, 18 June 1946," pp. 4, 5, in *America's Plans for War against the Soviet Union, 1945–1950: A Fifteen-Volume Set Reproducing in Facsimile 98 Plans and Studies Created by the Joint Chiefs of Staff* (hereafter referred to as *America's Plans for War*), ed. David Alan Rosenberg and Steven T. Ross (New York: Garland Publishing, 1989), vol. 2. The most thorough account of the war plans written between 1945 and 1950 is Steven T. Ross, *American War Plans, 1945–1950* (New York: Garland Publishing, 1988).

38. Joint Staff Planners, "Staff Studies of Certain Military Problems Deriving from Concept of Operations for Pincher, 13 April 1946," in *America's Plans for War,* 2: 19, 20, 31, 32; Joint Intelligence Committee, "Strategic Vulnerability of the U.S.S.R. to a Limited Air Attack," 3 November 1945, ibid., 2: 9–12; and Joint War Plans Committee, "Military Position of the United States in the Light of Russian Policy, 8 January 1946," ibid., 2: 20.

39. Ross, *American War Plans,* 6, 7; Joint Staff Planners, "Concept of Operations Pincher, 4 March 1946," in *America's Plans for War,* 2: 1.

40. Ross, *American War Plans,* 62.

41. Joint Strategic Planning Group, "Broiler, 11 February 1948," in *America's Plans for War,* 6: 6.

42. Ibid., 6: 175–82.

43. David Alan Rosenberg, "Toward Armageddon: The Foundations of United States Nuclear Strategy, 1945–1961," Ph.D. diss., University of Chicago, 1983, 156–60.

44. Joint Strategic Plans Group, "Crankshaft, 11 May 1948," in *America's Plans for War,* 7: 4.

45. Ibid., 7: 5.

46. Ibid., 7: 145–49.

47. Ibid., 7: 145.

48. Ibid., 7: 146; James Forrestal, "General Notes on the Question Naval Air," 27 October 1948, in Walter Millis, ed., *The Forrestal Diaries* (New York: Viking Press, 1951), 514.

49. Report by the ad hoc committee, "Evaluation of Effect on Soviet War Effort Resulting from the Strategic Air Offensive, 12 May 1949," in *America's Plans for War,* 2: 6–8, 41; also see [George A. Lincoln], "Rela-

tion of Atomic Power to Post-War Strategy," December 1946, box 3, Lincoln Papers; "The Theory of Atomic Bombing," 16 June 1947, box 197, RG 341, NA.

50. General Omar Bradley to Representative Carl Vinson, 18 July 1949, box 42, Vandenberg Papers; Admiral Louis Denfield to Chairman, 18 July 1949; "Agenda of B-36 Investigation," 9 June 1949, ibid; Barlow, *Revolt of the Admirals,* 218.

51. See, for example, memo, Ofstie to OP-05, "Naval Concept of Modern War," 10 March 1949, box 8, Ofstie Papers; "Memorandum by the Chief of Naval Operations," [undated], box 9, Symington Papers; memo for editors of navy publications in Washington area, "Monthly Basic Article," 23 March 1949, box 11, John L. Sullivan Papers (Sullivan Papers), Truman Library.

52. Symington to Forrestal, 1 October 1948, box 8, Symington Papers; summary of "B-36 Changes Europe's Air Plans," from *Aviation Week* (28 March 1949), box 11, Sullivan Papers.

53. Barlow, *Revolt of the Admirals,* 222–24.

54. Testimony by General Curtis L. LeMay, House Committee on Armed Services, *Investigation of the B-36 Bomber Program,* 81st Cong., 1st sess., 11 August 1949, pp. 152–53.

55. Ibid.

56. Testimony by General Hoyt S. Vandenberg, House Committee on Armed Services, *Investigation of the B-36 Bomber Program,* 12 August 1949, pp. 188–89. For examples of the "attempts" that General Vandenberg was referring to, see Blackett, *Political and Military Consequences of Atomic Weapons,* 26–27; Jerome B. Cohen, *Japan's Economy in War and Reconstruction* (Minneapolis: University of Minnesota Press, 1949).

57. W. Sterling Cole, House Committee on Armed Services, *The National Defense Program: Unification and Strategy,* 81st Cong., 1st sess., 19 October 1949, p. 496; David MacIsaac, "What the Bombing Survey Really Says," 63; Perera, *Leaves from My Book of Life,* 183.

58. Barlow, *Revolt of the Admirals,* 245.

59. Testimony by Commander Eugene Tatom, House Committee on Armed Services, *The National Defense Program: Unification and Strategy,* 10–11 October 1949, pp. 172–76.

60. USSBS, *The Effects of Atomic Bombs on Health and Medical Services in Hiroshima and Nagasaki,* 3.

61. USSBS, Chairman's Office, *The Effects of Atomic Bombs on Hiroshima and Nagasaki* (Washington, D.C.: USGPO, 1946), 3; USSBS, *Effects of Atomic Bombs on Health and Medical Services in Hiroshima and Nagasaki,* 15–20. Admiral Radford acknowledged in his memoirs that Tatom's statements caused great controversy, and he doubted the credibility of Tatom's assertions: *From Pearl Harbor to Vietnam: The Memoirs of Arthur W. Radford,* ed. Stephen Jurika, Jr. (Stanford: Hoover Institution Press, 1980), 194.

62. Ramsey Potts to Ball, 25 October 1949, box 43, Ball Papers.

63. [Author unknown], "The Strategic Bombing Myth," [summer 1949], box 6, Symington Papers. "The Strategic Bombing Myth," is also in box 167, Nitze Papers; also see "Analysis of Another Anonymous Attack on the Air Force and the Concept of Aerial Warfare by the Joint Chiefs of Staff," [undated], box 167, Nitze Papers.

64. Statement by Secretary of the Air Force Stuart Symington, House Armed Services Committee, *The National Defense Program: Unification and Strategy,* 18 October 1949, pp. 402–8.

65. Barlow, *Revolt of the Admirals,* 226.

66. Testimony by Admiral Radford, House Armed Services Committee, *The National Defense Program: Unification and Strategy,* 7 October 1949, pp. 40–52, 81, 107. It is also worthwhile to point out the intense dislike and mistrust between Symington and Radford. Symington cried to Forrestal that "no civilian" was going to tell Radford what "to do with respect to the Navy, that he [Radford] believes much of the future of the Navy lies in these attacks against the Air Force . . ." An assistant to Symington (probably Barton Leach) noted that Radford was "a brilliant and an unbalanced man—a dangerous man to have in any position of responsibility." See memo, Symington to Forrestal, 22 November [1948], box 52, Vandenberg Papers; [undated character description of Admiral Arthur Radford], box 7, Symington Papers.

67. Testimony by Brigadier General Vernon E. Megee, House Armed Services Committee, *The National Defense Program: Unification and Strategy,* 11 October 1949, pp. 196–97.

68. Testimony by Admiral W. H. P. Blandy, House Armed Services Committee, *The National Defense Program: Unification and Strategy,* 11 October 1949, p. 203. Fleet Admiral William F. Halsey argued along the same lines in his testimony to the committee, 12 October 1949, pp. 240–41. The evidence that both admirals drew on seems to have come

from a number of different Survey reports. For example the *Areas Studies Division Report,* from the European Survey, argued that area bombing "did not have a decisive effect upon the ability of the German nation to produce war material" (23). Two reports from the Pacific Survey, *The War against Japanese Transportation* (59) and *The Effects of Strategic Bombing on Japan's War Economy* (6), argue that Japan was a defeated nation before the main weight of the strategic bombing campaign was brought to bear against the Japanese home islands. The implicit argument in the latter two reports is that the antishipping campaign may have been the decisive factor in Japan's defeat. The European *Summary Report* (8–12) and the Pacific Survey *Summary Report* (19) argue that the ideal targets for strategic bombing were transportation and electrical power facilities.

69. Statement and testimony by Admiral Ralph A. Ofstie, House Armed Services Committee, *The National Defense Program: Unification and Strategy,* 11 October 1949, pp. 184–87.

70. Ibid., pp. 402–8.

71. Testimony by Admirals Radford, Kinkaid, and Blandy, House Committee on Armed Services, *The National Defense Program: Unification and Strategy,* pp. 56, 273, and 212 respectively.

72. Curiously, when discussing the B-36 and the "Admiral's Revolt" hearings in his memoirs, Admiral Radford makes no mention of the moral concerns over strategic bombing that he and other naval officers proclaimed during the hearings: see Radford, *From Pearl Harbor to Vietnam,* 175–216. Also see a critique of Radford's testimony (probably prepared for Symington by Leach) that notes a contradiction between the admiral's criticism of the air force's approach to strategic bombing on moral grounds and earlier arguments made by navy officers in favor of strategic bombing operations against Russian urban areas; "[Barton Leach], "Outline of Statement," [October 1949], box 7, Symington Papers.

73. Memo, Ofstie to Chairman, General Board, "General Board Serial 315," 8 April 1948, box 3, Ofstie Papers.

74. Ibid.; also see Address of Dr. R. E. Lapp, Acting Head of Nuclear Physics Branch, to Western Safety Conference, "Atomic Warfare and City Defense," 29 June 1949, box 6, Ofstie Papers.

75. For an analysis of the Bikini Tests, see Jonathan M. Weisgall, *Operation Crossroads: The Atomic Tests at Bikini Atoll* (Annapolis: Naval Institute Press, 1994).

76. Joint Chiefs of Staff, "The Final Report of the Joint Chiefs of Staff Evaluation Board for Operation Crossroads, 29 December 1947," in *America's Plans for War,* 9: 110, 111.

77. Joint Chiefs of Staff, "The Final Report of the Joint Chiefs of Staff Evaluation Board for Operation Crossroads, 23 September 1947," in *America's Plans for War,* 9: 10–12.

78. Ibid., 9: 97–101, 110–11, 114–15; memo, Ofstie to Compton, "Final Report of JCS Evaluation Board: General Considerations," 18 June 1947, box 3, Ofstie Papers.

79. Forrestal to President, 6 April 1948, box 201, President's Secretary Files, Truman Papers.

80. USSBS, *Air Campaigns of the Pacific War,* 68–69.

81. [Admiral Ralph Ofstie's marked copy of] *Air Campaigns of the Pacific War,* box 8, Special USSBS Folder, Ofstie Papers.

82. O. A. Anderson interview, 24–25 September 1943, file 168-7006-2, AFHRA; Anderson interview, 6 August 1945, file 168-7006-2, AFHRA.

83. [Lesson Plan by Orvil Anderson], [1947], file 168.7006-36, AFHRA; speech by O. A. Anderson to the American Legion, "The Role of Intelligence in America's Future," [1947], file 168.7006-11, AFHRA.

84. Allen Rankin, "U.S. Could Wipe Out Red A-Nests in Week, Gen. Anderson Asserts," *Montgomery Advertiser,* 1 September 1950. Allan Rankin, the author of the article that contained Anderson's interview, was reporting on another article by syndicated journalist Drew Pearson that was critical of Anderson's Air War College for purportedly teaching preventive war to its students. Pearson's article had appeared in a number of newspapers across the country, including the *Washington Post* on 31 August 1950. At the AFHRA there is a complete folder (168.7006-3) on the relief of General Anderson in September 1950. The folder contains statements made by the general in response to being removed from his post, along with many newspapers articles reporting on the general's relief.

85. The complete title is *Dr. Strangelove; Or, How I Learned to Stop Worrying and Love the Bomb*; for an analysis of *Dr. Strangelove* that places it in historical context, see Charles Maland, "'Dr. Strangelove' (1964): Nightmare Comedy and the Ideology of Liberal Consensus," in *Hollywood as Historian: American Film in Cultural Context,* ed. Peter C. Rallins (Lexington: University of Kentucky Press, 1983), 190–210.

86. Peter B. Young, "The Dismissal of General Anderson," 1959, file

168.7006-3, AFHRA. This short unpublished essay by Young appears to be a college research paper, though it is hard to tell. Young interviewed Anderson in 1959 for the essay. Young acknowledged that Rankin's Anderson interview in 1951 "stands as a remarkable summary of the theoretical work accomplished at the Air War College. All the main themes are there: the nation is at war; the power of the new weapons is such that the first blow will be decisive; therefore, this first (atomic) blow must be struck by the United States." Also see a 1949 essay by General Orvil A. Anderson, "Air Warfare and Morality," *Air University Quarterly Review* (winter 1949): 5–14. Anderson argues that atomic warfare against the Soviet Union would be moral because American bombers would not be attacking civilians directly, but rather the Soviet industrial "power" base (7). Bernard Brodie's *Strategy in the Missile Age* (227–32), has an excellent and still relevant passage on preventive war theory. Also see Marc Trachtenberg, "A 'Wasting Asset': American Strategy and the Shifting Nuclear Balance, 1949–1954," in Trachtenberg, *History and Strategy* (Princeton: Princeton University Press, 1992), 105.

87. USSBS, *Summary Report (Pacific War),* 30.

88. Bernard Brodie to O. A. Anderson, 2 September 1950, file 168.7006-3, AFHRA.

89. Barry H. Steiner, B*ernard Brodie and the Foundations of American Nuclear Strategy* (Lawrence: University Press of Kansas, 1991), 47.

90. Bernard Brodie, "Changing Capabilities and War Objectives," 17 April 1952, lecture to the Air War College, box 12; Bernard Brodie Papers (Brodie Papers), Special Collections, University of California, Los Angeles (UCLA); Bernard Brodie, "Possible U.S. Military Strategies," 11 October 1954 (RAND Corporation), box 13, ibid.; Bernard Brodie, "The Atomic Bomb and American Security," 1 November 1945, unpublished essay for Yale University, box 11; ibid.

91. Brodie, *Absolute Weapon,* 23–27, 71, 83.

92. Brodie to Turner, 28 January 1953, box 1, Brodie Papers. Also see Fred Kaplan, *The Wizards of Armageddon* (Stanford: Stanford University Press, 1983), 38.

93. Steiner, *Bernard Brodie and the Foundations of American Nuclear Strategy,* 94–98. For a more current use of the Survey's findings on electrical systems as targets for strategic bombing, see Thomas E. Griffith, Jr., "Strategic Attack of Electrical Systems" (Maxwell Air Force Base, Ala.: Air University Press, 1994).

94. Brodie to Tanham, 31 July 1957, "Comments on Professor Blackett's Letter," box 1, Brodie Papers.

95. Blackett, *Political and Military Consequences of Atomic Weapons,* 26–27.

96. USSBS, *Effects of Strategic Bombing on the German War Economy,* 13–14.

97. Blackett, *Political and Military Consequences of Atomic Weapons,* 26–27.

98. Ibid., 24, 55–56.

99. Hanson W. Baldwin, *The Great Mistakes of the War* (New York: Harper and Brothers, 1949), 101, 105–7.

100. Henry L. Stimson, "The Decision to Use the Bomb," *Harper's Magazine* (February 1947), reprinted in Bernstein, *Atomic Bomb,* 1–17 (italics mine). For another essay published around the same time as Stimson's that also uses the Survey to support an argument favoring the president's decision to use the bomb against Japan, see Karl T. Compton, "If the Atomic Bomb Had Not Been Used," *Atlantic Monthly,* December 1946, 54–56.

101. Bernstein, "Seizing the Contested Terrain of Early Nuclear History," 43, 49.

102. Fred Eastman to D'Olier, 13 March 1947, box 165, Nitze Papers; D'Olier to Eastman, 17 March 1947, ibid.; McMurrin to Nitze, 11 July 1947, ibid.

103. "Text of Address of Mr. D'Olier," 22 December 1944, box 39, file 350.001, RG 243, NA.

104. Alperovitz, *Atomic Diplomacy,* 286–87.

105. David Halberstam, *The Best and the Brightest* (New York: Random House, 1969, 1972), 161–72; I. F. Stone, "Nixon's Blitzkrieg," *New York Review of Books,* 25 January 1973, 13.

106. Editorial, *Nation,* 19 April 1999, 13.

Notes to Chapter 7

1. Few book-length studies have been written on the air force's experience in the Korean War. The best available accounts are Conrad C. Crane, *American Air Power Strategy in Korea, 1950–1953* (Lawrence: University Press of Kansas, 2000); Robert Frank Futrell, *The United States Air Force*

in Korea, 1950–1953 (Washington, D.C.: Office of Air Force History, 1983); and Futrell, *Ideas, Concepts, Doctrine.*

2. See for example Captain Robert H. McDonnell, "Clausewitz and Strategic Bombing," *Air University Quarterly Review* 6 (spring 1953): 51–53; Colonel John R. Maney, "The Support of Strategy," *Air University Quarterly Review* 6 (fall 1953): 46–47; Harry S. Truman, *Memoirs,* vol. 2: *1946–1952, Years of Trial and Hope* (New York: Smithmark, 1955), 341–42, 346–47.

3. Phillip S. Meilinger, "Alexander S. De Seversky and American Air Power," in Meilinger, *Paths of Heaven,* 269; Crane, *American Air Power Strategy in Korea,* 44–45.

4. Crane, *American Airpower Strategy in Korea,* 60; also see "Evaluation of the Effectiveness of the USAF in Korea (Barcus & Stearns Reports), 1 August 1951, file 168.041-1, pp. 1–5, AFHRA.

5. Curtis E. LeMay with MacKinlay Kantor, *Mission with LeMay* (Garden City, NY: Doubleday Books, 1965), 565.

6. Mark Clodfelter, *The Limits of Air Power: The American Bombing of North Vietnam* (New York: Free Press, 1989), x.

7. Dennis M. Drew, "Air Theory, Air Force, and Low Intensity Conflict: A Short Journey to Confusion," in Meilinger, *Paths of Heaven,* 334.

8. Quoted in Coldfelter, *Limits of Air Power*, ix.

9. Earl H. Tilford, Jr., *Setup: What the Air Force Did in Vietnam and Why* (Maxwell AFB, Ala.: Air University Press, 1991), 288–92.

10. Clodfelter, *Limits of Air Power*, xii.

11. Tilford, *Setup*, 294.

12. Colonel John A. Warden to AF/XO, 11 January 1991, file 0874792, miscellaneous (misc.) 56, volume 6, Gulf War Air Power Survey Collection (GWAPS Collection), AFHRA; General John M. Loh to CSAF, "Desert Shield/Storm Post-Game Analyses," 3 February 1991, ibid.; [Wayne Thompson to Eliot Cohen], 2 October 1992, ibid.

13. For some of Warden's pre– and post–Gulf War writings, see John A. Warden III, *The Air Campaign: Planning for Combat* (Washington: Brassey's, 1988); "The Enemy as System," *Airpower Journal* 9 (spring 1995): 40–55.

14. Richard T. Reynolds, *Heart of the Storm: The Genesis of the Air Campaign against Iraq* (Maxwell AFB, Ala.: Air University Press, 1995), 72–75; Michael R. Gordon and Bernard E. Trainor, *The Generals' War:*

The Inside Story of the Conflict in the Gulf (Boston: Little, Brown and Company, 1995), 82–84, 100–101; Eliot Cohen et al., *Gulf War Air Power Survey,* vol. 1: *Planning* (Washington, D.C.: USGPO, 1993), 108–9 (the published volumes of the Gulf War Air Power Survey are hereafter referred to as GWAPS followed by the respective volume number and title).

15. On the issue of the decisiveness of air power in the Gulf War, see James A. Winfield, Preston Niblack, and Dana J. Johnson, *A League of Airmen: U.S. Air Power in the Gulf War* (Santa Monica: Rand, 1994), 275–88; and Edward C. Mann III, *Thunder and Lightning: Desert Storm and the Airpower Debates* (Maxwell AFB, Ala.: Air University Press, 1995).

16. An example by a serving air officer is David A. Deptula, "Parallel Warfare: What Is It? Where Did It Come From?" in *The Eagle in the Desert: Looking Back on U.S. Involvement in the Persian Gulf War,* ed. William Head and Earl H. Tilford, Jr. (Westport, Conn.: Praeger, 1996), 127–56.

17. Donald B. Rice to Cohen, "Terms of Reference for the Gulf War Air Power Survey," 19 August 1991, file 0874745, misc. 37, GWAPS Collection, AFHRA; Cohen to Rice, 26 July 1991, file 0874792, misc. 56, v. 6, ibid.; Cohen to Rice, "GWAPS report #1," 16 August 1991, file 0874765, misc. 47.

18. This was Barry Watts's recollection on the matter. Considering the support that Rice would give to Cohen to keep the GWAPS impartial, Rice's "promise" does not seem unreasonable; e-mail comments from Watts to author, 21 December 1999.

19. Eliot Cohen in fact drafted the GWAPS "Terms of Reference" for Rice's memorandum: personal e-mail, Cohen to author, 20 December 1999; and Emery Kiraly to author, 10 January 2000.

20. GWAPS, *Summary Report,* ix. Each GWAPS volume contains the same forward.

21. At the beginning of each GWAPS volume there is a list of the respective task forces, primary authors, and contributors to each task force Volume, and a list of the review committee members.

22. Colonel L. E. Trapp, Jr., to Director, Joint Staff, "Gulf War Airpower Survey (GWAPS) Team Access to Joint Staff," 10 January 1992, file 0874792, misc. 56, v. 6., GWAPS Collection, AFHRA.

23. It should be noted that the Office of Air Force History has yet to publish a comprehensive history of the USAF's operations in the Vietnam War.

24. Loh to CSAF, "Desert Shield/Storm Post-Game Analyses," 3 February 1991, file 0874792, misc. 56, v. 6; GWAPS Collection, AFHRA; Sydell

Gold to Assistant Vice Chief of Staff, "Desert Shield/Desert Storm Lessons Learned," 14 June 1991, ibid.; Allan W. Howey, memorandum for record, 28 May 1991, ibid.

25. "Notes from SECAF Meeting," taken by LTC Kearney, 24 July 1991, file 0874792, misc. 56, v. 6, GWAPS Collection, AFHRA.

26. Thompson to Cohen, 2 October 1992, file 0874792, misc. 56, v. 6, GWAPS Collection, AFHRA; David A. Tretler to AF/XOX, "Historical Coverage of the Gulf War," 22 July 1991, ibid.; Eliot Cohen, "Draft Talking Points for Secretary Rice," 17 March 1992, file 0874758, misc. 42, v. 1, GWAPS Collection, AFHRA. Also see Richard H. Kohn, "History as Institutional Memory: The Experience of the United States Air Force," in *Military History and the Military Profession,* ed. David Charters, Marc Milliner, Brent J. Wilson (Westport, Conn.: Praeger, 1992), 159.

27. Spaatz to Arnold, 13 June 1944, box 225, Spaatz Papers; Kuter to Spaatz, June 1944, ibid.

28. Eliot Cohen, "GWSS Guiding Concepts," 7 August 1991, file 0874792, misc. 56, v. 6, GWAPS Collection, AFHRA.

29. Cohen to Rice, "GWAPS report # 19," 24 April 1992, file 0874765, misc. 47, v. 2, GWAPS Collection, AFHRA; e-mail, Cohen to GWAPS Staff (GWAPS e-mail messages were printed on paper and placed in folders in the collection), "Style Sheet, USSBS, leaks," 20 April 1992, file 0874789, misc. 56, v. 3, ibid.; memo by LTC Dale Hill, "SecAF Study of the Gulf War," 1 August 1991, file 0874792, misc. 56, v. 6, ibid.; personal e-mail from Colonel Emery M. Kiraly to author, 18 October 1999.

30. See for example GWAPS, *Summary Report*, ix–x.

31. "Eliot A. Cohen, Current as of 19 February 1992," file 0874754, misc. 41, GWAPS Collection, AFHRA. Cohen had published widely in the defense studies field. His most notable works prior to joining the GWAPS were *Military Misfortunes: The Anatomy of Failure in War* (co-authored with John Gooch) (New York: Free Press, 1990); and *Citizen Soldiers: The Dilemmas of Military Service* (Ithaca: Cornell University Press, 1985). Cohen also co-authored with GWAPS task force leader Thomas A. Keaney *Revolution in Warfare: Air Power in the Persian Gulf War* (Annapolis: Naval Institute Press, 1995). This book was originally published as the GWAPS *Summary Report* but with some added material.

32. Galbraith, *Life in Our Times*, 196.

33. Kiraly to author, 18 October 1999. A review of selected folders in

the GWAPS Collection reveals the extent of the intellectual and managerial involvement of Cohen. See for example the folders in GWAPS Collection files 0874788, 0874789, misc. 56, v. 3, AFHRA. Comparing the minutes of meetings of the GWAPS and USSBS can also shed light on the differences between Cohen and D'Olier. While at the USSBS meetings (especially the one held between USSBS members and the AAF staff in June 1945), D'Olier rarely contributed anything of substance during discussions. Cohen, conversely, during the briefings to the review committee, was closely involved in the dialogue.

34. E-mail comments from Watts to author, 21 December 1999.

35. "[Eliot Cohen] Comments," 27 May 1992, file 0874758, misc. 42, v. 1, GWAPS Collection, AFHRA; e-mail, Kiraly to task force leaders, "Expanding DS/DS knowledge base," 1 April 1992, file 0874791, misc. 56, v. 5, ibid.; "Minutes GWAPS Internal Review Session, Operations," 7 August 1992" (minutes were compiled by Wayne Thompson), file 0874788, misc. 56, v. 2, ibid.; Cohen to Daniel Kuehl, Thomas Hone, and Kiraly, "Interim Report," 18 March 1992, file 0874789, misc. 56, v. 3, ibid.

36. GWAPS Review Session, "Minutes," 7 August 1992, file 0874788, misc. 56, v. 2, GWAPS Collection, AFHRA.

37. E-mail, Cohen to all GWAPS staff, "Access to Our Reports," 27 October 1992, file 0874789, misc. 56, v. 3, GWAPS Collection, AFHRA; e-mail, Cohen to all GWAPS staff, "The Press," 17 November 1992, ibid.; letter (fax copy), Hallion to Administrative Assistant/Secretary of the Air Force (Bill Richardson), "GWAPS," 30 April 1993. Copy of letter provided to author by Mark Mandeles.

38. "Draft Review Committee Notes," 24 March 1992, file 0874758, misc. 42, v. 1, GWAPS Collection, AFHRA.

39. Biographical descriptions of GWAPS members are scattered throughout the GWAPS Collection. See, for example, files 0874754, misc. 41; 0874793, misc. 56, v. 7; and 0874755, misc. 41, AFHRA; e-mail from Watts to author, 20 December 1999.

40. Harry G. Summers, *On Strategy: A Critical Analysis of the Vietnam War* (Novato, Calif.: Presidio Press, 1982). In a recent essay historian Russell Weigley argues that Summers's book has caused confusion and mythmaking within the military as to why the United States lost the Vietnam War; see Weigley, "The Soldier, the Statesman and the Military Historian," *Journal of Military History* 63 (October 1999): 807–22.

41. It should be pointed out that John Warden's emphasis on operational art does not necessarily mean that he embraced all of Clausewitz's theory of war. Indeed, one could argue that in *The Air Campaign* and other writings by Warden he was actually more "Jominian" in the sense that he believed that modern technology and the application of air power in war could actually do away with the Clausewitzian notion of friction. Clearly, the overall importance of Warden's *Air Campaign* was to force American airmen in the late 1980s to conceptualize an air offensive in an operational, nonnuclear way; the air force had for the most part jettisoned that way of thinking through the many years of SAC dominance during the cold war; see Barry D. Watts, *Clausewitzian Friction and Future War* (Washington, D.C.: National Defense University, 1996); personal e-mail from Watts to author, 21 December 1999.

42. Joe Strange, *Centers of Gravity and Critical Vulnerabilities: Building on the Clausewitzian Foundation So That We Can All Speak the Same Language* (Marine Corps War College, 1996), 5.

43. Clodfelter, "The Limits of Air Power," p. xi. Barry D. Watts, *Clausewitzian Friction and Future War.*

44. See for example GWAPS, *Summary Report* ,ix.

45. John J. Mearsheimer, *Liddell Hart and the Weight of History* (Ithaca: Cornell University Press, 1988), 14.

46. MacIsaac, *Strategic Bombing in World War Two*, 161.

47. Eliot Cohen, memorandum for Secretary of the Air Force, "Presentation Strategy for GWAPS," 24 August 1992, file 074758, misc. 42, v. 1, GWAPS Collection, AFHRA.

48. The review committee members were Paul H. Nitze (Chairman) of the Paul H. Nitze School of Advanced International Studies at the Johns Hopkins University; General Michael J. Dugan (retired), former Air Force Chief of Staff; Admiral Huntington Hardisty (retired); Dr. Richard Kohn of the University of North Carolina at Chapel Hill; Dr. Bernard Lewis of Princeton University; Andrew Marshall of the Office of the Secretary of Defense; Phillip Merrill, former Assistant Secretary General for Defense Support, NATO; Dr. Henry Rowen of Stanford University; Honorable Ike Skelton, U.S. House of Representatives; General Maxwell Thurman (retired); Major General Jasper A. Welch (retired); and Dr. James Q. Wilson of the University of California at Los Angeles.

49. Frank Kistler to Cohen, "Review Board," 16 October 1991, file

0874759, misc. 42, v. 2, GWAPS Collection, AFHRA; memo to Secretary of the Air Force, "Survey of the Air Force Participation in the Gulf War," 24 July 1991, file 0874792, misc. 56, v. 6, ibid.; Cohen to GWAPS review committee, "Progress Report," 20 August 1992, file 0874791, misc. 56, v. 5, ibid.; Eliot Cohen, "Draft Talking Points for Secretary Rice," 17 March 1992, file 0874758, misc. 42, v. 1, ibid.

50. "Draft Review Committee Notes," 24 March 1992, file 9874758, misc. 42, v. 1, GWAPS Collection, AFHRA.

51. Cohen to Secretary of the Air Force, "GWAPS report # 17," 27 March 1992 (Rice's margin comments are on this memo), file 0874765, misc. 47, v. 2, GWAPS Collection, AFHRA; memo for record, "Briefing for Secretary of the Air Force and GWAPS Review Committee," 14 January 1993, file 0874787, misc. 56, v. 1, ibid.

52. "Briefing for Secretary of the Air Force and GWAPS Review Committee," 14 January 1993, file 0874787, misc. 56, v. 5, GWAPS Collection, AFHRA; e-mail, Cohen to senior staff and secretaries, "Review Committee post-mortem," 31 March 1992, file 0874791, ibid.

53. Memo for record, "Visit to Maxwell AFB," 27–28 August 1991, file 0874788, misc. 56, v. 2, GWAPS Collection, AFHRA.

54. GWAPS, *Effects and Effectiveness,* vol. 2, part 2 (Washington, D.C.: USGPO, 1993), 16–21.

55. "Minutes of Review Session for Task Force VI, Effects and Effectiveness," 9 June 1992 (notes taken by LTC Daniel Kuehl), file 0874788, misc. 56, v. 2, GWAPS Collection, AFHRA; Watts and Keaney to Cohen, "Pedantic Thunder: Task Force VI Research Agenda and Production Plan," [undated], file 0874790, misc. 56, v. 4, ibid.

56. GWAPS, *Effects and Effectiveness,* vol. 2, part 2, 27–31, 57–63.

57. Ibid., 30, 57–63.

58. USSBS, *Effects of Strategic Bombing on the German War Economy,* 13–14.

59. Overall Effects Division, "Memorandum on the Investigation of the Effects of Strategic Bombing," undated, box 18, file 300.6, RG 243, NA; Overall Economic Effects Division, "Brief Notes on the Conference with Overall Economic Effects Division at Bad Nauheim," 3 July 1945, box 14, file 300.6, RG 243, NA.

60. Personal e-mail from Watts to author, 22 December 1999.

61. See for example Galbraith, "Germany Was Badly Run"; John Ken-

neth Galbraith, "Albert Speer Was the Man to See," *New York Review of Books*, 10 January 1971); John Kenneth Galbraith, "Peace through Patience, Not Air Power," *New York Times*, 25 April 1999.

62. Galbraith, *Life in Our Times*, 226–27.

63. Except, ironically, Orvil Anderson's *Air Campaigns of the Pacific War*, which bombastically proclaimed the dominance of air power in World War II and beyond.

64. See, for example, MacIsaac, "What the Bombing Survey Really Says."

65. Memo from Galbraith, 19 October 1949, box 70, Harvard University File, Galbraith Papers; Potts to Galbraith, 22 March 1950, ibid.

66. GWAPS, *Effects and Effectiveness*, vol. 2, part 2, 262.

67. Ibid., 354–58, 370.

68. Richard P. Hallion, *Storm over Iraq: Air Power in the Gulf War* (Washington, D.C.: Smithsonian Institution Press, 1992), 253. It should be noted that the first three chapters and five appendices of *Storm over Iraq* are a masterful account of the history of technology and air power.

69. Letter (fax copy), Hallion to Administrative Assistant/Secretary of the Air Force (Bill Richardson), "GWAPS," 30 April 1993.

70. Letter (fax copy), Hallion to Administrative Assistant/Secretary of the Air Force (Bill Richardson), "GWAPS," 30 April 1993; personal e-mail, Mark D. Mandeles to author, 11 January 2000; Cohen to author, 20 December 1999; also see Mark D. Mandeles, Thomas C. Hone, and Sanford S. Terry, *Managing "Command and Control" in the Persian Gulf War* (Westport, Conn.: Praeger, 1996), 8.

71. Hallion, *Storm over Iraq*, 265–68 (italics mine).

72. E-mail, Cohen to senior staff and secretaries, 20 April 1992, file 0874789, misc. 56, v. 3, GWAPS Collection, AFHRA; e-mail, Cohen to all GWAPS staff, 21 October 1992, ibid.; Kohn to Cohen, 13 December [1992], file 0874791, misc. 56, v. 5, GWAPS Collection, AFHRA.

73. Eliot Cohen, memorandum for GWAPS review committee, "Progress Report," 20 August 1992, file 0874791, misc. 56, v. 5, GWAPS Collection, AFHRA; personal e-mail, Cohen to author, 18 October 1999.

74. GWAPS, *Command and Control*, vol. 1, part 2 (Washington, D.C.: USGPO, 1993), 337; also see Mandeles, Hone, and Terry, *Managing "Command and Control" in the Persian Gulf War*. This book by the three authors drew heavily on their GWAPS volume *Command and Control*.

75. GWAPS, *Operations*, vol. 2, part 1 (Washington, D.C.: USGPO,

1993), 326, 342; also see Williamson Murray's *Air War in the Persian Gulf* (Baltimore: Nautical and Aviation Publishing Company of America, 1995); this was a commercially published version of Murray's GWAPS volume.

76. For three reviews of the GWAPS, see *Air Power History* 41 (fall 1994): 51–54; *Armed Forces Journal* (April 1994): 51; *Naval War College Review* 48 (summer 1995): 115–16.

Notes to the Afterword

1. For a short monograph that argues that continuity exists between American air power theorists of the 1930s and 1990s, see Scott D. West, "Warden and the Air Corps Tactical School: Déjà Vu?" (Maxwell Air Force Base, Ala.: Air University Press, 1999).

2. Testimony of Lieutenant General Michael C. Short to the Senate Armed Services Committee, "Lessons Learned from Military Operations and Relief Efforts in Kosovo," 21 October 1999 (CIS, Congressional Universe, accessed 5 January 2000) available from http://www.lexis-nexis-com/cis.

3. Charles D. Link, "Why Airpower?" and "Airpower?—Why Not?" *Deadalus Flyer* (Summer 1999): 8–9. For a scholarly analysis of the air war over Kosovo, see Daniel A. Byman and Matthew C. Waxman, "Kosovo and the Great Air Power Debate," *International Security* 4 (Spring 2000): 5–38.

BIBLIOGRAPHY

✦ ✦ ✦ ✦ ✦ ✦ ✦ ✦ ✦ ✦ ✦

Manuscript Sources

Air Force Historical Research Agency, United States Air Force, Air University, Maxwell Air Force Base, Ala.

Orvil A. Anderson Papers
Muir S. Fairchild Papers
Gulf War Air Power Survey Collection
History of the Committee of Operations Analysts
Laurence S. Kuter Papers
Miscellaneous Records of the United States Strategic Bombing Survey
Records of the Joint Target Group

Hoover Institution on War, Revolution and Peace, Stanford University, Stanford, Cal.

Frederick L. Anderson Papers

John F. Kennedy Library, Boston, Mass.

John Kenneth Galbraith Papers

Manuscript Division, Library of Congress, Washington, D.C.

James H. Doolittle Papers
Ira C. Eaker Papers
Curtis E. LeMay Papers
Paul H. Nitze Papers
Carl A. Spaatz Papers
Hoyt S. Vandenberg Papers

Seely G. Mudd Library, Princeton University, Princeton, N.J.

George W. Ball Papers
Edward Mead Earle Papers

Ferdinand Eberstadt Papers
Adlai E. Stevenson Papers

Naval Historical Center, Washington, D.C.
Ralph A. Ofstie Papers
Arthur W. Radford Papers
National Archives and Records Administration, Washington, D.C.
Record Group 107: Office of the Secretary of War
Record Group 218: Joint Chiefs of Staff
Record Group 243: United States Strategic Bombing Survey
Record Group 340: Office of the Secretary of the Air Force
Record Group 341: Headquarters, United States Air Force Naval Historical Center, Washington, D.C.

Franklin Delano Roosevelt Library, Hyde Park, N.Y.
Map Room Files

Harry S. Truman Library, Independence, Mo.
Dan A. Kimball Papers
Edwin Locke Papers
Francis P. Matthews Papers
W. Stuart Symington Papers
John L. Sullivan Papers
Official File, Truman Papers
President's Secretary Files, Truman Papers

United States Military Academy, Special Collections, West Point, N.Y.
George A. Lincoln Papers

University of California, Los Angeles, Special Collections, Los Angeles, Cal.
Bernard Brodie Papers

Manuscript Collections on Microfilm
Diary of Henry L. Stimson
Miscellaneous Records of the United States Strategic Bombing Survey (Air Force Historical Research Agency)
Records of the United States Strategic Bombing Survey (National Archives)

Published Manuscript Collections

America's Plans for War against the Soviet Union, 1945–1950. A 15-volume set reproducing in facsimile 98 plans and studies created by the Joint Chiefs of Staff, ed. Steven T. Ross and David Alan Rosenberg (New York: Garland, 1989).

Beveridge, James. "History of the United States Strategic Bombing Survey." Boxes 24–26, RG 243, National Archives, and available on microfilm from the National Archives and the Air Force Historical Research Agency.

Congressional Hearings

U.S. Congress. Senate. Committee on Military Affairs. *Department of Armed Forces, Department of Military Security.* 79th Cong., 1st sess., October–December 1945.

———. Special Committee on Atomic Energy. *Atomic Energy.* 79th Cong., 2d sess., February 1946.

U.S. Congress. House. Committee on Expenditures in the Executive Department. *National Security Act of 1947.* 80th Cong., 1st sess., May 1947.

———. Committee on Armed Services. *Investigation of the B-36 Bomber Program: Hearings.* 81st Cong., 1st sess., August and October 1949.

———. Committee on Armed Services. *The National Defense Program—Unification and Strategy: Hearings.* 81st Cong., 1st sess., October 1949.

Published Reports of the United States Strategic Bombing Survey

United States Strategic Bombing Survey, Aircraft Division. *Aircraft Division Industry Report.* Washington, D.C.: USGPO, 1945.

———, Area Studies Division. *Area Studies Division Report.* Washington, D.C.: USGPO, 1945.

———, Area Studies Division. *A Detailed Study of the Effects of Area Bombing on Hamburg, Germany.* Washington, D.C.: USGPO, 1946.

———, Chairman's Office. *Over-all Report (European War).* Washington, D.C.: USGPO, 1945.

United States Strategic Bombing Survey, Aircraft Division. Chairman's Office. *Summary Report (European War)*. Washington, D.C.: USGPO, 1945.

———, Equipment Division. *The German Anti-Friction Bearings Industry*. Washington, D.C.: USGPO, 1945.

———, Morale Division. *The Effects of Strategic Bombing on German Morale*. Washington D.C.: USGPO, 1947.

———, Over-All Economic Effects Division. *The Effects of Strategic Bombing on the German War Economy*. Washington, D.C.: USGPO, 1945.

———, Transportation Division. *The Effects of Strategic Bombing on German Transportation*. Washington, D.C.: USGPO, 1945.

———, Utilities Division. *German Electric Utilities Industry Report*. Washington, D.C.: USGPO, 1945.

———, Chairman's Office. *The Effects of Atomic Bombs on Hiroshima and Nagasaki*. Washington, D.C.: USGPO, 1946.

———, Chairman's Office. *Japan's Struggle to End the War*. Washington, D.C.: USGPO, 1946.

———, Chairman's Office. *Summary Report (Pacific War)*. Washington, D.C.: USGPO, 1946.

———, Military Analysis Division. *Air Campaigns of the Pacific War*. Washington, D.C.: USGPO, 1947.

———, Morale Division. *The Effects of Strategic Bombing on Japanese Morale*. Washington, D.C.: USGPO, 1947.

———, Naval Analysis Division. *Campaigns of the Pacific War*. Washington, D.C.: USGPO, 1946.

———, Medical Division. "The Effects of Atomic Bombs on Health and Medical Services in Hiroshima and Nagasaki." Washington, D.C.: USGPO, 1947.

———, Overall Economic Effects Division. *The Effects of Strategic Bombing on Japan's War Economy*. Washington, D.C.: USGPO, 1946.

———, Transportation Division. *The War against Japanese Transportation*. Washington, D.C.: USGPO, 1947.

———, Urban Areas Division. *The Effects of Air Attack on Japanese Urban Economy*. Washington, D.C.: USGPO, 1947.

———. *Index to Records of the United States Strategic Bombing Survey*. Washington, D.C.: USGPO, 1947.

Published Volumes of the Gulf War Air Power Survey

Cocharan, Alexander S., Lawrence M. Greenberg, Wayne W. Thompson, Michael J. Eisenstadt, and Kurt R. Guthe (principal authors). *Planning the Air Campaign.* Vol. 1, Part 1. Washington, D.C.: USGPO, 1993.

Cohen, Eliot A., and Thomas A. Keaney (principal authors). *Summary Report.* Washington, D.C.: USGPO, 1993.

Hone, Thomas C., Sanford S. Terry, and Mark D. Mandeles (principal authors). *Command and Control.* Volume 1, Part 2. Washington, D.C.: USGPO, 1993.

Keaney, Thomas A., and Barry D. Watts (principal authors). *Effects and Effectiveness.* Vol. 2, Part 2. Washington, D.C.: USGPO, 1993.

Murray, Williamson (principal author). *Operations.* Vol. 2, Part 1. Washington, D.C.: USGPO, 1993.

Doctoral Dissertations

Crane, Conrad C. "The Evolution of American Strategic Bombing of Urban Areas." Ph.D. diss., Stanford University, 1990.

Rosenberg, David A. "Toward Armageddon: The Foundations of United States Nuclear Strategy, 1945–1961." Ph.D. diss., University of Chicago, 1983.

Scrivner, John Henry, Jr. "Pioneer into Space: A Biography of Major General Orvil Arson Anderson." Ph.D. diss., University of Oklahoma, 1971.

Author Correspondence

Cohen, Eliot A., Director, Gulf War Air Power Survey. E-mail correspondence, 22, 24, September 1999, 30 November 1999, 4, 5 January 2000.

Keaney, Thomas A., Gulf War Air Power Survey. E-mail correspondence, 21 December 1999

Kiraly, Emery M., Executive Director, Gulf War Air Power Survey. E-mail correspondence, 27 September 1999, 5, 10 January 2000.

Mandeles, Mark D., Gulf War Air Power Survey. E-mail correspondence, 11 January 2000.

Watts, Barry D., Gulf War Air Power Survey. E-mail correspondence, 20, 21, 22 December 1999, 5 January 2000.

Books

Alperovitz, Gar. *Atomic Diplomacy: Hiroshima and Potsdam*. New York: Penguin Books, 1965, 1985.

———. *The Decision to Use the Atomic Bomb and the Architecture of an American Myth*. New York: Alfred A. Knopf, 1995.

Ambrose, Stephen. *Citizen Soldiers*. New York: Simon and Schuster, 1997.

Arnold, H. H. *Global Mission*. New York: Harper and Brothers, 1949.

Baldwin, Hanson W. *The Great Mistakes of the War*. New York: Harper and Brothers, 1949.

Ball, George W. *The Past Has Another Pattern: Memoirs*. New York: W. W. Norton and Company, 1983.

Barlow, Jeffrey. *Revolt of the Admirals: The Fight for Naval Aviation, 1945–1950*. Washington, D.C.: Naval Historical Center, 1994.

Bernstein, Barton J., ed. *The Atomic Bomb: The Critical Issues*. Boston: Little, Brown and Company, 1976.

Blackett, P. M. S. *Political and Military Consequences of Atomic Weapons*. London: Turnstile Press, 1948.

Boia, Lucian, ed. *Great Historians of the Modern Age: An International Dictionary*. New York: Greenwood Press, 1991.

Borgiasz, William S. *The Strategic Air Command: Evolution and Consolidation of Nuclear Forces, 1945–1955*. Westport, Conn.: Praeger, 1996.

Borowski, Harry. *A Hollow Threat: Strategic Air Power and Containment before Korea*. Westport, Conn.: Greenwood Press, 1982.

Brodie, Bernard, ed. *The Absolute Weapon*. New York: Harcourt, Brace and Company, 1946.

———. *Strategy in the Missile Age*. Princeton: Princeton University Press, 1959.

Burns, James McGregor. *Roosevelt: The Soldier of Freedom*. New York: Harcourt Brace Jovanovich, 1970.

Carr, E. H. *What Is History?* New York: Vintage Books, 1961.

Chappell, John D. *Before the Bomb: How America Approached the End of the Pacific War*. Lexington: University of Kentucky Press, 1997.

Clodfelter, Mark. *The Limits of Air Power: The American Bombing of North Vietnam*. New York: Free Press, 1989.

Coffey, Thomas M. *Hap: The Story of the U.S. Air Force and the Man Who Built It*. New York: Viking Press, 1982.

Cohen, Eliot A. *Citizen Soldiers: The Dilemmas of Military Service*. Ithaca: Cornell University Press, 1985.

Cohen, Eliot A., and Gooch, John. *Military Misfortunes: The Anatomy of Failure in War.* New York: Free Press, 1990.

Cohen, Jerome B. *Japan's Economy in War and Reconstruction.* Minneapolis: University of Minnesota Press, 1949.

Cowdrey, Albert E. *Fighting for Life: American Military Medicine in World War II.* New York: Free Press, 1994.

Crane, Conrad C. *American Air Power Strategy in Korea, 1950–1953.* Lawrence: University Press of Kansas, 2000.

———. *Bombs, Cities and Civilians: American Airpower Strategy in World War II.* Lawrence: University Press of Kansas, 1993.

Craven, Wesley Frank, and James Lea Cate. *The Army Air Forces in World War II.* 7 vols., Chicago: University of Chicago Press, 1948.

Daniels, Gordon. *A Guide to the Reports of the United States Strategic Bombing Survey.* London, 1981.

Divine, Robert. *The Reluctant Belligerent: American Entry into World War II.* Austin: University of Texas Press, 1965.

Douhet, Guilio. *The Command of the Air.* Trans. Dino Ferrari. 1942; new imprint by the Office of Air Force History, Washington, D.C.: USGPO, 1983.

Dower, John W. *Embracing Defeat: Japan in the Wake of World War II.* New York: W. W. Norton & Company, 1999.

Drea, Edward. *McArthur's Ultra: Codebreaking and the War against Japan, 1942–1945.* Lawrence: University Press of Kansas, 1992.

Finney, Robert T. *History of the Air Corps Tactical School, 1920–1940.* Washington, D.C.: USGPO, 1955.

Futrell, Robert. *Ideas, Concepts, Doctrine: Basic Thinking in the United States Air Force, 1907–1960.* Maxwell Air Force Base: Air University Press, 1971.

———. *The United States Air Force in Korea, 1950–1953.* Rev. ed. Washington, D.C.: Office of Air Force History, 1983.

Galbraith, John Kenneth. *A Life in Our Times: Memoirs.* Boston: Houghton Mifflin Company, 1981.

Gaston, James C. *Planning the American Air War: Four Men and Nine Days in 1941—An Inside Narrative.* Washington, D.C.: National Defense University Press, 1982.

Gordon, Michael R., and Bernard E. Trainor. *The Generals' War: The Inside Story of the Conflict in the Gulf.* Boston: Little, Brown and Company, 1995.

Greer, Thomas H. *The Development of Air Doctrine in the Army Air Arm, 1917–1941.* Maxwell Air Force Base, Ala.: Air University Press, 1955.

Groves, Leslie M. *Now It Can Be Told: The Story of the Manhattan Project.* New York: Da Capo Press, 1962.

Halberstam, David. *The Best and the Brightest.* New York: Random House, 1969, 1972.

Hallion, Richard P. *Storm over Iraq: Air Power in the Gulf War.* Washington, D.C.: Smithsonian Institution Press, 1992.

Halperin, William. *Some 20th Century Historians: Essays on Eminent Europeans.* Chicago: University of Chicago Press, 1961.

Hansell, Haywood S. *The Air Plan That Defeated Hitler.* Atlanta: Higgins-MacArthur, 1972.

———.*Strategic Air War against Germany and Japan: A Memoir.* Washington, D.C.: USGPO, 1986.

———. *Strategic Air War against Japan.* Washington, D.C.: USGPO, 1980.

Hastings, Max. *Bomber Command: The Myths and Reality of the Strategic Bombing Offensive, 1939–1945.* New York: Dial Press, 1979.

Hayes, Grace Person. *The History of the Joint Chiefs of Staff in World War II: The War against Japan.* Annapolis: Naval Institute Press, 1982.

Hershberg, James G. *James B. Conant: Harvard to Hiroshima and the Making of the Nuclear Age.* New York: Alfred A. Knopf, 1993.

Hobsbawm, Eric. *On History.* New York: New Press, 1997.

Hughes, Thomas Alexander. *Over Lord: General Pete Quesada and the Triumph of Tactical Air Power in World War II.* New York: Free Press, 1995.

Hurley, Alfred F. *Billy Mitchell: Crusader for Airpower.* Bloomington: Indiana University Press, 1964.

Jurika, Stephen, Jr., ed. *From Pearl Harbor to Vietnam: The Memoirs of Arthur W. Radford.* Stanford: Hoover Institution Press, 1980.

Kaplan, Fred. *The Wizards of Armageddon.* Stanford: Stanford University Press, 1983.

Keaney, Thomas A., and Eliot A. Cohen. *Revolution in Warfare: Air Power in the Persian Gulf War.* Annapolis: Naval Institute Press, 1995.

Kennett, Lee. *A History of Strategic Bombing.* New York: Charles Scribner's Sons, 1982.

LeMay, Curtis E., with MacKinlay Kantor. *Mission with LeMay*. Garden City, NY: Doubleday Books, 1965.

McArthur, Charles W. *Operations Analysis in the U.S. Army Eighth Air Force in World War II*. Providence: American Mathematical Society, 1990.

MacIsaac, David. *Strategic Bombing in World War Two: The Story of the United States Strategic Bombing Survey*. New York: Garland Publishing, 1976.

———. *The United States Strategic Bombing Survey*. Vols. 1–10. Introduction by David MacIsaac, New York: Garland Publishing, 1976.

Mandeles, Mark D., Thomas C. Hone, and Sanford S. Terry. *Managing "Command and Control" in the Persian Gulf War*. Westport, Conn.: Praeger, 1996.

Mann, Edward C., III. *Thunder and Lightning: Desert Storm and the Airpower Debates*. Maxwell Air Force Base, Ala.: Air University Press, 1995.

Mearsheimer, John J. *Liddell Hart and the Weight of History*. Ithaca: Cornell University Press, 1988.

Meilinger, Philip S., ed. *The Paths of Heaven: The Evolution of Airpower Theory*. Maxwell Air Force Base, Ala.: Air University Press, 1997.

Mets, David R. *Master of Airpower: General Carl A. Spaatz*. Novato, Cal.: Presidio Press, 1988.

Mierzejewiski, Alfred C. *The Collapse of the German War Economy, 1944–1945: Allied Air Power and the German National Railway*. Chapel Hill: University of North Carolina Press, 1988.

Millis, Walter, ed. *The Forrestal Diaries*. New York: Viking Press, 1951.

Mitchell, William. *Winged Defense: The Development and Possibilities of Modern Air Power—Economic and Military*. Rpt. New York: Kennikat Press, 1971.

Moody, Walton S. *Building a Strategic Air Force*. Washington, D.C.: USGPO, 1995.

Murray, Williamson. *Air War in the Persian Gulf*. Baltimore: Nautical and Aviation Publishing Company of America, 1995.

Newman, Robert P. *Truman and the Hiroshima Cult*. East Lansing: Michigan State University Press, 1995.

Nitze, Paul H. *From Hiroshima to Glasnost: At the Center of Decision*. New York: Grove Weidenfeld, 1989.

Novick, Peter. *That Noble Dream: The "Objectivity Question" and the American Historical Profession.* Cambridge: Cambridge University Press, 1988.

Perera, Guido R. *Leaves from My Book of Life: Washington War Years.* Boston: privately printed, 1975.

Radford, Arthur W. *From Pearl Harbor to Vietnam: The Memoirs of Arthur W. Radford.* Ed. Stephen Jurika, Jr. Stanford: Hoover Institution Press, 1980.

Reynolds, Richard T. *Heart of the Storm: The Genesis of the Air Campaign against Iraq.* Maxwell Air Force Base, Ala.: Air University Press, 1995.

Rhodes, Richard. *The Making of the Atomic Bomb.* New York: Simon & Schuster, 1986.

Ross, Steven T. *American War Plans, 1945–1950.* New York: Garland Publishing, 1988.

Scales, Robert H., Jr., et al. *Certain Victory: United States Army in the Gulf War.* Washington, D.C: Office of the Chief of Staff, U.S. Army, 1994.

Schaffer, Ronald. *Wings of Judgment: American Bombing in World War II.* New York: Oxford University Press, 1985.

Sereny, Gita. *Albert Speer: His Battle with Truth.* Alfred A. Knopf: New York, 1995.

Sherry, Michael S. *Preparing for the Next War: American Plans for Postwar Defense, 1941–1945.* New Haven: Yale University Press, 1977.

———. *The Rise of American Air Power: The Creation of Armageddon.* New Haven: Yale University Press, 1987.

Shiner, John F. *Foulois and the U.S. Army Air Corps, 1931–1935.* Washington, D.C.: USGPO, 1984.

Speer, Albert. *Inside the Third Reich: Memoirs.* New York: Collier Books, 1981.

Steiner, Barry H. *Bernard Brodie and the Foundations of American Nuclear Strategy.* Lawrence: University Press of Kansas, 1991.

Strange, Joe. *Centers of Gravity and Critical Vulnerabilities: Building on the Clausewitzian Foundation So That We Can All Speak the Same Language.* Marine Corps War College, 1996.

Summers, Harry G. *On Strategy: A Critical Analysis of the Vietnam War.* Novato, Cal.: Presidio Press, 1982.

Talbott, Strobe. *The Master of the Game: Paul Nitze and the Nuclear Peace.* New York: Alfred A. Knopf, 1988.

Tilford, Earl H., Jr. *Setup: What the Air Force Did in Vietnam and Why.* Maxwell Air Force Base, Ala.: Air University Press, 1991.

Truman, Harry S. *Memoirs,* vol. 2: 1946–1952, *Years of Trial and Hope.* New York: Smithmark, 1955.

Warden, John A., III. *The Air Campaign: Planning for Combat.* Washington, D.C.: Brassey's, 1988.

Watts, Barry D. *Clausewitzian Friction and Future War.* Washington, D.C.: National Defense University, 1996.

Webster, Charles, and Noble Frankland. *The Strategic Air Offensive against Germany, 1939–1945,* vol. 2: *Endeavour.* London: Her Majesty's Stationary Office, 1961.

Weisgall, Jonathan M. *Operation Crossroads: The Atomic Tests at Bikini Atoll.* Annapolis: Naval Institute Press, 1994.

Winfield, James A., Preston Niblack, and Dana J. Johnson. *A League of Airmen: U.S. Air Power in the Gulf War.* Santa Monica: Rand, 1994.

Wright, Gordon. *The Ordeal of Total War, 1939–1945.* New York: Harper & Row, 1968.

Zuckerman, Solly. *Scientists and War: The Impact of Science on Military and Civil Affairs.* London: Scientific Book Club, 1966.

Articles

Anderson, Orvil A. "Air Warfare and Morality." *Air University Quarterly Review* 2 (winter 1949): 5–14.

Asada, Sadao. "The Shock of the Atomic Bomb and Japan's Decision to Surrender—A Reconsideration." *Pacific Historical Review* 67 (November 1998): 477–512.

Bernstein, Barton J. "The Alarming Japanese Buildup on Southern Kyushu, Growing U.S. Fears, and Counterfactual Analysis: Would the Planned November 1945 Invasion of Southern Kyushu Have Occurred?" *Pacific Historical Review* 68 (November 1999): 561–609.

———. "The Atomic Bomb and American Foreign Policy, 1941–1945: An Historiographical Controversy." *Peace and Change* (spring 1974): 1–16.

———. "Compelling Japan's Surrender without the A-bomb, Soviet Entry, or Invasion: Reconsidering the US Bombing Survey's Early-Surrender Counterfactual." *Journal of Strategic Studies* 18 (June 1995): 101–48.

Bernstein, Barton J. "Reconsidering Truman's Claim of 'Half A million American Lives' Saved: The Construction and Deconstruction of a Myth." *Journal of Strategic Studies* 22 (1999): 54–95.

———. "Roosevelt, Truman, and the Atomic Bomb, 1941–1945." *Political Science Quarterly* 90 (spring 1975): 23–69.

———. "Seizing the Contested Terrain of Early Nuclear History: Stimson, Conant, and Their Allies Explain the Decision to Use the Atomic Bomb." *Diplomatic History* 17 (winter 1993): 35–72.

———. "The Struggle over History: Defining the Hiroshima Narrative." *Judgment* at the Smithsonian: The Bombing of Hiroshima and Nagasaki, ed. Philip Nobile (New York: Marlowe and Company, 1995): 127–256.

Biddle, Tami Davis. "British and American Approaches to Strategic Bombing: Their Origins and Implementation in the World War II Combined Bomber Offensive." *Journal of Strategic Studies* 18 (March 1995): 91–144.

Brodie, Bernard. "Critical Summary of War Department Paper." In *The Atomic Bomb and the Armed Services,* ed. Bernard Brodie and Eileen Galloway. Washington, D.C.: Library of Congress, 1947. 86–97.

Brower, Charles F., IV. "Sophisticated Strategist: General George A. Lincoln and the Defeat of Japan, 1944–1945." *Diplomatic History* 15 (summer 1991): 317–37.

Byman, Daniel A., and Matthew C. Waxman. "Kosovo and the Great Air Power Debate." *International Security* 4 (spring 2000): 5–38.

Clodfelter, Mark L. "Molding Airpower Convictions: Development and Legacy of William Mitchell's Strategic Thought." In Meilinger, *Paths of Heaven,* 79–114.

Crane, Conrad C. "The Cigar Who Ignited the Fire Wind: Curtis LeMay and the Incendiary Bombing of Urban Areas." Unpublished and undated. Personal copy provided by Crane to author.

Compton, Karl T. "If the Atomic Bomb Had Not Been Used." *Atlantic Monthly,* December 1946, 54–56.

Deptula, David A. "Parallel Warfare: What Is It? Where Did It Come From?" In *The Eagle in the Desert: Looking Back on U.S. Involvement in the Persian Gulf War,* ed. William Head and Earl H. Tilford, Jr. Westport, Conn.: Praeger, 1996. 127–56.

Drew, Dennis M. "Air Theory, Air Force, and Low Intensity Conflict: A Short Journey to Confusion." In Meilinger, *Paths of Heaven,* 334.

Faber, Peter R. "Interwar US Army Aviation and the Air Corps Tactical School: Incubators of American Airpower." In Meilinger, *Paths of Heaven,* 183–238.

Galbraith, John K. "Albert Speer Was the Man to See." *New York Review of Books,* January 10, 1971. 173–200.

———. "Germany Was Badly Run." *Fortune,* December 1945.

———. "Peace through Patience, Not Air Power." *New York Times,* 25 April 1999.

Gentile, Gian P. "A-Bombs, Budgets, and Morality: Using the Strategic Bombing Survey." *Air Power History* 44 (spring 1997): 18–31.

———. "Advocacy or Assessment? The United States Strategic Bombing Survey of Germany and Japan." *Pacific Historical Review* 66 (February 1997): 53–79.

Griffith, Thomas E., Jr. "Strategic Attack of Electrical Systems." A thesis presented to the faculty of the School of Advanced Air Power Studies. Maxwell Air Force Base, Ala.: Air University Press, 1994.

Haskell, Thomas. "Farewell to Fallibilism." *History and Theory* 37 (1998): 347–69.

Kohn, Richard H. "History as Institutional Memory: The Experience of the United States Air Force." In *Military History and the Military Profession,* ed. David Charters, Marc Milliner, and Brent J. Wilson. Westport, Conn.: Praeger, 1992.

———. "History at Risk: The Case of the Enola Gay." In *History Wars: The Enola Gay and Other Battles for the American Past,* ed. Edward T. Linenthal and Tom Engelhardt. New York: Metropolitan Books, 1996, 140–70.

Link, Charles D. "Why Airpower?" and "Airpower?—Why Not?" *Daedalus Flyer* (summer 1999): 8–9.

Lorenz, Chris. "Can Histories Be True? Narrativism, Positivism, and the 'Metaphorical Turn.'" *History and Theory* 37 (1998): 309–29.

MacIsaac, David. "A New Look at Old Lessons." *Air Force Magazine* (September 1970): 121–27.

———. "What the Bombing Survey Really Says." *Air Force Magazine* 56 (June 1973): 60–63.

———. "Voices from the Central Blue: The Air Power Theorists." In *Makers of Modern Strategy,* ed. Peter Paret. Princeton: Princeton University Press, 1986. 624–47.

McDonnell, Robert H. "Clausewitz and Strategic Bombing." *Air University Quarterly Review* 6 (spring 1953): 43–54.

Maland, Charles. "'Dr. Strangelove' (1964): Nightmare Comedy and the Ideology of Liberal Consensus." In *Hollywood as Historian: American Film in Cultural Context,* ed. Peter C. Rallins. Lexington: University of Kentucky Press, 1983. 190–210.

Maney, John R. "The Support of Strategy." *Air University Quarterly Review* 6 (fall 1953): 42–51.

Meilinger, Philip S. "Alexander S. De Seversky and American Air Power." In Meilinger, *Paths of Heaven,* 239–77.

———. "Guilio Douhet and the Origins of Airpower Theory." In Meilinger, *Paths of Heaven,* 1–40.

Newman, Robert P. "Ending the War with Japan: Paul Nitze's Early-Surrender Counterfactual." *Pacific Historical Review* 64 (May 1995): 176–94.

Rosenberg, David A. "American Postwar Air Doctrine and Organization: The Navy Experience." In *Air Power and Warfare: The Proceedings of the 8th Military History Symposium United States Air Force Academy, 18–20 October 1978,* ed. Alfred F. Hurley and Robert C. Ehrhart. Washington D.C.: USGPO, 1979. 245–78.

———. "The Origins of Overkill: Nuclear Weapons and American Strategy, 1945–1960." *International Security* 7 (spring 1983): 3–71.

Spaatz, Carl A. "Strategic Airpower: Fulfillment of a Concept." *Foreign Affairs* 24 (April 1946): 385–96.

Stone, I. F. "Nixon's Blitzkrieg." *New York Review of Books,* 25 January 1973.

Trachtenberg, Marc. "A 'Wasting Asset': American Strategy and the Shifting Nuclear Balance, 1949–1954." In Trachtenberg, *History and Strategy.* Princeton: Princeton University Press, 1992. 100–152.

Walker, J. Samuel. "The Decision to Use the Atomic Bomb: A Historiographical Update." *Diplomatic History* 14 (winter 1990): 97–114.

Warden, John A., III. "The Enemy as System." *Airpower Journal* 9 (spring 1995): 40–55.

Watson, Frank C. "United States Strategic Bombing Survey: A Look to the Future" (research report submitted to the Air War College Faculty, Air University, February 1983. Available at the Maxwell Air Force Base Library.

Weigley, Russell. "The Soldier, the Statesman and the Military Historian." *Journal of Military History* 63 (October 1999): 807–22.

West, Scott D. "Warden and the Air Corps Tactical School: Déjà Vu?" Maxwell Air Force Base, Ala.: Air University Press, 1999.

INDEX

ABOUT THE AUTHOR

✦ ✦ ✦ ✦ ✦ ✦ ✦ ✦ ✦ ✦ ✦

Gian P. Gentile is an active duty army officer who holds a B.A. in history from the University of California, Berkeley, an M.A. and Ph.D. in history from Stanford University, and an M.M.A.S. from the School of Advanced Military Studies. He has served in command and staff positions in armored units in Korea and Germany. He commanded a tank company in Korea in the 2nd Infantry Division from 1991–1993 and taught American history at West Point from 1995 to 1998. He is presently serving with the 4th Infantry Division at Fort Hood, Texas.